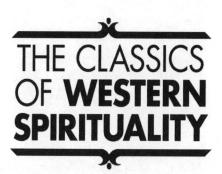

THE CLASSICS
OF **WESTERN**
SPIRITUALITY

THE CLASSICS OF WESTERN SPIRITUALITY
A Library of the Great Spiritual Masters

(V. III)

President and Publisher
Lawrence Boadt, C.S.P.

EDITORIAL BOARD

Sor Juana Inés de la Cruz
SELECTED WRITINGS

TRANSLATED AND INTRODUCED BY
PAMELA KIRK RAPPAPORT

PREFACE BY
GILLIAN T. W. AHLGREN

PAULIST PRESS
NEW YORK • MAHWAH, NJ

Cover art: *Sister (Suor) Juana Inés de la Cruz* by Miguel Cabrera (1695–1768), painted ca. 1750. Used by permission of Schalkwijk/Art Resources, NY.

All of the texts in this volume have been translated from the following source: Alfonso Mendez Plancarte and Alberto Salceda, eds., *Obras completas de sor Juana Inés de la Cruz*, 3rd ed. (Mexico City: Fondo de Cultura Economica/Instituto Mexiquense de Cultura, 1990), copyright Fondo de Cultura Economica/Instituto Mexiquense de Cultura. Used with permission.

Cover and caseside design by A. Michael Velthaus
Book design by Lynn Else

Library of Congress Cataloging-in-Publication Data

Juana Inés de la Cruz, Sister, 1651–1695.
   [Selections. English. 2005]
   Sor Juana Inés de la Cruz : selected writings.
      p. cm. — (The classics of Western spirituality)
   Includes bibliographical references and index.
   ISBN 0-8091-4012-8 (pbk. : alk. paper); ISBN 0-8091-0530-6 (hardcover : alk. paper)
   1. Theology. 2. Nuns' writings, Mexican. 3. Juana Inés de la Cruz, Sister, 1651–1695—Translations into English. I. Kirk Rappaport, Pamela. II. Title. III. Series.
   BX4705.J728A25 2005
   861'.3—dc22

                                 2005009269

Published by Paulist Press
997 Macarthur Boulevard
Mahwah, New Jersey 07430

www.paulistpress.com

Printed and bound in the
United States of America

CONTENTS

CONTENTS

To Edward
With Love

Translator of This Volume

PAMELA KIRK RAPPAPORT is an associate professor of theology at St. John's University, New York. She holds a doctorate in theology from the University of Munich. With research interests in the history of women in the Christian tradition, she has written extensively on Sor Juana. She has also written about Karl Rahner's friend Luise Rinser.

Author of the Preface

GILLIAN T. W. AHLGREN, PhD, is professor of theology at Xavier University in Cincinnati, Ohio, and frequently offers public talks and retreats. She is also the author of *Teresa of Avila and the Politics of Sanctity* (Cornell University Press, 1996) and of *Entering Teresa of Avila's* Interior Castle: *A Reader's Companion* (Paulist Press, 2005).

ACKNOWLEDGMENTS

Thanks are due to many people who have helped bring this, my second book on Sor Juana, to completion. St. John's University has been generous in granting me teaching reductions, and Provost Julia Upton, RSM, was crucial in making sure I had a year of absence (2001–2) that enabled me to work full time on the translations. Departmental Chair Jean-Pierre Ruiz obtained funding for my participation in the semester-long interdisciplinary seminar "Gender and Sanctity in Counter-Reformation Europe" held at the Folger Institute in 1998. My graduate assistant Maryellen Sullivan was of great help with the bibliography and notes. Administrative assistant Frances Fico's skill in word processing and unfailing patience and good humor have moved the manuscript through its many versions.

Diana Villegas, convener of the Spirituality Program Group of the Catholic Theological Society of America, read the draft of my introduction and gave incisive and constructive criticism. Bernard McGinn, Editor-in-Chief of the Classics of Western Spirituality series, contributed invaluable advice and meticulous editing. Maria Pilar Aquino, Elizabeth A. Johnson, and William Thompson have supported this project with letters of recommendation. To all, my heartfelt gratitude.

My family has been supportive of this effort through its enthusiasm, interest, and knowledge. Victor Abeyta, my brother-in-law, has guided me through difficult patches in Sor Juana's poetry and prose. My husband, Edward, encouraged me every day in more ways than I can count.

PREFACE

Gillian T. W. Ahlgren

Juana Inés de la Cruz is already well-known in a surprising nexus of circles—academic, artistic, and popular. After successive waves of "rediscovery" of her works, she has achieved significant recognition in recent years, but such public acclaim is not new to her. Hailed as the Tenth Muse during her day, her literary genius was prized at court as a great novelty, and her works circulated throughout New Spain and beyond. Often characterized, in the past and the present, as a woman of "singular" and exceptional talent, Sor Juana remains perhaps as enigmatic now as she was in her own day: born in obscurity, self-taught, prolific, and progressively more celebrated, until finally, embroiled in controversy over the public circulation of her provocative ideas, she fades once more into anonymity.

What has probably attracted the most scholarly attention over the past several decades is her eloquent defense of the role and place of women as authoritative religious teachers, structured around a careful appropriation of elements of the Christian tradition. When coupled with her reflections on the active, redemptive role of Mary, students of Sor Juana have seen in her a prophetic witness to a more egalitarian understanding of human personhood and community. The fact that her *apologia* for women's right to theologize and interpret scripture was followed by silence and obscurity only begs more interpretive questions that perhaps we are now in a better position to answer.

Born of unmarried parents in a small village outside Mexico City, Sor Juana's rise to international fame was not entirely predictable. We can credit her own deep thirst for learning and the material support of her maternal grandparents for her first steps

1

away from obscurity. Her desire for education led her to Mexico City, where she eventually came to live under the protection of the viceroy. In 1667, responding to her "aversion to marriage," she entered the discalced Carmelite Convent of San José and then transferred to the Hieronymite Convent of St. Paula, where she professed her vows in 1669. Thus, at a relatively early age Sor Juana found herself, perhaps surprisingly, settled in a context uniquely suited to enable the development of her spiritual, literary, and religious interests, particularly as they coalesced in her passion for writing.

Convent life in the late seventeenth century took many forms. Without idealizing Sor Juana's circumstances, it is clear that her situation at St. Paula provided her with the fundamental needs of a dedicated writer: resources for her ongoing study, time and space to compose her works, and contact with others in academic and court circles, which allowed for the cultivation and circulation of her ideas. This was particularly true by the 1680s, her most prolific period as a writer, when support by the vicereine María Luisa Manrique de Lara y Gonzaga ensured that Sor Juana's works would see new light in Spain. A versatile and "natural" writer, not unlike her self-proclaimed mentor Teresa of Avila, Sor Juana's works span many genres: poems, liturgical contributions, dramas, comedies, treatises, and hundreds of letters, most of which have been lost. Both the quantity and the style of these works testify to Sor Juana's creativity and seemingly boundless energy, and, while she is not at all immune to the literary and cultural conventions of her day, the reader can discern, centuries later, a certain *joie de vivre* and freedom of spirit embedded in her words. In the act of writing, Sor Juana clearly took full possession of herself—reveling in all of the dimensions of personal development, intellectual exploration, and self-sharing that writers are graced to experience.

As she grew more self-revelatory, however, Sor Juana also became more vulnerable to the vicissitudes of public life. When her patron María Luisa left Mexico for Spain in 1688, Sor Juana fell prey to manipulation and criticism; the explosion of works during the 1680s was followed by controversy surrounding the unauthorized publication of her famous *Carta Athenagórica* (1690), in which she set down in writing some christological views she had shared with the bishop of Puebla, Manuel Fernández de Santa Cruz. Her attempts to clarify her intellectual positions and to renegotiate her position vis-à-vis the religious hierarchy resulted in the spirited and much-cited *Response to Sor Philotea de la Cruz* (1691). Read in the context of this new collection of her works, the latter can be seen not only as a carefully reasoned and passionate argument for women's equality but also as a scripturally based rationale for a theological anthropology that assumes women's authority as spiritual and theological teachers. The *Response* has all the qualities of an explosive tour-de-force: clarity of thought, citation of and debate with theological authorities, nuanced integration of scripture, and theological positions that beg further conversation. Indeed, the *Response* invites the reader into the very process of theology itself—a process of reflection, contemplation, debate, and ongoing refinement. Sadly, this process of speculation and conversation was cut off immediately; the *Response* became Sor Juana's last major work. We can only make educated guesses about her own disposition and agency during the period of Juana's silence, from 1692 until her death in 1695, but it speaks at least as loudly as the rest of her works.

Like many Hispanic religious women, Sor Juana saw herself as part of a larger tradition of female writers. However, Sor Juana appears less interested than many of them in chronicling her subjective religious experience. Autobiographical information emerges in her *Response*, but never does she characterize or analyze her experience of prayer or her understanding of God. We gain, through her writings, little sense of the landscape of her internal life; instead, Sor Juana chooses the theater of human history as the arena to chronicle her relationship with God. Sor Juana theologizes more as an astute observer of life around her, attempting to capture, in words, the dynamics of divine activity within human interactions, past and present. Her reflections on human nature and the human-Divine relationship were shaped as much by social interactions, her keen sense of social and religious structures, and her understanding of history as by her attunement to her own internal world. The literary genres she chooses reflect this orientation to larger social, historical, and even ethical questions. Sor

Juana was consciously aware of the social and political dimensions of her writings, and she sought a public voice. Thus, in some very real ways, Sor Juana's literary works gave her a unique role as a socio-political, religious, and even theological commentator of no little authority and influence.

Re-creating and understanding all of the nuances and complexities of that specific context is somewhat difficult. Like all female religious writers, as a woman she was self-taught. But her educational milieu in the New World was quite different from that of her European foremothers. In particular, the multiplicity of cultural and religious influences and the context of colonial Christianity with its triumphalist overtones provided Sor Juana with a host of theological issues (and assumptions) that might not have played out quite so consciously or immediately in the minds of some of her predecessors. Certainly, she, like all of us, is marked by the specificity of her circumstances and lenses of context and personal idiosyncrasies that shape her exploration of how God can be seen and known in the here-and-now. Indeed, Sor Juana's synthesis of the Christian tradition cannot help but raise anew profound and interesting questions about how theological ideas translate and are appropriated across cultures and religious traditions. For that reason alone, we should welcome this new translation of her works, designed to facilitate our appreciation of Sor Juana's contributions as a theologian.

But there are other reasons to be grateful for this new look at Sor Juana. Locating her works among the many classics of western spirituality provides her with a much needed home. Read within the context of a larger tradition of philosophical, theological, and spiritual inquiry, Sor Juana loses nothing of her originality, but the label of singularity that has dogged her for centuries can now slip gracefully away. As a voice in a larger conversation about human meaning, it becomes easier to assess and appreciate Sor Juana's contributions and limitations. Finally, she is able to take her rightful place in a chorus of voices that seeks to shed light and bear witness to the myriad manifestations of the Divine in the drama of human history.

INTRODUCTION

In 1689, with the publication of the first volume of her collected works, *Castalian Inundation,* the Mexican nun of the Order of St. Jerome, Sor (Sister) Juana Inés de la Cruz (1648–95) was called "tenth muse," indicating that she, a mere mortal, was like Sappho in antiquity, worthy of the company of the nine goddess of the arts, the muses.[1] Another favorite epithet reflecting the baroque age's love of expressions of astonishment applied to Sor Juana was "phoenix," a reference to a mythical bird that regenerated from its own ashes every five hundred years. But in this case, epithets such as "muse" and "phoenix" were not mere baroque hyperbole. It is an irony of history, or perhaps rather a fitting symmetry, that five hundred years earlier, we find—as if she were the previous incarnation of the phoenix—the only other woman whose writings exhibit a comparable complexity and variety of genre, and universal curiosity: Hildegard of Bingen (1098–1179). Like Hildegard, whose music, after centuries of obscurity, reached best-selling levels in the late twentieth century, Sor Juana has experienced a revival of interest since the publication of Nobel laureate Octavio Paz's biography, *Sor Juana Inés de la Cruz, or The Traps of Faith,* in 1988. Her life has been the subject of a feature film, several plays, and a novel.[2] Her work has also been the subject of many scholarly conferences, books, and countless articles.[3]

Known today primarily among Latin American literary scholars, but enough a part of Mexican popular culture to be the face on Mexico's 200–peso bill, Sor Juana Inés de la Cruz was a writer of astonishing range and versatility. Octavio Paz has called her one of the great poets of the Spanish language.[4] He also considers her *Response to Sor Philotea de la Cruz* to be the first intellectual autobiography in the Hispanic world. One of her religious dramas (or *auto sacramentales*), *Divine Narcissus,* in which Christ is configured as the Narcissus of classical mythology, is considered an outstanding example of the genre. Though it is not known if she composed music, the vast majority of her religious poems were written for a typically Hispanic form of liturgical music, the *villancico*. We also know that she wrote a now lost treatise on music, *"La Caraccole"* (conch, or spiral). Her first biographer, Diego Calleja, SJ, recounts that, for the benefit of her religious sisters, she developed a method of teaching music that "achieved its goal without all the detours of the old method."[5] Sor Juana's philosophical poem *First Dream* reflects her contemporaries' ideas about the functioning of the body and intellectual and sensory perception. The Jesuit explorer and scientist Eusebio Francisco Kino visited her when he came to Mexico, and she wrote a sonnet in his honor. She also wrote a theological treatise on the benefits of divine love based on her critique of a sermon of the famous Portuguese Jesuit Antonio Vieira.

When she died in an epidemic in April 1695, she was known as a poet, dramatist, and religious writer in places as far flung as Lima,[6] Colombia, Stockholm, and, of course, Spain. Numerous editions of the first two volumes of her collected works had been published there (Madrid, Seville, Barcelona, Majorca), making her one of the most widely published writers of the period. Her reputation was only enhanced by the posthumous publication of a third volume of her collected works in 1700. This third volume contains three of the prose works translated here (*Offerings for the Sorrows of Our Lady, Devotional Exercises for the Feast of the Incarnation,* and *Response to Sor Philotea of the Cross*).

Feminist literary scholars and historians have been fascinated by Sor Juana's ability to achieve fame in her own lifetime as a nun who did not base her claim to wisdom on mystical insight. Rather, Sor Juana maintained that both her drive to learn and her intellectual gifts were God given, but that her arguments were open to rational scrutiny and her poetry subject to the critique of good taste. Until recently, there has been little serious attention paid to the content of her religious work.[7] Scholars of Latin American literature are fascinated almost exclusively by her person and secular works, or have tended to see her religious works as perfunctory exercises, vehicles to secure her reputation. Theologians have been reluctant to deal with the literary nature of much of her religious writing. Those who do not read Spanish have been hampered by the absence of translations of her religious writings. It is my hope that this translation of a significant portion of Sor Juana's religious works will be an invitation to theologians beyond the Spanish-speaking world to become acquainted with her writing.

Life

Whether she was considered a phoenix or a "fair-ground freak," as one feminist scholar has suggested, Sor Juana came from humble beginnings.[8] On December 2, 1648, near the tiny village of Nepantla, she was registered for baptism as a "daughter of the church" (a euphemism for an illegitimate child). Very little is known about her father except that he was the father of two of her sisters, that he was Basque, that his name was Asbaje or Avuaje, and that he may have been a soldier. Her godparents were Miguel and Beatriz Ramírez, Sor Juana's mother's brother and sister.[9] Her early childhood was spent on a small farm in Panoayán, a few leagues away from her birthplace. When she was three years old she learned to read from a local woman who gave individual instruction to girls. Such women were known as *amigas* (women friends) and seem to have constituted an informal network through which girls could get the rudiments of literacy even in relatively remote regions. Though she does not mention the name of her teacher in her autobiography, she does mention that "she is still with us," honoring a connection that went back nearly forty years.

Learning to read brought with it knowledge of the wider world, and literacy fueled a desire to study the world and the world of books. She writes of herself as a small child: "I heard that in Mexico City there was a university and many schools where many subjects were studied. Hardly had I heard this when I began to pester my mother to death with constant and inopportune pleas to dress me as a boy and send me to Mexico City to the home of some of her relatives so that I could study and take courses at the university" (OC 4:446). Her mother did not allow her to go, but Juana Inés was able to satisfy her hunger for knowledge to a certain degree by reading the books in her grandfather's library. By the age of eight she had learned enough to enter a competition to compose a short play *(loa)* for the feast of Corpus Christi, motivated in part, according to her earliest biographer, Diego de Calleja, SJ, because the prize was a book.[10]

It was probably in 1656 that she was sent to the capital to live with her maternal aunt, María Ramírez, who had married the wealthy merchant Juan de Mata. There, after the arrival in 1664 of the new viceroy, the Marquis of Mancera, her aunt and uncle presented her to the viceregal court. The court in Mexico as a reflection of the court in Madrid was supposed to suggest the glitter and power of the far-off ruler. As a result, when the marquis's wife, Leonor Carreto, invited Juana Inés to become one of her ladies in waiting, it meant access to more education, social and intellectual, for the girl. The viceroy was the king's representative and as such very powerful. In order that he not become powerful in his own right his term was limited generally to six years, and he could not take any of his children with him to New Spain, as Mexico was called at the time. It was in this setting that Sor Juana achieved her reputation as a child prodigy, dazzling members of the court. Calleja recounts an anecdote he learned from the marquis, in which the young Juana Inés was examined by learned university professors and other scholars, with the marquis commenting: "She defended herself like a galleon against a slew of canoes."[11]

By all accounts she was very beautiful, but for reasons that remain unclear she chose not to marry and entered the convent instead. Calleja, in a striking sentence, alludes to the dangers awaiting unmarried women of modest means in the world: "The face of a beautiful woman is a blank slate on which every man wants to make his mark."[12] Later the nun, in a much debated phrase, says she entered the convent because of a disinclination to marriage and because, given her thirst for learning, the convent seemed the best way for her to work out her salvation. She was helped in this decision by the influential Jesuit Antonio Núñez de Miranda, who encouraged her in her studies. She was financially supported by Pedro Velázquez de la Cadena, who helped with her dowry. Brother Martín de Olivas gave her instruction in Latin to prepare her for reading the breviary, but Latin was also the key to higher learning in philosophy and theology. In August 1667 she entered the discalced Carmelite convent of San José but left after three months, apparently for reasons of health.[13] Shortly thereafter she entered the Order of St. Jerome in the convent of St. Paula, where she became a professed nun on February 24, 1669. Sor Juana's entry into the prestigious, wealthy convent gave her status she would not have had as the illegitimate daughter of an itinerant soldier and a woman who ran a small farm.[14] Even had she been able to marry into wealth and respectability, she would not have had the institutional prestige that accompanied being a member of the large Hieronymite convent. The nuns were teachers in a school attached to the convent where they taught secular and religious subjects, music, dance, and drama to daughters of those who could afford the cost.[15]

Because Sor Juana's reputation as a poet and scholar was already established among those influential at court and among the clergy, she continued to receive commissions to compose plays and poems for court occasions as well as for religious celebrations, writing, among other things, twelve sequences of hymns for major feasts that were set to music and performed in the cathedrals of Mexico City, Puebla, and Oaxaca.[16] Although some of the sisters disapproved of her fame, the majority must have respected her, because three times they elected her to the important office of *contadora* (bookkeeper/financial officer). She held this office at her death.[17] It was an office that required the mathematical skills of a bookkeeper and the organizational skills of a savvy manager.

From within the convent Sor Juana maintained a vast correspondence (now lost) with friends and admirers in Spain and the New World.[18] She was also able to receive many visitors in the convent parlor. These included the other multi-talented personality of Mexico City at the time, the scholar-priest, astronomer, mathematician, chronicler, journalist, and anthropologist Carlos Sigüenza y Góngora. Others acquaintances included her sometimes confessor, Núñez de Miranda, SJ, and the Bishop of Puebla, Manuel Fernández de Santa Cruz, as well as the scientist and explorer of the U.S. Southwest, missionary Eusebio Kino, SJ. She enjoyed not only the patronage of the viceroy, the Marquis of Mancera, and his wife, Leonor Carreto, but of all subsequent viceroys as well. This included the Franciscan archbishop and viceroy Payo Enríquez de Rivera and especially his successor and relative, the Marquis of Laguna, and his wife, Maria Luisa, Countess of Paredes. The Countess of Paredes may have been fascinated by Sor Juana in part because she was reminded of her own grandmother on her mother's side, Luisa Enríque de Lara. In addition to being correspondent of King Phillip IV over many years, Luisa Enríque had, before entering the convent on the death of her husband, written a considerable amount of poetry, some of which had been published when she was a lady at court. As a nun she also wrote religious reflections for her sisters in the Carmelite convent where she was abbess.[19] Some have argued that the importance of the friendship between Sor Juana and the Countess of Paredes for posterity lies in the countess's publication, on her return to Madrid, of *Castalian Inundation,* the first volume of Sor Juana's collected works. It was highly unusual for a woman to publish another woman's works.[20]

It would be this publication, with its numerous poems to her patroness, that would fuel speculation in the twentieth century about the nature of their relationship and the seriousness of Sor Juana's commitment to her religious vocation. Because this issue has affected the public persona of Sor Juana to a considerable degree, it needs further consideration here.[21] A number of the poems in question are written as if the poet is painting the countess's portrait. Of these, most are written to the countess after her return to Spain. One argues that "pure love can be expressed in the same language as profane love" and maintains: "neither your being a woman, nor absent, is an impediment to loving you, since as you know souls ignore distances and gender *(sexo)*" (OC 1:57). Another speaks of the power of the countess's beauty to enslave and enrapture (OC 1:221–24). In a third the poet describes her emotions while contemplating the portrait (OC 1:240–42). A fourth poem begins with a description of the sitter's hair, her forehead, eyebrows, nose, cheeks, neck, arms, fingers, waist, and feet—all the flesh that would be visible in a formal portrait (OC 1:171–73). This poem especially has been interpreted as an indication of a sexual attraction or even more explicit sexual relationship between the Countess of Paredes and Sor Juana. What militates against this is that we find this same conceit in two other poems published in *Castalian Inundation*. One is to the Countess of Galve, the wife of the viceroy after the Countess of Paredes had left (OC 1:119–20). In it the Countess of Galve's features are compared to male heroes, so that the portrait will turn out to be *"valiente."* "Ulysses is your hair, with Alexander; because the one is subtle, and the other long." Finally, one of over four hundred lines is a burlesque rendering of the genre (OC 1:320–30). There Sor Juana is the inexperienced painter who takes brush in hand and forges fearlessly ahead. The poem describes the inept and foolish mistakes of the painter and her surprise at the way things are turning out. For example, when beginning with the obligatory description of the sitter's hair, the painter suddenly finds herself thinking of the hair of David's son Absalom, which becomes caught in a tree as he is fleeing and results in his death (2 Sam 18:9–17). She makes fun of worn-out metaphors and comments that being able to lie about the sitter's features is the true sign of the accomplished artist.[22] All that being said, however, affection and love are evident to a greater degree in the poems to the Countess of Paredes than to the Countess of Galve, the subsequent viceroy's wife.

Beyond literary form, another dimension that needs to be considered is the expected relationship between artist and patron. While the publication of *Castalian Inundation* in Spain has been seen primarily as a tribute to Sor Juana by the countess, it can equally be seen as a tribute to the countess and her family. The countess, though undoubtedly a friend, was also a member of one of the most powerful families in Spain, as was her husband. Moreover, though it contains many expressions of friendship for the countess, the volume as a whole has more works written for court festivities on the occasions of birthdays of the viceregal family and those of the members of the royal family in Spain. It concludes with *Neptuno Alegórico*, a philosophical essay with accompanying poem written in honor of the arrival of the marquis as the new viceroy. Against this background Merrim seconds Paz's judgment that the poems "express her affection more for the body politic than for the body of the vicereine."[23] This need not be seen as a cynical manipulation but rather reflects the political realities of the time, a time in which court literary entertainment was highly prized and convents could benefit from good relationships with the court. Even a writer as celebrated as Calderón de la Barca, after he was ordained a priest in 1651, was pressured by the Spanish court to continue producing plays for royal occasions. He was also subject to much criticism for doing so. To his critics he responded: "Either it is bad or good: If good, there should be no objection, if bad, I should not be ordered to write them."[24]

Literary Genres

Sor Juana, of course, was not only "ordered to write" poems for the court but received numerous commissions to compose cycles of hymns to be sung for special feasts. In fact, the vast majority of Sor Juana's religious poems were written for public celebrations and are liturgical in nature. That she regarded these commissions as merely routine, which some of her interpreters maintain, is belied by her assessment of the importance of liturgical prayer in *Devotional Exercises:* "That which is most pleasing is the prayer of many united in one method and formula in the manner that our Holy Mother Church recites the Divine Office, with the same prayers, psalms, and supplications" (OC 4:477).

Poetry

The twelve sets of eight or more hymns for major feasts make up over half of Sor Juana's religious poetry. Known as *villancicos,* they were designed as musical accompaniment for solemn vespers in the cathedrals and were a major dimension of Hispanic religious music of the sixteenth to the eighteenth centuries. Six of her *villancicos* are for feasts honoring Mary: four for the feast of the Assumption (1676, 1679, 1685, 1690), and two for the feast of the Conception of Mary (1676, 1689). One is for Christmas (1689). The other five are in honor of saints: St. Joseph (1690), two for the apostle Peter (1677, 1683), one for St. Peter Nolascus (1677), and one for St. Catherine of Alexandria (1691).[25]

Villancicos had evolved from folk music into high baroque liturgical music with chorus, soloists, and orchestra. The music for

INTRODUCTION

Sor Juana's *villancicos* has still not been found, but we do know the names of some of the composers, and it is possible to hear this type of music on contemporary recordings today.[26] Though some of the hymns are in Latin, most are in Spanish. This reflected a trend in Spain since the mid-sixteenth century to replace the Latin responsories with Spanish ones for public celebrations of major feasts. This practice continued in spite of resistance in Rome and the example of King Phillip II, who prohibited the use of the vernacular in the liturgy of the royal chapel.[27] One of the vestiges of their origin in folk traditions was that many different voices were represented in the hymns, especially in the last song, the *ensalada*, which was also expected to be humorous in order to wake people up at the end of the long service. It was the accepted space for mild ironic asides about possible misunderstandings of doctrine or time to poke fun at overly serious sacristans or overzealous theology students.

Sor Juana's *villancicos* reflect the multilingual vernacular of colonial Mexico. Two are in Nahua, the Aztec language, several in the Spanish dialect of African slaves, one partly in Portuguese, one partly in Basque.[28] Sor Juana's two *villancicos* in Nahua demonstrate her ability to write with great subtlety and poignancy in the language she would have heard growing up in the country and would have continued to hear among the servants in the convent.[29] These poems were part of a literary tradition in the colonial period of hymns and dramas in indigenous languages.[30] In the *ensalada* for the feast of the Assumption, 1685, Sor Juana includes Basque as the "language of my ancestors/grandparents" (OC 2:97–98). It is possible that she learned it from her father, the Basque Pedro Manuel de Asbaje. The most obvious evidence of Sor Juana's connection to the Portuguese culture is her critique of the sermon of the Portuguese Jesuit Vieira, but her *villancicos* for the feast of St. Peter (1977) contain a poem of twenty-four lines in Portuguese. There were many Portuguese in colonial Mexico. Many were in attendance at the viceregal court where Sor Juana had been a companion of the vicereine Leonor Carreto.[31]

I have selected a small, somewhat representative sample of the *villancicos* for translation based on those I liked best, namely, those of a lyrical rather than a satirical nature, and among these, those that best lent themselves to translation. One is from a small cycle of three hymns for the feast of the Presentation of Mary; one for the feast of the Conception of Mary; one for the feast of the Assumption. I have included one on St. Peter because it is typical of her portrayal of his weaknesses and strengths. In her autobiographical *Response* she compares herself to Peter, who followed wisdom from afar as he sat in the courtyard outside the high priest's house where Jesus was being tried. Peter is also an example of a weak instrument through whom God works great things, and Sor Juana is well aware of her own frailty as well as her remarkable intellectual and artistic gifts. The last three poems are from the feast of St. Catherine of Alexandria, whose wisdom converted the sages of Egypt who were initially her accusers and whose bloody martyrdom is represented by the Catherine wheel. There are obvious autobiographical references in some of the poems, which were written at a time when Sor Juana was experiencing criticism from detractors. They are also a wonderful tribute to a female saint who was the patron saint of the University of Mexico at the time.[32] I have also included a dedicatory poem of Sor Juana's to *Mary Conceived without Sin*, from the *villancicos* for the feast of the Assumption (1679), in which we hear her expressing her devotion to this teaching, at the time still under dispute. Three poems describing the effects of divine love are included (two under the title *"In which she expresses the effects of Divine Love and proposes to die loving, despite all risk,"* and one *"Of the loving effects of Christ in the sacrament on the day of communion").*[33] They are unique among her poems insofar as they appear to be explorations of Sor Juana's subjective state of religious devotion. Though connections to St. Teresa have been noted,[34] their level of paradox and terminological abstraction give them more the flavor of the metaphysical poets of England, especially John Donne, than of Spanish mystics. In addition, I have included one of the meditative poems on the Incarnation and a related piece, for the feast of the nativity.[35]

Sor Juana's most famous poem is *Primero Sueño* (first dream). Over nine hundred lines long, it has been interpreted as philosophical and less frequently as theological in nature.[36] I consider it a philosophical reflection in the form of a dramatic poem on the limits of human knowledge, and for that reason I do not include it here. It exerts a fascination all its own because of the complex beauty of the poetry and the density of mythological references. The poem exists in several translations, which I list in the bibliography. It is also one of the three works Sor Juana mentions in her autobiography as having written solely of her own volition, that is, not at the request of others.

Drama

Sor Juana's dramatic *oeuvre* resembles her poetic one in that it contains both secular and religious dimensions. Her secular poetry includes cycles of poems on the nature of love and flirtation popular in court circles, which shock readers today when coming from a nun, but which Sor Juana's editors in the 1690s let pass with minimal comment. Merrim makes a compelling case that these cycles, when viewed within the broader context of courtly love and poetic virtuosity collectively, can be considered an interrogation of "the passionate world of *un*reason and *not*-knowing."[37] As such, they represent Sor Juana's analytical mind at work when confronted with the human psyche rather than the expression of personal sentiments. Similarly, Sor Juana's comedies *The Trials of a Noble House* and *The Second Celestina* as well as *Love Is the Greater Labyrinth* attest to her delight in the analysis of human character and in the portrayal of human emotions. These works are not mere trifles written for convent entertainment. Sor Juana is considered the last great dramatist of the Spanish Golden age *(siglo de oro)*.[38] She wrote six full-length dramas and numerous short plays. The three just mentioned are comedies of manners. Two are in contemporary settings: *The Trials of a Noble House* and *The Second Celestina*. The third, *Love Is the Greater Labyrinth*, is based on the myth of Theseus and the Minotaur. The other three are religious dramas called *autos sacramentales*. As a type they were originally intended to be performed on the feast of Corpus Christi, the feast celebrating the presence of Christ in the Eucharist. In general, the dramatization of biblical stories and saints' lives predominated, but it was not unusual to use myths from ancient Greece and Rome as allegories for Christian truths. Calderón de la Barca, for example, in his play *El verdadero Dios Pan* (the true god Pan) takes advantage of the multiple meanings of *pan*, Spanish for "bread." Pan was also the Greek god of woodlands and fields. In Greek his name signified "all," and by extension, the universe. Another of his mythological *autos* was *El Divino Orfeo* (divine Orpheus).[39] Sor Juana wrote three of these *autos sacramentales*. Her St. *Hermenegild: Martyr for the Sacrament* is based on the life of an early Spanish martyr who died rather than take sacrilegious communion from the hands of an Arian bishop.[40] *Divine Narcissus* conflates Ovid's story of the proud and vain Narcissus with the figure of Jesus. In Ovid, Narcissus, doomed by the goddess of the hunt, Diana, for scorning the nymph Echo, falls in love with his reflected image in a pool and pines away foolishly. In Sor Juana's play Narcissus falls in love with the image he sees in the still waters of a woodland pool which symbolizes the Virgin Mary. *The Scepter of Joseph* is a retelling of the Genesis story of Joseph, who was sold into slavery by his brothers only to redeem them from hunger and desolation many years later.[41] The three plays explore the doctrine of the Eucharist from three complementary perspectives: *The Scepter of Joseph* from the perspective of Old Testament prophecy and fore-shadowing; *St. Hermenegild: Martyr for the Sacrament* from the per-spective of the believers in the mystery of the Real Presence; and *Divine Narcissus* within a broad frame of salvation history leading up to the scene of temptation in the desert, after which Narcissus finds perfect human nature reflected in the perfect humanity of Mary, falls in love, and dies for the unblemished image of human-ity in female form.

   Divine Narcissus is considered by some to be the greatest of all the *autos sacramentales* of the Spanish golden age because of the beauty of its language, the unity of conception, and the depths and complexity of its theology.[42] This is the play I have selected to translate for this volume. This does not mean that *St. Hermenengild* and *The Scepter of Joseph* are not worthy of study but merely that *Divine Narcissus* is the most complete. Indeed, it could be argued that Sor Juana meant for the three to be considered a unity, since in 1692 they were published together in the second volume of her collected works. Another indication of their belong-ing together is that each of them was prefaced by a short play, known as a *loa*, that dealt with some aspect of the meeting of cultures in the Americas. This volume appeared in the bicentennial of Columbus's first voyage. Columbus even makes an appearance in the *loa* preceding *St. Hermenengild.*

For the most part the *loas* that accompanied longer dramas were unrelated or only tangentially related to the longer *auto* that followed, much as a short movie is used to precede the feature. Sor Juana's *loas*, preceding her *autos*, however, are designed to introduce the longer play.[43] In the *loa* to *Divine Narcissus*, also included in this volume, Spain's and America's religions meet in the guise of the two couples: America and Occident, and Christian Religion and the conquistador Zeal. Though in the course of the play America and Occident are conquered, they maintain they will never surrender their own religious faith without understanding why the new religion is superior to the old. After hearing of their devotion to a god who is present in the grain and blood of the sacrificial victims of the Aztec rites, Religion undertakes to show them how the Christian God is willing to suffer, to die as sacrifice, and to become food for the faithful. In order to make it more acceptable to the New World pagans, Religion says she will combine Old World pagan myths and holy scripture to make her points. Accordingly, *Divine Narcissus* has been set up as a catechetical tool, but one that in actuality will not be performed for an indigenous audience but at the Spanish court. Not unaware of this discrepancy, Religion, who is one of the director/authors[44] of the play, declares:

> Since my only goal is to
> celebrate the Mystery,
> and since the persons
> in question are nothing more
> than abstractions depicting
> the intended meaning,
> there is nothing to contradict
> their being taken to Madrid.
> For intellectual notions
> are not hampered by distance
> or hindered by oceans. (OC 3:20)

17

SOR JUANA INÉS DE LA CRUZ

Devotional Works

As is clear by now, most of Sor Juana's religious work was written not at the request of her confessor, as in the case of so many other women religious, but due to the wishes and needs of other ecclesial constituencies.[45] Her longest cycle, thirty-one hymns, was written for the dedication of a church for Bernardine Sisters in Mexico City and was commissioned by laymen who had funded its construction.[46] In her *Response* Sor Juana mentions having written two pieces anonymously for the use of her sisters in the convent. She tells "Sor Philotea" (the pseudonym used by Bishop of Puebla Manuel Fernández de Santa Cruz) that she will send her one of them but that the other is out of print. "Only the *Exercises for the Incarnation* and the *Offerings for the Sorrows* were printed with my permission for public devotion, but without my name. I will send you some copies of them so that, if it seems good to you, you can distribute them among our sisters, the religious of your holy community, and moreover of your city. I can only send you one copy of *Sorrows* because the rest have been used up and no more can be made. I only wrote them for the devotion of my sisters many years ago, and afterward they were published" (OC 4:474). The full text reveals that Sor Juana was being disingenuous when she describes *Exercises* as being only for cloistered sisters, since she addresses variously "Reverend Fathers and Reverend Sisters" and in other places the equivalent of "ladies and gentlemen." As the *Exercises* develop, she also makes a point of directing priests who are engaged in these *Exercises* to read the Divine Office and even to engage in their customary penitential practices.

Designed as a novena leading up to the feast of the Annunciation (March 25), Sor Juana's *Exercises* build on an idea put forth in María of Ágreda's *Mystical City of God* that Mary was given knowledge of the creation of the world as a preparation for becoming the Mother of God. Sor Juana transforms this idea into a reflection on creation and its relationship to God, on God's relationship to humanity, and on Mary as the image of perfect humanity.[47] The first six days of the novena become reflections on the creation in Genesis, the last three on the order of the angels. All creation is involved in joyful praise of Mary. *Offerings for the Sorrows of Our*

18

Lady, in contrast to the *Exercises*, is very short.[48] It was extremely popular and was reprinted many times. Designed to accompany three cycles of the Rosary dedicated to Mary's suffering at the crucifixion of her Son, it combines the five sorrowful mysteries of the Rosary, a meditation on the Way of the Cross's fourteen stations, and the five words spoken at the foot of the cross. However, the starting point is at the cross itself. Mary sees the cross taken off her Son's shoulders and his stripping in preparation for being nailed to the cross. Though Mary's suffering is assumed to be greater than that of any other person, because of the transparency of her being conceived without sin, the perfection of her compassion, and the extraordinary nature of the Son she sees suffer, the prayers become a meditation on the suffering of all who watch their beloveds suffer. Mary is tormented by the suffering of her Son but also by her knowledge that for some this suffering will not be redemptive because of the hardness of their hearts. Both *Exercises* and *Offerings* contain elements of the Ignatian meditations. They call upon participants to use their imagination to focus on biblical events and inspire religious feelings. They use both to motivate participants to moral resolve to glorify God in the world through prayer and action. Both are translated here for the first time.

Theology

Sor Juana was connected to prominent churchmen through her life in various ways. As mentioned before, her reputation as a poet at court also won her commissions to write *villancicos* from the clerics who sat in the cathedral chapters of Mexico City, Puebla, and Oaxaca. When published, these works required yet another level of ecclesiastical approval from censors.[49] The first two volumes of her collected works published in Spain contain laudatory prefaces from members of nearly all the major religious orders including Jesuits, as well as other clerics in high offices, all in addition to the praises of the censors.[50] However, the views of important churchmen about Sor Juana were sometimes at odds. In 1680 she received her first major commission for a work that included poetry, but that was primarily a work of political philosophy. This literary construction was to accompany the erection of a triumphal arch welcoming the incoming viceroy, Tomás Antonio de la Cerda, Marquis de la Laguna. Fray Payo Enríquez de Rivera, at the time both archbishop and viceroy, requested that she write what became *Allegorical Neptune (Neptuno Alegórico)*[51] (OC 4:355–409). Her confessor, Antonio Núñez de Miranda, was incensed at her acceptance of the commission, which he considered too worldly for a nun, and he was not reticent about making his views known to others. Sor Juana defended herself in a recently discovered letter to him. The "arch for the church" was "my unpardonable offense, which was preceded by my having been asked three or four times and my having as many refused, until two lay magistrates came who before calling upon me called first upon the Mother Prioress and then upon me, and commanded in the name of His excellency the Archbishop that I do it because the full chapter had so voted and His Excellency approved." In this letter she also dismisses Núñez as her confessor.[52]

Ten years after the publication of *Allegorical Neptune* differing views on Sor Juana's place as a nun and writer emerged into the public arena once more. This time they coalesced around the publication of her critique of the sermon of a renowned Portuguese writer Antonio Vieira, SJ. The Bishop of Puebla, Manuel Fernández de Santa Cruz, who seems to have been a frequent visitor of Sor Juana's in the convent parlor, had requested she put in writing her views of positions taken by Vieira in a sermon on the benefits of Christ's love.[53] The theme and the issues involved allow Sor Juana to explore dimensions of the relationship of Christ to his disciples and of God to humanity as well as to critique Vieira's arguments. The final section moves beyond issues raised specifically in Vieira's sermon to an additional question of the bishop: Which was the greatest benefit of God's love, beyond those of Christ in his lifetime? There she sketches out basic arguments of a theodicy. God grants us "negative benefits" that allow suffering for our own good as well as giving us some control of our own destiny, even though this may have negative consequences for us. She concludes: "Thus I judge this the greatest demonstration of love that God does for us. May his Majesty give us the grace to recognize his benefits, and to respond to them, which shows a greater understanding. May he grant that when we consider benefits we do not remain at the level of speculative argument but go on to practical service, turning negative benefits into positive ones creating a disposition worthy to open the dam of our ingratitude, which restrains and holds in check the torrents of divine generosity" (OC 4:439).[54]

Publishing this text in November 1690 without her permission, Bishop Fernández de Santa Cruz prefaced it with a letter using the pseudonym Sor Philotea de la Cruz.[55] He also gave it a new title. Sor Juana had called it *Critique of a Sermon*. The bishop changed this to *Athenagoric Letter*, implying that it was worthy of Athena, the Greek goddess of wisdom. The letter is a curious mixture of praise and condemnation, almost as if it represents the views of two different people. It praises Sor Juana's God-given intellectual talents but condemns her for wasting them on secular rather than sacred studies. This is a strange objection since the work he is publishing is a theological one. Four months after receiving *Athenagoric Letter* Sor Juana had finished her *Response to Sor Philotea de la Cruz*. Paz has called this her "intellectual autobiography," and it is that. However, it is much more than that. Explicitly and implicitly it brings more general issues to bear: the education of women, the tradition of learned women honored for their contribution to the church, alternative interpretations of passages in scripture that diminish women. All this is implicitly based on a Christian anthropology that sees men and women as equal. The *Response* advocates for the study of the created world through reason as a preparation for the study of revealed texts. Jesus, divine beauty and wisdom incarnate, is the model for those who would search for wisdom.[56]

I am including the complete translations of these three interlocking texts. The *Critique/Athenagoric Letter* has only been translated once, in the early 1950s. The *Response* exists in several translations, but I believe linking it with the *Critique/Athenagoric Letter* in one volume is a sufficient justification for another translation. The second volume of Sor Juana's collected works (1692) opened with the *Critique/Athenagoric Letter*, a sign of the high esteem in which it was held. The letter of "Sor Philotea" (Bishop Manuel Fernández de Santa Cruz), after its initial publication in Mexico, was not published again until the posthumous third volume appeared in 1700; this volume also contained Sor Juana's *Response*. I am placing a translation of the bishop's letter before the *Response* rather than before the *Critique/Athenagoric Letter* because that was the order in which they were written. I have decided to include the bishop's letter because of the controversy surrounding it and Sor Juana's response to it. This will allow for an easier examination of the cause-and-effect relationship of the three "letters," which has been the subject of intense analysis and speculation by twentieth-century readers of Sor Juana, including myself.[57]

There has been so much written about Sor Juana's life after the publication of *Critique/Athenagoric Letter* that a summary of the discussion can hardly do it justice. A few points here must suffice. Some interpreters maintain that Sor Juana was convinced by the bishop's arguments and withdrew from the world.[58] The majority of critics see the publication of the *Critique/Athenagoric Letter* as provoking a negative response among the clergy in Mexico City in spite of the support obvious in Spain, where the second volume of her collected works had been published in 1692. Núñez de Miranda, who was also head of the Inquisition, and whom Sor Juana had dismissed a decade earlier, may have been offended by this vigorous attack on the arguments of his fellow Jesuit, Vieira. The archbishop at the time, Francisco Aguiar y Seijas, known for his aversion to women, may have taken offense that an author whose sermons he had published in Spanish in Mexico would come under such sharp critique from a woman. Sor Juana's friend the countess had returned to Spain. All these factors would contribute to Sor Juana's feelings of isolation and could have led to discouragement and eventual capitulation to the pre-dominating view of the limitations of a nun's vocation.

The text of Sor Juana's *Response* deflects both positions, at least in the immediate aftermath of the publication of *Critique/Athenagoric Letter*. First she says that the bishop cannot mean she should stop writing works such as the *Critique/Athenagoric Letter*, because it is "dealing with the book of Jesus Christ." Second, it is clear throughout Sor Juana's narrative of her life's struggle for wisdom that this struggle has taken place under difficult circumstances, many of them caused by those close to her who have not understood her vocation. However, the overall tone of the *Response* is not fear of impending punishment but anger and indignation at the wrong done her by the publication of her work without her permission. It is clear that the bishop's letter provoked Sor Juana's indignation and resulted in her writing the *Response to Sor Philotea*, which some would argue is her most brilliant work.[59] Many scholars have emphasized Sor Juana's critique of misogynist attitudes and practices in the church as an indication of her condemnation of the church itself. Such a position, however, fails to consider seriously Sor Juana's many statements of loyalty to the church. Indeed, in the *Response* she argues that church tradition supports her advocacy for women since it honors and values the wisdom of women—Mary being the stellar example, but also many women saints "canonized or not."

In my opinion it has not yet been conclusively proven that the writing of *Critique/Athenagoric Letter* precipitated a life crisis.[60] Was she forced by ecclesiastical pressure to withdraw from public life at a later point in time?[61] Beginning with Octavio Paz, who found that there is no evidence that for her part Sor Juana made a decision to stop writing, scholars have begun to move her "withdrawal from public life" to a date two years after the publication of *Critique/Athenagoric Letter*. Several short documents in the convent archives, as well as the account of her earliest biographer, Calleja, placed this withdrawal or conversion in 1693. More recently, Trabulse has developed the theory of a secret ecclesiastical administrative threat that led Sor Juana to retreat unwillingly from activities that were considered by some too worldly for a cloistered nun.[62]

There is another way to understand her withdrawal from public life. That is to understand it as temporary.[63] According to the series of short documents in the convent archives written in 1693 and 1694, Sor Juana decided to celebrate the twenty-fifth anniversary of her monastic profession by reaffirming her vows. She took the surprising step of returning to Núñez, the confessor she had dismissed a decade earlier, but he was also her confessor at the time of her first pronouncement of vows. There may have been an intended symbolic symmetry in her return to him. She made a general confession and formally applied to be accepted to the process of renewal. She gave most of the books in her famous library to the archbishop, according to her first biographer, Calleja, to be sold to raise money for the poor and so that others would have the benefit of reading them. Such an act reflects sacrifice and almsgiving, part of penitential practice. In 1694 convent records attest that she completed the process, as it registers her renewal of vows.[64] I find it plausible to attribute the apparent diminishing of her literary activity in the last years of her life as due in part to this year-long spiritual retreat.[65] Also, the degree to which this year was in all senses a retreat from the world has to be set in the context of Sor Juana's continuing activity as the nun responsible for the financial workings of the convent, a position necessitating regular contact with the major domo of the convent and involvement in mundane affairs, such as supplying the convent with food, directing construction projects or repairs, and administering convent properties.[66] When she died a year later during an epidemic that swept through the convent, a poem, "To the Pens of Europe" (OC 1:158–61), her reflection on the critical acclaim that the second volume of her collected works was receiving, was found in her cell. A list of books from the convent archives indicate that she had begun rebuilding her collection. Both of these are signs that the scope of her concerns embraced both the secular and the sacred even to the very end of her life.

Though in many respects Sor Juana's works do not seem particularly self-revelatory, if one looks at them in their entirety they reveal a multidimensional personality participating intensely with both faith and reason within the ecclesial community and the world. Though not a mystic, she was a poet, religious writer, theologian, and faithful Catholic. Her experience of self, both within the cloister and through her relations with those "in the world," is reflected back to us through the prism of her faith as well as the inevitable influences of the age in which she lived. Her religious reflection makes great use of the imagination through her dramatic and poetic works. This reflection moves her to action, that is, to the writing of her works, to the defense of women, and to complex relationships with the rulers of Mexico. In short, Sor Juana's works reflect an understanding of her experience of herself as a creature of God, a daughter of the church, an intellectual, a poet, and a woman.

An Invitation to a Theological Reading of Sor Juana Inés de la Cruz

Sor Juana's religious writings contain numerous themes that are of interest to contemporary theologians. She is fascinated by the relationship between religion and culture, as is obvious in the *loa* to *Divine Narcissus* as well as the other *loas* preceding her sacramental dramas. She has a nuanced view of the relationship of the artist and the representation of doctrine in art, as we see in *Divine Narcissus* where one of the "authors" of the play is "fallen angelic nature." The scope and variety of her work as an artist allow much room for exploration of the aesthetic dimension of theology and the relationship between beauty and doctrine. She is aware of the interlocking of secular disciplines and also of the interrelatedness of theological disciplines. All of the formal theological topics are represented in some form in her work: creation, Christology, ecclesiology, the sacraments, veneration of the saints, missiology, anthropology. Development of these themes in Sor Juana's work is waiting to be done. In the following section I consider briefly three themes central to Sor Juana's thinking: Mary's conception free of sin; God's loving relationship with humanity; and the call of God to wisdom and learning.

Mary, Conceived without Sin

There are several indications that this teaching was an important part of Sor Juana's personal devotional life. One may be deduced from the habit she wore. Hieronymite nuns wore a large papier-maché medallion fastened to the front of their formal habit. Each nun could choose a saint or biblical scene to which she had a particular devotion. In the most famous portraits of Sor Juana, one by Juan de Miranda and another by Miguel Cabrera, both painted after her death, the scene on the medallion is of the annunciation, depicting Mary and the angel Gabriel.[67] However, in an engraved portrait in the opening pages of the second volume of her collected works, published in 1692, the figure on the medallion is Mary Immaculate. This would have been the only depiction of her medallion Sor Juana herself would have seen, and it is a good indication of the importance this doctrine had for her. There are also numerous other indications. In 1694 Sor Juana twice entered a vow to defend the doctrine of the Immaculate Conception into convent archives, one in conjunction with her renewal of vows, which she signed with her blood. Contemporary readers may find this repulsive and indicative of an unhealthy desire for self-abnegation, but it was a common practice at the time.[68] She made these vows in part because the doctrine had been under attack, and Spanish theologians had petitioned Rome again and again to settle the disputed issue. It was not until 1661 during the papacy of Alexander VII that the teaching that the Virgin Mary "had been preserved from the stain of original sin from the first instant of her conception" was declared an object of faith. And it was not until 1696 that Rome mandated a feast for the Immaculate Conception be celebrated in the universal church, as were Christmas and the Assumption.[69] However, Sor Juana's interest in and devotion to the Immaculate Conception is not limited to the two documents in the convent records. Mary's "conception," as it was still called at the time, was the subject of two of Sor Juana's *villancicos*, one in 1676, the other in 1689, comprising sixteen poems in all. She also wrote a short play the subject of which was the debate over the doctrine (OC 3:259–79).[70] We find a text similar to that in the vow in the early *Devotional Exercises*, one of the three works she claims in the *Response* to have written wholly of her own volition. There she calls upon the participants to "vow to defend it [the Immaculate Conception] to the fullest extent possible, even to the point of spilling our blood in defense of this doctrine, and we hope, our Lady and our supreme good, to merit dying in your service" (OC 4:491–92).

In addition to being part of her religious devotion, the Immaculate Conception is central to Sor Juana's theology. We see this in the *Devotional Exercises*. Building on María of Agreda's idea that one of the favors God granted Mary because of her sinlessness was to "show her the creation of the universe," Sor Juana structures her novena to follow the seven days of creation. Mary is introduced as "Princess Immaculate" in the first paragraph. The second paragraph speaks of "the incarnation of the Eternal Word

INTRODUCTION

in the pure womb of most holy Mary, conceived without stain of original sin." As such, she is worthy of the honors God showered upon her and has a unique bond to the Creator. At each step what is created on that day praises Mary, exulting in that connection. "Earth sees herself the envy of the heavenly gardens, which, though they have pure angelic substances springing forth eternally from them, have never produced a rose with beauty to equal this one of royal purple. Earth rejoices because as the center of the universe she can represent most Holy Mary as the center of all virtues. She rejoices in being called the common mother of all living things, as our most sweet mother Mary is called with more justification" (OC 4:482).[71] Something analogous occurs in the *villancicos* for the feast of the Conception when the elements are personified and engage in debates about who is more worthy to be associated with Mary: the stars because they are her crown, the moon as her footstool, and so on. This personification is more than a literary device. By implication other creatures have a voice in creation and actively participate in a relationship with God. After Adam's transgression he was "rejected by his inferiors. The elements and the rest of the creatures rebelled against him" (OC 4:490).

It is through Mary that "the perfection of all the universe was restored" (OC 4:495), and "for this reason it is not only human beings who are in Mary's debt but all the other creatures as well because she gives them perfection and nobility" (OC 4:490). At the end of the sixth day of the *Devotional Exercises*, which completes the creation of the physical universe, the faithful are called upon to praise her: "Long live the queen of all humanity, the honor of nature, the crown of the human race, the restorer of our honor lost through Adam, the glory of Jerusalem, the joy of Israel, the supreme honor of our Christian people, the restorer of the image of God in nature, the ultimate perfection of all creation" (OC 4:491). We find this same idea expressed in the poetry of the *villancicos* for the feast of the Conception in 1689 (OC 4:100–101). All creatures remain indebted to Mary, for perfection, joy, grace, and loveliness.[72] Mary is greater than the angels. "She keeps and shelters humankind with more care and love than the angels; she participates in the divine secrets and proclaims them better than the archangels; she performs greater marvels and miracles than the virtues. Her majesty alone represents the incomprehensible mystery of the most blessed Trinity with a perfection greater than the three sovereign choirs of angels" (OC 4:495).

Participation in divine life, or the life of grace, and the corresponding transformation are linked especially to Mary. In the play *Divine Narcissus* Mary must be conceived without sin in order to mirror Narcissus perfectly and to be the object of Divine "falling in love." On the one hand, God willingly became like us so that we could love him; on the other hand, as Grace says in *Divine Narcissus*, it was God's "own likeness" that God had to love "because only God can be a worthy object of God's love" (OC 3:93). God became human "for all, from compassion,/ for her, from love's passion," as she writes in one of her poems on the Incarnation. In one of the hymns for Bernadine nuns she includes the expression "Mary is not God, but she is the one who most resembles God" (OC 2:211). In one of her *villancicos* for the feast of the Assumption, 1679, a poem that appears to describe a painting of the Assumption, she has the three Divine Persons coming out to greet Mary as "Daughter, Mother, and Spouse" (OC 2:71). However, it is in the last four days of *Devotional Exercises* where the connection of Mary to the Trinity is most developed. There the angels swear allegiance to her as "the one who enjoyed the unutterable favors of the blessed Trinity…according to the three prerogatives…communicated to her by the three divine Persons: power, wisdom, and love" (OC 4:503).

Mary is Mother of God and mother of humanity. Sor Juana presses all the implications of the ancient title Mother of God as a vehicle to express the relationship of Mary's humanity to divinity.

> Oh, may that same Lord help me, who enclosed himself in this phrase: Mother of God! Mother of God? No wonder she is the queen of the world! Mother of God? Of course all people must render her homage! Mother of God? No wonder the elements become her vassals! Mother of God? For this reason the heavens bow down before her! Mother of God? It is only just that the angels swear her allegiance as their queen! All this is

INTRODUCTION

appropriate, all is included, all is embraced, all is merited in the one who is Mother of God! (OC 4:503)

Mary is "mother of the eternal Word" but also the second Eve, not in the traditional sense of the *ave/Eva* comparison, in which Mary's obedience is contrasted to the disobedience of Eve, but a second Eve as "mother of all living." Sor Juana praises Mary for deigning to "be the mother of humankind" (OC 4:505). She thanks Mary for being "so merciful" and enabling humanity to become related to her Son. "It is through you that we see ourselves, as entitled to be part of the royal house of the Lord, who treats us as and calls us his kin" (OC 4:505). She underscores this in a rare personal aside: "I, for myself, know that if it were possible to exchange the miseries of my human nature for the privileges and perfections of angelic nature, thereby losing the relation we have of family ties with Mary most holy, I would not accept them, even if I could, in view of this, and in consideration of the fact that I cherish and appreciate with all my heart being of her lineage" (OC 4:500–501).

The faithful are inspired to become ethically and spiritually transformed in view of their relationship to Mary and Christ's humanity. An especially poignant passage is on the sixth day of the novena when the faithful are asked

> to abstain from envy, because if we need to love the image of God and if this image is in other people, it is clear that we need to love them, and loving them and envying them are in no way compatible. Let us consider how if an image of the Lord made of wood or bronze moves us to veneration and reverence, how much more the living image and likeness which is that of our neighbors? Do you dare to wish evil to a child of God and of the Virgin, and a brother or sister of Christ? Furthermore all of us are, although not naturally, sons and daughters of God and Mary and brothers and sisters of Christ our Lord. They are images made in the likeness of God, and Christ is the image of God made in the likeness of humankind. Behold this mutual loving rela-

29

tionship! So how can you hate and desire evil for someone whom God loves and desires the good? (OC
4:493–494)

God's Loving Relationship with Humanity

Sor Juana's understanding of the nature of the loving relationship between God and humanity as one of *relative* equality is
most explicitly worked out in her theological treatise,
Critique/Athenagoric Letter. The discursive, even polemical, nature
of this work allows her to develop her position more directly than
is possible in her poetic and dramatic works. However, it is present by implication wherever there is the metaphor of spousal love,
as in *Divine Narcissus*, especially in her reworking of the *Song of
Songs.* We also find it in abundance in the *Devotional Exercises* and
in many of her poems celebrating Mary, where she elaborates on
God's fascination with the beauty of Mary/humanity. Many other
of the *villancicos*, such as #306 and #309 for the feast of the
Assumption, 1690, celebrate Mary's loveliness in the midst of
celestial and earthly creatures (OC 2:152–57). This beauty, though
a reflection of Narcissus's (Christ's) own beauty, is unique or different enough to evoke feelings of yearning, joy at encounter, sorrow at separation.

Her metaphors of spousal love in *Critique/Athenagoric Letter*
contrast sharply with that of her discussion partner, the Jesuit
Antonio Vieira, whose metaphor for the relationship of Christ to
his disciples is that of master/slave. From the Old Testament, Sor
Juana compares God/Christ's love to Jacob's courtship of Rachel
and contrasts it to Ahasuerus's of Esther. For God, as for human
lovers, the perfect gift or benefit *(fineza)* must "cost the lover and
profit the beloved" (OC 4:416). This idea is already evident in her
earlier *Devotional Exercises:* "Since he [God] knew that all things
love their equal, and since he so desired that we love him, he did
not spare himself the effort of becoming like us so that we would
love him" (OC 4:493). It is Christ's death that is his perfect gift
because it cost him more than any other demonstration of love,
and it benefited humanity more by bringing with it redemption
(OC 4:415–18). Sor Juana, while not maintaining that God needs

our response in an absolute sense, points out that scripture is full of evidence that God desires our response. Indeed, not only does scripture show that God/Christ desires to be in relationship with us, but God insists on it, coaxes, rages, pleads, and finally becomes incarnate in order to die for it. "Oh, the beauty of divine Love that calls what is a benefit to us an honor for you! Oh, the wisdom of God! Oh, the generosity of God! And, oh, what a demonstration of love worthy only of God! For this God wants our love for our good, not for his. The beauty of his gift of love is not, as the author maintains, to desire our love in return, but that he desires this very thing for our sake" (OC 4:432).

The loving response involves obligation voluntarily assumed on the part of lover and beloved. Thus because God through Christ willingly assumed equality with humanity, humanity has the capacity and the responsibility to respond. Christ's love for humanity differs from the love of human lovers for each other in two respects: Christ does not need our love; his love alone is sufficient for our good. Why then, Sor Juana asks, "would he solicit our love at all since without it he can still benefit us by loving us?" (OC 4:431). The answer is that God solicits the response of our love freely given. In giving us free will God has given us "the power to desire or not to desire to do good or evil" (OC 4:431). And she insists: "When we do not exercise it we suffer violence to ourselves, because it is a tribute that God has granted us and a deed of authentic liberty that he has awarded us....This liberty is the reason that it is not enough for God to desire to be ours, if we do not desire to be God's" (OC 4:431).

A corollary of this liberty is that we can express our love for God in ways that not even Christ could do: resist temptation and fear the dangers of sin (OC 4:429). Sor Juana sees the apostle Paul's idea of completing the sufferings of Christ (Col 1:24) as support for her point. Paul's struggles against temptation and sin are demonstrations of love that Christ himself cannot give. Here she draws support from Gregory the Great, who connected original sin to the act of conception. Thus all humans are burdened with the *fomes peccati*, which inclines them to sin by consent or pleasure, but Christ, whose natural origin was of "miraculous conception" did not participate in humanity's fallen nature.[73] There

31

was no willing against the good within him, and thus the temptations he did experience were of an "extrinsic" nature. The temptation scene in *Divine Narcissus* shows Narcissus supremely self-confident when, without a moment's hesitation, he rebukes Echo (Fallen Angelic Nature).

Beyond obligation and responsibility, the relationship of loving response presupposes a willingness to suffer for the beloved. Mary's suffering because of the torments inflicted on her Son, but also because of the sins of humanity, is the subject of *Offerings for the Sorrows*. Christ's suffering unto death is the greatest gift of God's love, greater than the Incarnation, according to *Critique/Athenagoric Letter*. "The Word became flesh and for love of us overcame the immense distance between God and humanity. He died and overcame the bounds of death. Clearly he perceived his death as overcoming the greater distance, since when he reminded us of his love and entrusted his memory to us, he did not remind us of his incarnation and did emphasize his death" (OC 4:416). In *Divine Narcissus* this emphasis on the suffering and death of Christ has an added nuance. Though the scene of Narcissus's plunge into death in the fountain is constructed to include the last words of Jesus from the gospels, in a curious twist Narcissus "gives permission to death" (OC 3:78), leaving the impression that it is not only the humanity of Christ that suffers but God himself. Strengthening this impression are the words coming from offstage after the death of Narcissus, the subsequent earthquake, eclipse, and so on:

Either the Author of the universe is suffering,
Or the machinery of the world is perishing. (OC 3:81)

If Mary's beauty is that of the original human *imago Dei*, Christ is the beautiful image of God incarnate. "If we behold his image which quality is more lovable than divine beauty? Which with more power to enrapture the heart? If mere human beauty holds sway over free will, subjecting it with sweet, alluring violence, what would Christ's beauty with its many prerogatives and sovereign gifts not have had the power to do?" (OC 4:453–54). And in a description that is clearly meant to be a reference to

Teresa's image of the presence of God as a diamond at the center of the soul, she continues: "What would the incomprehensible beauty of his lovely face, which as through a prism renders transparent the glory of the Divinity, do, or not do, move or not move?" In fact, it is in connection with this portion of the *Response* that Sor Juana makes one of her rare explicit references to St. Teresa: "The holy mother, my mother Teresa, said that after she saw the beauty of Christ she remained free of all inclination to any creature (OC 4:453–54).[74] In *The Interior Castle* Teresa writes of the Lord as being the most beautiful and delightful person imaginable as experienced in imaginative visions. The pains of hell, she writes, would be nothing compared to the pain inflicted by seeing anger at one's sins reflected in his beautiful eyes.[75] Yet in stark contrast to the Christ of judgment in *The Interior Castle*, Sor Juana's Christ is being judged and condemned by the Pharisees: "If merely conversing with God face to face made Moses' countenance unbearable to behold (Ex 34:29–30), what would be the impact of this same God incarnate?…How could they not love him? O my God, for these very reasons they did not love him; for these reasons they hated him! They themselves have born witness to it" (OC 4:453–54). This image of vulnerability of the Divine in the world finds expression also in *Divine Narcissus* when Grace comments:

Even for God in the world
there is no love without danger. (OC 3:93)

The Call to Wisdom and Learning

Sor Juana's greatest argument for her intellectual activities is that God has given her the gift of an insatiable desire for knowledge and wisdom. It is a drive or a call, she repeats again and again in the *Response*, a curse and a joy, and she compares it to Paul's "thorn in the flesh." On another level it is more than a personal call. It reflects God's desire that creation be understood by the human mind. To underscore this Sor Juana calls upon an idea her contemporaries would have found familiar: the world as God's book. At one time, as she recounts in the *Response*, when she was prohibited from reading for reasons of health, she writes: "Although I did not study in books, I directed my study to all the things God has made. They became my letters, and my book was the machinery of the universe. There was nothing I saw that I did not reflect upon. There was nothing I heard that I did not ponder, even the smallest and most material of things. Because there is no creature, no matter how lowly, in which the *me fecit Deus* [God made me] cannot be found. There is not one that does not fill the mind with wonder if considered as it deserves. And so I, I repeat, observed and admired them all" (OC 4:458). By implication even the smallest physical object is worthy of study for religious reasons.

Not only are the objects in creation worthy of study and wonder, but their interrelationship as investigated in the various disciplines give witness to the will of the Creator that the human mind strive for understanding of the natural world and the world of human affairs. Far from obstructing one another, the abstract disciplines "help one another, giving light and opening paths to one another through variations and hidden connections. The wisdom of their Author put them in a universal chain, in such a way that they appear to correspond to one another and to be united with admirable consistency and agreement. This is the chain that the ancients imagined came from the mouth of Jupiter, through which all things were linked together....All things come from God, who is the center and at the same time the circumference from which the lines of all created things come and to which they all tend" (OC 4:450).[76]

An idea less accepted but not unknown at the time was that the Creator also wanted the mind of woman to engage in learning. In *Response* she refers to "our Arce," a scriptural scholar in Mexico who answered the question of whether women should study scripture in the affirmative.[77] Sor Juana's own experience is that her intellect is a divine gift from God. Based on this experience she argues against a simplistic suspicion of learning that would see it as, by definition, detrimental to women's salvation. In the 1682 letter to Father Núñez she writes: "That St. Anthony was saved in his holy ignorance is well and good. St. Augustine chose the other path, and neither of them went astray."[78] Her defense of women's learning is also based on her experience of God's relationship to women as human beings. "Like men, do they not have a rational soul? Why then shall they not enjoy the privilege of the enlightenment of letters? Is a woman's soul not as receptive to God's grace and glory as a man's? Then why is she not as able to receive learning and knowledge, which are the lesser gifts? What divine revelation, what regulation of the church, what rule of reason framed for us such a severe law?"[79] Indeed, one of the main points of the *Response* is that the church is missing a great deal by not letting women be of greater service. There is also a tradition of religious women arguing that their religious insights, visions, and prophecies are from God and therefore cannot be disobeyed. In her sequence of hymns for the dedication of a church for Bernadine nuns, Sor Juana even speaks of her own desire to preach, at the same time insisting in the refrain that she "is not cut of such fine cloth" (OC 2:202–3). In her partly autobiographical *villancicos* for the feast of Catherine of Alexandria she writes of Catherine using the present tense:

> She studies, argues, and teaches,
> All in service of the church,
> Since the one who gave her the gift of reason
> did not mean for her to be ignorant. (OC 2:171)

But it is Mary above all who is a model for women's wisdom, learning, and creativity. The invocation of Mary in language typical of the titles and functions of the Holy Spirit has been typical of Marian piety for centuries. Sor Juana plays along this vast register with skill and dexterity. A few examples among many must suffice here. On the first day of the *Devotional Exercises* Mary is introduced as advocate (OC 4:121–22), and so she is also in the *villancicos* (OC 2:10–13). "Her eloquence knows how to move the Eternal Judge to clemency" (OC 2:13). The faithful implore her to keep them in peace and justice and to "defend us with spirit against the infernal opposite" (OC 2:15). The *villancicos* are replete with references to Mary as comforter, help, refuge, and healer (OC 2:60–62). "She is the blessed herb," the "antidote to all poisons" (OC 2:21–22). However, in view of Sor Juana's own personal concerns, Mary is associated with wisdom to an extraordinary degree. She is invoked as a guide on the way to wisdom: "Queen of Light, more beautiful than material light, since you illumine the heavens with your splendor, illumine our souls with your gifts; and because you are the nearest to the faultless, inaccessible Light of the divine Essence, send us a ray of this divine Light to enlighten our understanding, so that freed from the darkness of human ignorance, we may contemplate heavenly things" (OC 4:478). Celebrated for her possession of the wisdom of heavenly things, she is "Queen of Wisdom, more learned and wise than the Queen of Sheba" (1 Kgs 10:1–13; 2 Chr 9:1–12), having "enjoyed the instruction of the true Solomon." She is called upon to help the faithful acquire "from His Majesty…true wisdom, which is virtue and the intelligence of heavenly things in order to inflame us with love of you and of your Son. For nine months your most pure womb was the chamber and sanctuary of Eternal Wisdom. Illumine our souls, most gracious teacher, and liberate us from all error" (OC 4:486). More generally, she shares the light of divine insight with the "Sun of Justice" and communicates it to the souls of those who turn to her.

In a less conventional sense Mary is portrayed as having the equivalent of contemporary scientific knowledge of the heavens. In one *villancico* she is celebrated as the great astronomer, who knows the celestial realm, the constellations of the Zodiac, the moon, and the sun (OC 2:65–66). Her scientific wisdom exceeds that of all the learned men throughout history:

> What a sight to behold our great Lady's supreme wisdom, through which she knew with perfect intuition all the natures and qualities of these luminous bodies: their influences, rotations, motions, retrogradations, eclipses, conjunctions, the waning and waxing of the moon, and all the effects that can be produced in sublunary bodies, the generation of rain, hail, ice and the terrifying flash of thunderbolts. She knew with absolute clarity and understanding all the causes of these marvelous effects that for so many centuries have held in abeyance and fatigued the understanding of the most scrupulous of

men without their arriving at a perfect knowledge of them. (OC 4:485)

Mary is also Sor Juana's ultimate justification for her calling as a poet: "The Queen of Wisdom and our Lady with her holy lips intoned the Canticle of the Magnificat (Luke 1:46–55). Since I am using her as an example, it would be insulting and goes beyond necessary proof to use profane examples, even though they be by serious and learned men" (OC 4:470).

Whereas Mary represents the transformation of the individual to participation in divine life through searching and finding wisdom under a joyful, hopeful aspect, the dark side, or the difficulties inherent in following this path, are represented by Christ and Peter. In the *Response* the pain Christ suffers from the crown of thorns in his "mock coronation" is contrasted to the mere shamefulness of the "crimson cloak" and "hollow reed."

> Why was it only the crown that was painful? Was it not enough that, as was the case for the other devices, it resulted in scorn and ignominy, since that was its purpose? No, because the sacred head of Christ and that that divine brain were the deposit of wisdom. And for the world, it is not enough that wise brain is scorned; it has to be injured and mistreated. A head that is a storehouse of wisdom can hope for no other crown than that of thorns. What garland can human wisdom expect, seeing what divine wisdom attained? (OC 4:455)

The weeping women accompanying Jesus through their tears attest their sorrow at this injury done to wisdom: "Coming out to see this sorrowful triumph, reminiscent of the triumph of that other Solomon, the daughters of Zion (Luke 23:28), then joyful, but now sorrowful, celebrated him with weeping, corresponding to the manner in which wisdom triumphs" (OC 4:456). Sor Juana's concluding remark emphasizes Christ's emblematic role: "Christ, as king of wisdom, wearing that crown for the first time, sanctified it on his temples and took away the horror of it for those who are wise, demonstrating that they should aspire to no greater honor" (OC 4:456).

Two sequences (1677 and 1683) of Sor Juana's *villancicos* are dedicated to Peter, the prince of the apostles, who was chosen to lead the church in spite of his weakness. In the *Response* Sor Juana sees Peter as inspirational in an unusual interpretation of the classic passage of his denial of Christ in the courtyard of the high priest's residence. Here Christ is Wisdom personified, and Peter is following, albeit "at a distance."

> There was a time when the prince of the apostles found himself far removed from wisdom as this phrase emphasizes: *Petrus vero sequebator eum a longe* [Peter then followed him at a distance—Luke 22:54]. So far from the applause of the learned was he, that he was given the title of ignorant. *Nesciens quid diceret* [Not knowing what he said—Luke 9:33]. Even when examined about his knowledge of Wisdom, he said that he did not have the slightest notion: *Mulier, nescio quid dicis. Mulier, non novi illum* [Woman, I do not know what you are saying—Luke 22:60. Woman, I do not know him—Luke 22:57]. And what happened to him? In spite of his reputation as one of the ignorant, he did not have their good fortune but suffered the afflictions of the wise. Why? No other reason is given than this: *Et hic cum illo erat* [And he was with him—Luke 22:56]. He loved wisdom and carried it in his heart; he walked according to her ways; he prized himself on being a follower and lover of wisdom. Even this was so much *a longe* [at a distance] that he had not understood or attained it. Even this proximity was sufficient for him to incur its torments. There was no lack of a soldier to afflict him, or of a servant woman to affront him. I confess that I have found myself very distant from the goals of wisdom and that I have desired to follow her, although *a longe*. However, everything has conspired to draw me closer to the fire of persecution, to the crucible of torment. (OC 4:457–58)

INTRODUCTION

Though Sor Juana does refer to St. Teresa as her mother, her relationship to that outstanding Spanish seeker and sufferer for mystical wisdom, as well as to her friend, John of the Cross, has yet to be explored. In addition to their fascination with the beauty of Christ mentioned above, both women understood the *imago Dei* as the foundation of humanity's dignity, even glory. Teresa considered the soul as *imago Dei* an idea so marvelous as to be only accessible through divine revelation. In as far as the soul is the image and likeness of God, who is ultimately unknowable, she writes that it is "almost impossible for us to understand the sublime dignity and beauty of the soul."[80] An additional reference to Teresa may be seen in Sor Juana's *Divine Narcissus*, where Narcissus falls in love with his image reflected in the crystal pool where Grace and Human Nature become one. In the opening chapters of *The Interior Castle* Teresa develops the image of the soul as a castle "made entirely out of a diamond or of a very clear crystal.[81] At the center of the castle the sun (God) "does not lose its beauty and splendor; it is always present in the soul, and nothing can take away its loveliness."[82] Sor Juana goes beyond this to envision not only the soul but the entire person, body and soul, as imaging the Divine because both were willed at the creation to reflect this image back to the Creator. Teresa also compares the soul of the just person to a "crystal-clear fount."[83] In *Divine Narcissus* Mary, again, is the clear pool allowing human nature and grace to reflect a clear image of God's original intent toward humanity. Hers is also the reflection in the pool with which Narcissus/Christ/God falls in love. He is willing to die for this image:

> the divine image
> of the one who is full of grace.
> O divine Fountain, O wellspring
> of life-giving waters!
> From your life's first instant
> you were spared
> the primal poison
> of the transcendental fault
> infesting all other rivers. (OC 3:54)

There are passages in *Divine Narcissus* in which the language clearly relates to that of John of the Cross's *Spiritual Canticle*, in which the bride asks the "crystalline fountain" *(Oh cristalina fuente)* if it has ever reflected back the eyes of the bridegroom, which are imprinted deep in her heart.[84] In his theological commentary on the poem John of the Cross explains that the Bride is the Soul and Christ is the bridegroom. The fountain is faith, which is crystalline, coming from Christ. Faith is a font of truth leading to all other spiritual goods.[85] In *Divine Narcissus* Grace has just urged Human Nature to place herself in a position at the fountain so "seeing your face reflected in the waters he will recognize his image and fall in love with you" (OC 3:55), after which both characters invoke the fountain: "Oh, siempre cristalina, / clara y hermosa Fuente." [Oh, fountain ever crystal/clear and lovely]. Though apparently inspired by John of the Cross's language and images, Sor Juana attributes different meanings to the images. In *Divine Narcissus* the fountain is not faith, but is, as mentioned before, the Virgin Mary, perfect image of humanity as created by God in the original goodness of creation. By honoring her, the faithful "are drawn up as on a cord" into the divine life (OC 2:17). And not just the faithful, but the potential faithful are meant to be included. The *Divine Narcissus* and its accompanying *loa*, which serves as a preface to the longer drama, stress that the peoples of the Americas are also intended to be caught up in this love affair between God and humanity.

This brief comparison with St. Teresa and St. John of the Cross illustrates that Sor Juana's writings do not stress interior states to the same extent that theirs do. If she deals with mystical themes, it is always based on scriptural argument or on the analysis of traditional authorities, church doctrine, or through the appreciation of the voices from popular culture.[86] Just as in her life she remained involved both in the world and in the convent, in her religious writing interiority is dependent on exteriority. Her piety, fervor, devotion, and ethical response are inspired by what God has made: the things of creation, and the words of divine revelation, including the incarnation of the Word in Jesus and its continuance in the church. Sor Juana's writing is also informed and inspired by the things women and men have made in response to

God's working through nature and revelation in governance, sciences, the arts.

Note on Translations

The translations have been based on the critical edition of *Obras Completas* edited by Alfonso Méndez Plancarte (vols. 1–3) and Alberto G. Salceda (vol. 4). This has been an invaluable resource, not only for consultation of variants from different editions, but because of the extensive scholarly notes, especially in volumes 1–3 by Alfonso Méndez Plancarte, who devoted his life to the edition, dying before finishing the fourth volume, which his admirer and collaborator Alberto Salceda brought to completion. Méndez Plancarte chose to divide Sor Juana's work into volumes based on genre rather than to edit and annotate the original editions of her collected works. The original editions included *Volume 1, Castalian Spring (Inundación Castalida)* (1689); *Volume 2* (Seville, 1692); and *Volume 3, Fame and Postumas Works (Fama y obras Póstumas)* (1700). Each of these contains poetry, plays, and prose. In the Méndez Plancarte/Salceda edition, published between 1951 and 1957, volume 1 contains *lírica personal* (poetry of a personal nature); volume 2, *villancicos y letras sacras* (*villancicos* and religious poetry); volume 3, *autos y loas* (religious dramas and short plays); and volume 4, *comedias, sainetes, y prosa* (comedies, light dramatic skits, and prose).

As a general principle I have tried to make the translation as clear and readable as possible without sacrificing entirely Sor Juana's sense of style. I have often shortened extremely long sentences, but not to the extent of losing all the dramatic effects of her way of composition. In translating the individual poems, as well as the verse of the dramas, I have not attempted to rhyme but have tried to do a line-by-line translation using alliteration and poetic turns of phrase that convey the flow of the verses without trying to imitate the meter. Though I have tried to stay as close to a literal translation as possible, I have taken poetic license when I felt it necessary to maintain some of the beauty of the original.

I have made the decision to use inclusive language in certain cases. For the Spanish equivalent of *man* I use "humanity," and depending on the context, I use "we" or "they" in order to avoid masculine pronoun referents to humanity. When *brothers* are obviously inclusive, I have used "brothers and sisters." Sor Juana was acutely aware of the power of language to define women, and it seems to me appropriate that a contemporary translation of her work would follow her in this direction. I have translated Sor Juana's Latin references from the Vulgate myself.

Section 1

Villancicos and Devotional Poems

VILLANCICOS in Praise of the Virgin Mary and the Saints

Poem II for the Feast of the Presentation of Our Lady[1]

Refrain

Ay, ay, ay, beautiful girl
in your lovely attire!
Ay, ay, ay, what lovely
steps you take!   (Song 8:1)

Verses

Girl, hardly had you
begun to walk,
when you had
the desire to fly,
Ay, ay, ay, what lovely
steps you take!   10

Up the high steps
ceaselessly you climb,
since ascending is for you
a natural inclination.
Ay, ay, ay, what lovely
steps you take!

Those who brought you,
you leave behind,
as you do all

Adam's children.   20
Ay, ay, ay, what lovely
steps you take!

Seeing you go up
leaves us in admiration
even though we don't know
your final destination.
Ay, ay, ay, what lovely
steps you take!

Blessed your parents
who bring as a present   30
the best offering
the world has ever seen.
Ay, ay, ay, what lovely
steps you take!

At this rate, girl,
I assure you, if you're
heading for heaven,
you'll be there in no time.
Ay, ay, ay, what lovely
steps you take!   40

Now enter the temple,
if it's God you're seeking,
And one day he will come
in search of you.
Ay, ay, ay, what lovely
steps you take!   (OC 2:218–20)

Villancico VII for the Feast of the Conception[2] of Mary, 1689

Refrain

Black is the bride.
The sun shines on her face. (Song 1:5–6)

Stanzas

Ebony against a red sky
she calls herself black
not for being in the shade,
rather constantly
her purity is fired
in the furnace of the sun.

Black is the bride.
The sun shines on her face. 10

Comparing the pure light
of the one to the other,
in the sun's divine light,
all creatures are dark;
but their beauty grows
as they draw closer to him.

Black is the bride.
The sun shines on her face.

Bathed by the sun,
the bride is inflamed, 20
and ever more lovely
in his company.
Her purity never fades,
for the sun never departs.

Black is the bride.
The sun shines on her face.

No horror of sin
could have had such effect,
rather the cause,
of her radiant color
is such, she claims   30
it adds to her grace.

Black is the bride.
The sun shines on her face.

Black she is, she confesses.
But this blackness, she says,
brings even greater beauty.
For in the first day's first light
Grace was morning star
to her first step.   40

Black is the bride.
The sun shines on her face.

A result and no small one,
the more she humbled herself,
confessing herself a slave,
the more she revealed the Master
who had purchased her freedom,
and so was free of any other.

Black is the bride
The sun shines on her face.   (OC 2:105–6) 50

Villancico VI for the Feast of the Assumption,[3] 1676

Clear the way for the entrance
of the bold adventuress
who undoes injustice
who smashes insults.[4]

The sun's rays are her
resplendent armor,
the stars her helmet,
the moon her boots.   (Song 6:10; Rev 12:1)

On her shining shield
with which she dazzles hell,   10
a mountain is emblazoned
and golden letters: *Tota Pulchra.*[5]

Celebrated for her beauty,
feared for her ferocity
she is jaunty and valiant,
and angelic is her beauty:
When the wind undoes
her blond curls' skein,
each cascading lock
draws a Roland to her side.[6]   20

She dispelled the charms
of the ancient serpent
whose conspiracy
set us under slavery's yoke.

She avenges wrongs
and annuls unjust laws,
gives refuge to orphans[7]
and shelter to widows.

She liberated prisoners
from that prison where,   30
were it not for her daring spirit,
still they'd await their release.

All hell trembles at the mere
mention of her name.
And they say its very kings
fast on her vigil.

She's the one who bore for us
a Lion whose fierce roar
has put to shameful flight
the Dragon and his sorcery.   (Rev 12:3–18)   40

Warrior most valiant
amid the cheering throng,
her service to the Holy Empire
entitles her to the imperial crown.

The celebrated champion
who with spirit and skill
won over the Holy Land,
where she triumphs forever.

She is the one, whose tread
no demon can endure.   50
When he sees her feet,
He takes to his heels.   (Gen 2:15)

Crowned with glory and honor,
the deeds that brought her fame,
since they cannot be contained on earth,
send her riding out of this world.

As knight errant of the spheres
on a new adventure,
she finds the hidden treasure
sought by so many.   (Matt 13:44)   60

There with a certain virtue
secretly sheltering her,
she is assured
of life eternal.

She comes just in time,
and it would be only just,
for her not to die like the others
who lived like no other.   (OC 2:10–12)

Villancico IV for the Feast of St. Peter the Apostle, 1683

Bright shepherd divine
of noble humility,
the humble who see you,
as sovereign, applaud you.

Solid foundation
on whose eternal marble
are set the church's
walls of diamond.

Rock wounded by the blows
of pain so penetrating
as to dissolve ice   10
into two pure torrents,

Fisherman so blessed
that you find yourself
master of a boat,
pilot of a ship,

Sovereign keeper
of those holy keys,
you close the door on sin
and open it to virtue,   20

Your Sacred Master
arranged it thus in your honor:
your permission we need
to pass over to heaven.

Refrain

Grant,
loving shepherd,
your erring flock
a swift passage
from earthly
to heavenly pastures.   (OC 2:78–79)   30

St. Catherine of Alexandria,
November 25, 1691

Villancicos for matins of the feast of the glorious martyr St. Catherine
of Alexandria, 1691, celebrated in the cathedral of the city of
Antequera, in the Valley of Oaxaca.[8]

First Nocturne

Refrain

Pure waters of the Nile,
cease, cease,
carrying
your tribute to the sea,
for the sea could envy
your good fortune.
No, no, don't flow
since now you can aspire
to nothing greater!
Cease, cease!   10

VILLANCICOS AND DEVOTIONAL POEMS

Stanzas

O River Nile, suspend
your rippling streams!
Halt, halt!
Behold with joy
the beauty you created, fertile
union of heaven and earth, a rose and a star.

Compassionate, your currents flowed,
coming just in time,
becoming, becoming
cradle to Moses,   20
his lullaby
the sounding surge and splash of surf.   (Exod 1:3)

More fortunate now,
the profusion of gifts
you possess. You possess,
one who gilds your shores
with a beauty more luxuriant
than Abigail, Esther, Rachel, Susanna.

Lovely Catherine,
whose Egyptian glory though   30
vain, vain,
was raised up to be divine
exchanging its virtues
for those of Deborah, Jael, Judith, Rebecca.

Not in the fragile loveliness
that values mad misuse,
did she place, place
hope secure,
although her face surpassed
that of Ruth, Bathsheba, Tamar, and Sarah.   40

To her, holy Nile,
Let your sounding streams

53

sing, sing,
and in concerted accord
your waves be swift
syllables, tongues, notes, and voices.   (OC 2:163–64)

Villancico II

Refrain

This, yes this,
is what it means to shine,
white, the carnation,
purple, the jasmine!
This, yes this,
is what it means to shine!

Stanzas

Rose of Alexandria,
you brought together
palm tree and laurel
white and scarlet.   10
Yes, this is what means to shine!

To one whose beauty
Made sumptuous display:
over Tyrian scarlet,
a gossamer of gold!
Yes, this is what it means to shine!

To the veil's candid white,
you gave an elegant tinge
with the crimson clouds
of your blood.   20
Yes, this is what it means to shine.

If ruddy and white
your tender Amadis be,   (Song 5:10, Vulgate)

you, rosy and white,
desire to follow him.
Yes, this is what it means to shine!

Your source of life
is that other Nile
that knows no beginning,
and has no end.   30
Yes, this is what it means to shine!

You, cut from
a beautiful garden,
best know how to
spread his fragrance.
Yes, this is what it means to shine!

Your triumph was greater
than that of Judith:
for hers was to kill
and yours was to die.   40
Yes, this is what it means to shine!

Live on then, since your prudence
knew to acquire
through a brief death
eternal life.
Yes, this is what it means to shine.   (OC 2:164–66)

Villancico **III**

Refrain

Hark, Hark as I sing
of two gypsies'
contrasting triumphs
linked by Egypt.

SOR JUANA INÉS DE LA CRUZ

Stanzas

An asp to her white breast
Cleopatra lovingly applied.
Oh, how superfluous, the asp
where the poison of love had been!
Oh, what a pity, O God!
Oh, what disgrace!   10

But a heroic descendant
of her generous line
wounded by a better love
aspired to a higher death.
She cannot die
whose love has no end.

Courageous Cleopatra
gave up her breast to poison,
her body immune to pain,
so wounded was her soul.   20
So perished most
what suffered least.

Copying this love and valor
Catherine suffered for
a better cause,
having this advantage:
Who dies for Christ,
prolongs her life.

To foil Augustus's triumph
Over her sovereign beauty,   30
Cleopatra killed herself,
Apprising life less
than reputation, death less long
than slavery.

So Catherine, heroic,
Baring her ivory throat

to the sword, foiled hell's
triumph over her resolve,
and so dying, prevailed
over those who killed her.   40

They threatened with shame,
O Death, the sweet life of Cleopatra,
but she chose as lesser evil
death, preferring it to shame,
loving honor
more than life.

Offering her beautiful body
to the cutting blades,
the better Egyptian,
aspired bravely to prevail,   50
and so by means of death
to attain life.   (OC 2:166–67)

DEVOTIONAL POEMS

Dedication to the Queen of Heaven, Mary, most holy, conceived in grace from the first moment of her being.[9]

Today, beautiful virgin, my love
prostrate before you
desires to offer you that same gift
I received from you.

Extend your hand, my Lady,
to this love that I feel.
Though the offering be unworthy
the affection is true.

The talent given me
I bring. Graciously receive
the little I've achieved
and pardon what has gone astray.

In you, not in me, I place my trust,
affirming to all the world
whatever here is good is yours,
whatever bad is mine.   (OC 2:60)

In which she expresses the effects of divine Love and proposes to die a lover, despite all risk.[10]

A care I carry within me
so elusive, though I believe
I sense it near, within
Myself I sense it not.

It is love, but a love
lacking in blindness,
so its sight serves
to increase its torment.

It is not the object
causing the grief I see,   10
for goodness is the object,
but all this pain—the means.

If this affection that I feel,
be lawful, even rightly due,
why am I punished
for returning what I owe?

Oh, how much kindness, how many
tokens of tenderness have I known!
For love that comes from God
is attribute without opposites.   20

What is true cannot contain
contradictory concepts.
Just so love cannot live
in the face of forgetting.

I remember (oh, had it never been!)
in another age the love I wanted
was beyond madness,
exceeding all extremes.

Since it was a bastard love,
composed of opposites,   30
easily it dissipated,
defective in its own being.

But now, woe is me, this love
is so much in its natural element,
that virtue and reason
fuel its flames.

Hearing this one might say
if this be true why do I suffer?
But my yearning heart
would say, for that very reason.   40

Oh, how weak our humanity
where even the purest affection
knows not how to strip itself
of natural emotion!

So indispensable is
this desire to be loved,
that, even knowing it's no use,
we will never give it up.

Though my response
add nothing to this love,   50
try as I might, I cannot
cease desiring to respond.

If it is a crime, I admit it.
If a sin, I confess it;
but repent I cannot,
try as I might to do so.

Well does he see who
penetrates my inner secrets
how I fashion myself
the sorrows I suffer.   60

Well does he know I am
my desires' executioner.
Dead among my longings,
Their tomb is my heart.

I die (who will believe it?) at the hands
of what I most love,
and the motive for my murder,
is the love I have for it.

Thus feeding, dejected,
my life with poison,   70
the very death I'm living
is the life I of which I'm dying.

But take courage heart,
for in such sweet torture,
in the midst of misfortune
I will not cease professing love.   (OC 1:166–68)

Ballad with the same intention.

The more grace prompts me
to move up to heavenly sphere,
the more the weight of my wretchedness
casts me into the depths.

Virtue and custom
struggle in the heart,
and the heart is in agony,
while they do combat.

And however strong virtue be,
I fear it may be vanquished,   10
since custom is very great,
and virtue very green.

The intellect is clouded
In dark confusion.
Who can light the way
if reason itself is blind?

I am my executioner.
And myself's own prison.
Who saw that sin and suffering
Are one and the same?   20

I am reluctant to do that thing
I most desire to do;
and for this reluctance
suffer the penalty.   (Rom 7:15–24)

I love God and sense myself in God,
But my very will makes
what is comfort, a cross,
what is haven, a storm.

Suffer, then, since God commands,
but let it be such,   30
that my sins bring suffering
not my suffering sin.   (OC 1:168)

Of the loving effects of Christ in the sacrament, on the day of communion.

Gentle lover of the soul,
supreme good to which I aspire.
You who understand to punish
offenses with benefits.

Divine Magnet whom I adore,
today, I see you so well disposed
that you animate in me the audacity
to call you mine.

Today, in loving union
your fondness has deemed it   10
a slight thing to be myself,
were you not here with me.

Today, to test
the love with which I serve you,
into my heart in person
you have entered.

I ask you: Is love or jealousy
the cause of this scrutiny?
He who needs examine all
reveals a suspicious nature.   20

Oh, how ignorant this view!
What errors just expressed!
As if human stubbornness
could obstruct divine Perspicacity.[11]

To see into our hearts,
you need not our assistance,
for you the secrets of the abyss
are as clear as day.

With one embracing vision
you hold present in your mind,
the infinite past,
up to the finite present.   30

Therefore you do not need
me to bare my heart to you.
Since your wisdom sees it,
you enter with loving devotion.

Therefore it is love, not jealousy
that I behold in you.   (OC: 1:169–70)

Hymn for the Feast of the Incarnation[12]

Divine Love this day
became incarnate,
a gift so precious as to give
all other gifts their worth.

Though those firstborn's
first good was to be formed,
what good to be created,
and not to be redeemed?

Nor can the mere partaking
in being bring pleasure.   10
What purpose to be,
if only to suffer?

The mysteries are linked
and for our salvation:
redemption, the means;
creation, the crown.

How great was the good
of the loving Incarnation,
if even its justification,
the fault, was fortunate?   20

Sin alone could not be the cause,
nor to mend the fault the reason,
since Mary alone sufficed
for God to become incarnate.

The opposite I will not admit
and find it strange to conceive
any power to be crime's cure
greater than her beauty.

What consolation this,
to a world in lamentation: 30
How much greater worth a world
with her of greater worth than heaven?

The mystery of the Incarnation
Could have twofold motivation:
for all, from compassion,
for her, from love's passion.

And thus the descent to earth
this day, for different reasons,
was caused by the sin of all
and by the grace of Mary.   (OC:2:221–22)   40

Song for the Nativity

Refrain

How can it be my God
that I believe in you
and believing what I see,
do not see all that I believe?

VILLANCICOS AND DEVOTIONAL POEMS

Verses

If faith and sight are so
conflicted, why
does sight need faith here,
and faith not need sight?

Child, I see you, and to know
what you are I need to believe,   10
but I also know you are great,
though my eyes do not see it.

To see you in the Eucharist
is easier for me, for there
I know I must believe
what goes counter to what I see.

But here, what do you command?
That in simplicity I believe
what I see and do not see,
what is and what is not.   20

You seem human and are,
Lord, what you seem to be,
but though I see not God in you,
I know you to be God.

Finally, the senses now
do not deceive,
but infinitely more is here
than ever sight perceived.   (OC 2:225–26)

Section 2

Drama

Loa to *Divine Narcissus*

An Allegory

Characters

America	[Christian] Religion
Music	Soldiers
Musicians	Zeal
Occident	

(Enter OCCIDENT, as a handsome Indian man, with a crown, and AMERICA, at his side as gorgeously attired Indian woman. They wear elaborate cloaks and tunics like those worn when the tocotín is danced. They sit down on two chairs. From both sides enter Indian men and women, dancing with feathers and bells in their hands, as they ordinarily do in this dance. While they dance MUSIC sings:)

Scene i

MUSIC
Noble Mexicans
whose ancient line
traces its origin
to the sun's clear rays,
since today is that happy day
of the year
when we consecrate
the greatest relic of all,
come adorn

69

yourselves with tribal emblems[1]   10
so that devotion
unites with joy
to celebrate with festive pageantry,
the great God of the Seeds.
And since the abundance
from our provinces
is owed the One
who fertilizes them,
offer with devotion,
since they are his due,   20
from the new fruit,
above all the first fruit.
Give the finest blood
from your veins
so that, mingled,
it may serves his cult;
and with festive pageantry,
celebrate the great God of the Seeds!

(OCCIDENT *and* AMERICA *sit down, and the music stops.*)

OCCIDENT
Among all the gods
my religion worships   30
in this city alone,
Royal City of lights,
over two thousand are
offered a sacrifice,
a bloody sacrifice
of human blood spilling,
from pulsating entrails,
from palpitating hearts.
Though the gods are (I repeat)
many, the one in my view,   40
the greatest of all, is
the great God of the Seeds!

AMERICA
Rightly so! He alone
sustains our monarchy,
and so the harvest's abundance
is destined for him.
Since this of all gifts
is the greatest,
and summation of all others
conserving life itself,   50
we count him greatest.
For what matter that rich
America abounds
in the gold of her mines,
if her fields are sterile
from their poisonous fumes,
which hinder the fruits
of fields abundantly sown
from springing forth?
Moreover, his protection   60
is not restricted to nurture
of material food,
but later by eating
his very own flesh
(purified in advance
of bodily dross),
we may be cleansed of the
stains on our souls. And so
intent on his worship,
all together repeat: 70

AMERICA AND MUSIC
With festive pageantry
celebrate the great God of the Seeds!

Scene ii

(Exit dancing. Enter [CHRISTIAN] RELIGION, as a Spanish lady, and ZEAL, as Commander in Chief, armed. Spanish soldiers follow them.)

[CHRISTIAN] RELIGION
Zeal, given your nature,
how can your righteous anger,
bear to see arrogant,
blind Idolatry worship
with superstitious rites
an idol, to the disgrace
of Christian Religion?

ZEAL
Religion, do not be so quick   80
to complain of my omission.
You grumble at my welcome.
Already my arm is raised,
already my sword
drawn to avenge you.
Step aside, while I
right the wrong done you.

(Enter OCCIDENT and AMERICA dancing. MUSIC and her MUSICIANS enter from the other side.)

MUSIC
With festive pageantry,
celebrate the great God of the Seeds!

ZEAL
Since they have arrived, I go to meet them.   90

RELIGION
I will go also, moved by
compassion to arrive before

they taste the onslaught of your fury,
and to invite them in peace
to consent to my cult.

ZEAL
Let us go then, while they are
engaged in their lewd rites.

MUSIC
With festive pageantry,
celebrate the great God of the Seeds!

(ZEAL and RELIGION approach them.)

RELIGION
Occident, you are powerful,   100
and you, America, beautiful and rich,
yet living miserably
in the midst of these riches.
Abandon this profane worship
to which the devil incites you.
Open your eyes! Follow
the true doctrine
persuaded by my love.

OCCIDENT
Heavens! What unknown
people are these I see   110
trying to impede the
course of my festivities?

AMERICA
What nations never seen
want to challenge the privileges
of my ancient domain?

OCCIDENT
O you, foreign beauty
O you, woman wanderer!

Tell me who you are, now come
to disturb my delight.

RELIGION
I am Christian Religion   120
and intend for your provinces
to be subject to my cult.

OCCIDENT
What a task you are undertaking!

AMERICA
What madness courting!

OCCIDENT
What impossibility plotting!

AMERICA
Of course she's crazy! Leave her,
and let our celebration continue!

MUSIC, OCCIDENT, AND AMERICA
And with festive pageantry
celebrate the great God of the Seeds!

ZEAL
What, barbarous Occident,   130
what, blind Idolatry,
you scorn Religion,
my gentle, beloved spouse?
Clearly your wickedness
surpasses all measure.
God will not permit
you to continue with your crimes
and has sent me to punish you.

OCCIDENT
Who are you? The very sight
of your face strikes fear in me.   140

ZEAL
I am Zeal. Why are you surprised?
When you have the audacity
to scorn Religion,
Zeal arrives to avenge her,
punishing your temerity.
I am a minister of God, who,
seeing your abuses
reach the heights,
and weary of your living
so many years in error,   150
has sent me to punish you.
And, therefore, these armed hosts,
whose steel rods shake,[2]
are ministers of his anger,
are instruments of his wrath.

OCCIDENT
What god, what error, what blunders,
what punishments are you hinting?
I do not understand your reasons
nor have the remotest idea
of who you are, who dares   160
to attempt such a task
as prohibiting my people
from worthy worship saying:

MUSIC
With festive pageantry,
celebrate the great God of the Seeds!

AMERICA
Barbarian, madman, how blind
with reasons incomprehensible,
you want to trouble the quiet,
peace, and serenity we enjoy
in tranquility! Cease your plan   170
if you do not want to be reduced

to ashes, so that even the winds
will not give news of your existence!
And you, my Spouse with your vassals

(To OCCIDENT)

close eyes and ears
to her reasoning. Take
no notice of her fantasies
and proceed in your worship,
without permitting upstart
nations the audacity   180
of claiming to interrupt it.

MUSIC
And with festive pageantry
celebrate the great God of the Seeds!

ZEAL
Since the first proposal
of peace from pride you scorn,
you will need to accept
the second, that of war.
To arms! War! War!

(Drums and bugles sound.)

OCCIDENT
What monsters is heaven
sending against me? What weapons   190
are these that my eyes have never seen?
Ah, my guards! Soldiers!
Release your ever ready
arrows!

AMERICA
What beams is heaven hurtling
against me? What fierce balls
of burning lead rain down?

What monstrous centaurs
combat my people?

(Off stage:)

To arms! To arms! War! War!   200

(Fanfare)

Long live Spain! Long live her king!

(Joining the battle, entering by one door, and exiting by another, the fleeing Indians and the Spaniards in pursuit. After them OCCIDENT retreating from RELIGION, and AMERICA from ZEAL.)

Scene iii

RELIGION
Surrender, proud Occident!

OCCIDENT
Now I must yield to
to your force, not your reason.

ZEAL
Die, insolent America!

RELIGION
Wait, don't put her to death,
I need her alive!

ZEAL
How can you defend her,
when you are the one offended?

RELIGION
Yes, the conquest of America   210
is due to your bravery,

but my piety
will save her life.
Your role was to conquer
by force; mine to subdue her
by reason and gentle persuasion.

ZEAL
After you have seen the perverse
blind desecration
of your cult, is it not
better for them all to die?   220

RELIGION
Restrain your justice,
Zeal. Do not put them to death!
My kind disposition
does not want their death,
but that they convert and live.   (Ezek 18:23, 32)

AMERICA
If your request for my life
and display of compassion,
is because you expect
to conquer me, proud one,
as once with physical,   230
now with intellectual arms,
you deceive yourself.
As a captive, I mourn
my lost freedom, yet my free will
with still greater liberty
will adore my gods!

OCCIDENT
I have already said force of arms
obliges me to surrender to you.
But for the rest, it is clear
that neither force nor violence   240
can impede the will

in its free operation.
So although I groan as a captive,
you cannot prevent me
from saying in my heart
I worship the great God of the Seeds!

Scene iv

RELIGION
Wait, it is not power
but concern motivating us.
What is this god that you adore?

OCCIDENT
A god who fertilizes   250
the fields so that they bear fruit,
a god to whom the heavens bow down
a god the rain obeys,
and finally he is the one
who cleanses our sins, to then
become the food he offers us.
See if you have
a deity more gentle,
granting so many benefits,
many more than I can recount.   260

RELIGION
(Aside)
Good Lord! What traces,
what imitation or what emblems
of our holy truths
in these lies may be contained?
O cunning serpent!
O venomous asp! O hydra!
From seven mouths   (Rev 12:3, 15)
you pour your poison,
deadly as hemlock!

how far will your malice   270
go to parody
God's holy wonders?
But the tools of your deception,
(God granting me a clever tongue)
shall serve me to convince you.

AMERICA
What confused thinking is this?
Can't you see there is no
God but this one, who confirms
his works through benefits?

RELIGION
Like Paul I have to convince   280
through their own doctrine,
as when he preached to the Athenians.   (Acts 17: 22–23)
He saw they had a law
condemning to death those
who introduced new gods,
and also knew that
they had an altar dedicated
to an unknown god.
So he said to them: "No new god,
rather the unknown one you   290
worshiped at this altar
is the one my voice proclaims."   (Acts 17:22–26)
So I...Occident, listen;
hear me, blind Idolatry,
because my words contain
the basis of all your bliss!
These miracles you recount,
these prodigies you impart,
these appearances, these features,
glimpsed beneath   300
the veils of superstition,
these portents you distort
by attributing to your

mendacious gods, are works
caused by the true God
and his Wisdom.
Because if the flowering
meadow is fertile,
if the fields are abundant
if the fruit trees flourish,   310
if what is sown increases,
if the rains fall, everything
is the work of his right hand.
For neither the arm that sows,
nor the rain bringing fruit
nor the heat bringing life
would give green increase
should his bountiful Providence   (1 Cor 3:7)
cease from conferring
their vegetative soul.   320

AMERICA
If that is so,
tell me if this deity is
so kind as to let himself
be touched by these very hands,
like the figure here
made by my own hands
from seeds and innocent
blood shed for
this purpose only?

RELIGION
Though his Divine Essence   330
is invisible and immense,
as such he is also united
to our oh so human
nature, and dwells
among us, allowing
the unworthy hands of
priests to touch him.

AMERICA
On that point, we agree
because no one
is permitted to touch my god
except for those who
serve him as priests.
Not only not touch him,
even entry in his chapel
is forbidden to laity.

ZEAL
Oh, reverence, more worthily
rendered to the true God!

OCCIDENT
Tell me, in detail if you must,
is this god made of materials
as rare, as exquisite
as blood, which has been
offered in sacrifice,
and grain, which sustains life?

RELIGION
As I've said already, his infinite
majesty is immaterial;
but his blessed humanity,
unbloody, is there in the holy
sacrifice of the Mass,
in simple accidents,
like the seeds of
grain, which are converted
into his own body and blood;
and his blood in the chalice,
blood sacrificed
on the altar of the cross,
pure, clean, and innocent
was the redemption of the world.

340

350

360

AMERICA
Now I want to believe
these things unheard of.
Is this deity you depict   370
so loving that he would
offer himself to me as food,
like the one that I adore?

RELIGION
Yes, because his Wisdom,
for this goal alone,
came to live among us.

AMERICA
Can I not see this god
to be persuaded?

OCCIDENT
And with one stroke
be cured of my obsession?   380

RELIGION
Yes, when you are washed
in the crystalline fountain
of baptism.

OCCIDENT
I know already
I have to bathe before
I approach the bountiful table.
Such is our ancient custom.

ZEAL
That is not the bath
your sins require.

OCCIDENT
Which one then?

SOR JUANA INÉS DE LA CRUZ

RELIGION
The bath of a sacrament
that by virtue of living waters   390
cleanses you of your sins.

AMERICA
As you are giving me news
of things so great, surpassing
my understanding, I would like
to receive them in full
since now divine inspiration
moves me to desire to know them.

OCCIDENT
And I too would also know the life
and death of this great God
whom you affirm is in the bread.   400

RELIGION
Let us go then. We will bring
into view a metaphor,
an idea dressed
in rhetorical colors,
to show you, since I know
you are more inclined
to visible objects, than
to what faith will inform you
through hearing. And so
you must use your eyes   410
and through them
receive the faith.

OCCIDENT
Very true. I'd much prefer to see it,
than to have you tell me about it.

Scene v

RELIGION
Let's proceed then.

ZEAL
Religion, tell me:
in what form have you determined
to represent the mysteries?

RELIGION
In the form of a play. Through allegory,
I want to show them in visible form,
so that she, and all the Occident   420
will be instructed in that
which they have asked
to know.

ZEAL
What title will you give
your allegorical play?

RELIGION
Divine Narcissus, because
if these unfortunates had
an idol that they adored,
of such strange currency
through which the devil claimed
to feign the high mystery   430
of the holy Eucharist,
know that among other pagans,
there have been similar
signs of exalted wonders.

ZEAL
Where will it be performed?

RELIGION
In the crown city
of Madrid, which is the center
of the faith, the royal seat
of her Catholic kings,
to whom the Indies owe   440
the light of the gospel
as it shines in the Occident.

ZEAL
Isn't it unseemly
for something written in Mexico
to be performed in Madrid?

RELIGION
Has it never been the case
that something done in one
place can serve in another?
Moreover, writing it
was not a capricious idea of mine   450
but due to obedience
attempting even the impossible.
So that the work, although it be
coarse and unpolished,
is the result of obedience,
and not born of audacity.

ZEAL
So tell me, Religion, since
you have broached this issue,
how do you respond to the objection
that you introduce the Indies   460
and want to take them to Madrid?

RELIGION
Since my only goal is to
celebrate the Mystery,
and since the persons

in question are nothing more
than abstractions depicting
the intended meaning,
there is nothing to contradict
their being taken to Madrid.
For intellectual notions
are not hampered by distance
nor hindered by oceans.

ZEAL
Since that is so at the royal feet
that bridge two worlds,
we beg pardon on our knees:

RELIGION
and of his illustrious queen,

AMERICA
whose sovereign feet
the Indies humbly kiss;

ZEAL
and of his supreme councils;

RELIGION
and of the ladies who
illuminate his hemisphere.

AMERICA
To his bright courtiers
of whom my own wit
humbly begs pardon
for wanting to describe
in rough lines such a mystery.

OCCIDENT
Let us go. I'm dying
to see what this God
is like whom they will give me as food,

470

480

SOR JUANA INÉS DE LA CRUZ

(AMERICA, OCCIDENT, and ZEAL sing:)

As we say, already
the Indies know   490
who is the true
God of the Seeds!
And with tender tears
that pleasure distills,
let us joyfully repeat
with festive voice:

ALL
Blessed the day
I came to know the great God of the Seeds!

(They exit dancing and singing.)

DIVINE NARCISSUS

Characters

Divine Narcissus   Paganism
Echo, Fallen Angelic Nature   Pride
Grace   Self-Love
Human Nature   Synagogue
Music   Choir I and Choir II
Nymphs, Shepherds

ACT 1

Scene i

(Enter from one side PAGANISM dressed as a nymph, accompanied by nymphs and shepherds; from the other side SYNAGOGUE (also as a nymph) with her retinue, who will be the musicians. In the rear of the stage HUMAN NATURE dressed in great splendor listens to their song.)

SYNAGOGUE
Praise the Lord, all you peoples.   (Ps 116:1, Vulgate)

CHOIR I
Praise the Lord, all you peoples!

SYNAGOGUE
Sing a new song   (Ps 149:1, 9)
To his divine Beauty
with the first light of day,
may eternal praise sound
to the glory of his name.

CHOIR I
Praise the Lord, all you peoples!

PAGANISM
Applaud Narcissus, fountains and flowers.

Since his divine beauty   10
has no mortal equal, is
beyond all loveliness
seen in other creatures,
it inspires love in them all.

CHOIR II
Praise Narcissus, fountains and flowers

SYNAGOGUE
Praise

PAGANISM
Acclaim!

SYNAGOGUE
with hymns,

PAGANISM
with voices,

SYNAGOGUE
the Lord

PAGANISM
Narcissus,

SYNAGOGUE
all you peoples.

PAGANISM
fountains and flowers.

(*HUMAN NATURE moves forward between the two choirs.*)

HUMAN NATURE
Paganism and Synagogue,
in sweet metrical voices
one of you applauds God,   20

the other celebrates a man.
Listen to what I tell you.
Pay heed to my reasons
since I'm mother to you both
and by virtue of nature's law
it is good for you both to hear me.

SYNAGOGUE
Long has my love recognized you,
O Nature, common
mother of all humanity.

PAGANISM
I too obey you.   30
Though Synagogue and I
are at odds, that is no reason
to deny you my love;
rather, I revere you.

SYNAGOGUE
Only on this do we agree.
Since we both observe, she
over there with her errors,
and me here with my truths,
that rule which says that you don't   40
impose on others what
you yourself cannot endorse.
And just as no father
wants his son to offend him,
so there can be no reason
for us to neglect our duty
by refusing to heed your words.

PAGANISM
Very true. So that everyone
would know this rule
you have written it   50
in your children's hearts.

SOR JUANA INÉS DE LA CRUZ

HUMAN NATURE
It is good so. This rule
suffices, for you to be aware
that as your common Mother
you owe me your attention.

SYNAGOGUE
Well then, tell us your purpose.

PAGANISM
Well then, tell us what you propose.

HUMAN NATURE
Having listened to
your well-versed words
and the different objects   60
of your praise, I say,
Paganism, you are blind,
in error, ignorant, and dull.
With your praise you glorify
a faded beauty past his prime.
And you, Synagogue, certain
of the truths you have
heard through your Prophets
render homage to God.
Leaving aside discussion   70
of your differences
(to PAGANISM) it is clear that you are in error
(to SYNAGOGUE) and clear that you know,
although a time will come when
you will exchange places.
Paganism will know,
and Synagogue will be unknowing,
but now this is not the case.
And, therefore, returning to the order
of our discourse, I say when   80
I heard your songs,
it occurred to me to consider

how mysterious it is
that certain truths hide
beneath fictions such as these.
Since you in your Narcissus find
perfection to such a degree
that you say his beauty
draws all hearts like a magnet,
not only is he followed   90
by nymphs and shepherds
but by birds and beasts
hills and mountains,
streams and fountains,
grasses, flowers, and plants.   (Dan 3:52–90)
So much more reason that
these exalted attributes
prove true of God,
whose beauty the celestial spheres
consider themselves   100
unworthy reflections.
To him all creatures
(though there could be no valid reason
deserving of such kindness,
of such singular favor)
for his loveliness alone
owe adoration.
As Human Nature to him
as my center I am
drawn by obligation. Him,   110
I follow as my North.

Thus as mother to you both
through allegorical colors
I will try to construct
ideas as part of a play,
which takes from one of you
the sense *(turns to SYNAGOGUE)* and
from the other the sound *(turns to PAGANISM)*.
So that by taking both expressions

and metaphorical idiom
through the figure of Narcissus   120
I will solicit the love
of God, and see if
these opaque scribblings
sketch the clarity of his plan.
For many times divine and
human letters in concert
show us that even from
pagan pens God
lets flow ideas,
offering glimpses   130
of his most exalted mysteries,
what do you say *(to SYNAGOGUE)* to being the body
of the idea, and you *(to PAGANISM)* to cutting the cloth
for her dress?

SYNAGOGUE
For my part as much as
I am involved in your plan,
I will serve you by giving you
everything that you need:
the verses of my Prophets
and the choirs of my cantors.

PAGANISM
Though I hardly understand you   140
since all you ask is
that I contribute material
that you then will inform
with another soul, another sense
that my eyes have not seen,
I give you from my store
of human letters the poetic
perfection of the story of Narcissus.

HUMAN NATURE
Then return to the musical

accord where I found you,   150
now to attain insight
from the metaphors found
in these loving voices
where one thing is heard,
another understood.

Scene ii

SYNAGOGUE
Praise the Lord, all you peoples!

CHOIR I
Praise the Lord, all you peoples!

PAGANISM
Acclaim Narcissus, flowers and fountains!

CHOIR II
Acclaim Narcissus, flowers and fountains!

SYNAGOGUE
All peoples praise him   160
and angels unceasingly laud
him in highest heaven.
As do the celestial bodies
as they rotate in the lovely sky.

CHOIR I
Praise the Lord, all you peoples!

CHOIR II
Acclaim Narcissus, flowers and fountains!

PAGANISM
And because his beauty, lovely,
sovereign and prodigious,

is of all the greatest,
above all excelling,
all the ends of the earth acclaim him.   170

CHOIR II
Acclaim Narcissus, fountains and flowers!

CHOIR I
Praise the Lord, all you peoples!

SYNAGOGUE
The waters above the heavens
forming crystalline ice
and the exalted virtues
in heavenly heights
all praise him with one accord.

CHOIR I
Praise the Lord, all you peoples!

CHOIR II
Acclaim Narcissus, fountains and flowers!

PAGANISM
Heaven's lantern, the sun,   180
stands stunned by his radiant
splendor. Seeing his face
the fiery chariot stops
to stare at his perfection.

CHOIR II
Acclaim Narcissus, fountains and flowers!

CHOIR I
Praise the Lord, all you peoples!

SYNAGOGUE
Sun, moon, and stars,
fire with flash of flame,

fog with silver spray,   190
snow, ice, and cold
all the days and all the nights

CHOIR I
Praise the Lord, all you peoples!

CHOIR II
Acclaim Narcissus, flowers and fountains!

PAGANISM
His magnetic charm
draws not only shepherd
boys and girls alike
in attendance, but rocks
and woodlands and fields as well.

CHOIR II
Acclaim Narcissus, fountains and flowers!

CHOIR I
Praise the Lord, all you peoples!   200

HUMAN NATURE
Oh, how beautifully united
does their harmonious praise
resound as they celebrate
his divine beauty's perfection!
Though my disgrace keeps
me banished from his sight,
it cannot prevent me
from adoring his beauty.
Though angered in justice
by my crimes beyond measure   210
he may disdain me, I have no lack
of pious intercessors
continually pleading
that he grant me pardon
since his image is present

in me still, though the vile
rushing waters of my sins
have dissolved all my beauty.
On many occasions the sacred
text calls sins waters, as   220
when it says: "Let me not   (Ps 68:162, Vulgate)
drown in the waters of the
stormy sea." In another place
when praising God's favors,
David recounts that the God
who helps him liberates
him from many waters;   (Ps 17:17)
and again, when he asks that
help arrive at an opportune
time, but not in the furor   230
of flooding waters.   (Ps 31: 6)
That is why I call my
sin muddy waters
whose dirty colors
interposed between him and me
so distort my being,
so blemish my beauty,
so alter my features,
were Narcissus to see me,
he would deny his own image.   240
So tell him that since the
first man's sin, sin became
like a sea whose foamy waves'
soaking no one escapes.
Many are the fountains,
many the rivers darkened
with sinners, where Nature
submerged hides her
beauty. Oh, may heaven grant
my hope and I stumble upon   250
some fountain free
of these filthy waters,
revealing Narcissus

in all his perfection!
Though to touch its crystal
clarity would be all my delight,
so as to soften the
sternness of Narcissus,
repeat his praises
in soft acclamations   260
phrasing with floods of tears,
music pleasing to his ears.
Tell him of my suffering.
May your melodious voices
move him to compassion
and merciful forgiveness.
And because in no age
have I ever lacked an advocate,
let us all go in search for
the Fountain where my stain   270
will be washed, and not
leave behind music's
sweet sound that with tears
and voices proclaims:

CHOIR I
Praise the Lord, all you peoples!

CHOIR II
Acclaim Narcissus, flowers and fountains!

(Exit all.)

Scene iii

(Enter ECHO, a nymph excited and out of breath; PRIDE, as a shepherdess; SELF-LOVE, as a shepherd.)

ECHO
Pride, Self-Love, friends,

do you hear voices
in this forest?

PRIDE
I heard   280
their words, though they penetrated
my heart less through what they signified
than through their sound.

SELF-LOVE
I, too, as I listened
to their sweet cadences,
was driven quite mad.

ECHO
Well, and what do you conclude from these voices?

PRIDE
Nothing since I only know
that what bothers me,
since I am pride,
is to hear others praised.   290

SELF-LOVE
I only know that I am fatigued by
reciprocal sweet nothings.
since I am Self-Love,
unable to love any other than myself.

ECHO
Well, I'll tell you what I understood
and how I can distinguish
my infused knowledge from
my Self-Love and my Pride.
There is not much that they miss,
and so it is natural that they fear it.   300
And so Self-Love, who
reigns inseparably in me,
can cause me to forget myself,

in order to make me love myself
(because Self-Love's
character is such,
like a fool, he forgets
the same thing he remembers).
Self-Love, first in my affections
since you are their source.   310
And you are their goal, Pride,
since they end up with you.
(When Self-Love from
reason strays, he
terminates in pride.
This is the affect he generates,
and he intends that
all things be
directed solely to
his advantage.)   320
Hear me now. You have seen
that beautiful shepherdess
representing the communality
of all Human Nature.
In the figure of a nymph,
a metaphorical notion,
she pursues a beauty she adores
despite his disdain for her.
So that human letters
may serve the Divine,   330
let us make use of both,
and their conformity compare,
taking from one the sense,
from the other the shape.
Let us proceed then with phrases
that paint freely
in rhetorical colors, being
one thing, yet revealing another,
and call Narcissus God
because his beauty   340
knows no equal,

nor anyone worthy of him.
Well then, since my character
represents angelic being, not
as commonly understood, but only
that reprobate part
that dared drag a third
of the stars into the abyss.   (Rev 9:1; 12:4)
I now, like Human Nature,
following her metaphor, will   350
create another nymph who
nymphlike follows Narcissus.
What role remains for me
but that of unhappy Echo,
in love and lamenting Narcissus?
What greater beauty
than his beauty beyond measure?
What greater scorn
than that which he shows to me?   360
Thus though you know already
what causes my torment
(my nature is such that
not even my pain is the greatest),
I will tell you the tale
using the same allegory,
to see if the myth of Echo
suits my tragedy.
From this vantage point
let the curious onlooker   370
judge if truth and fiction,
meaning and letter coincide.

Now you know I am Echo,
the unhappy beauty
who from wanting to be
more lovely became
more ugly.
Seeing myself endowed
with beauty and nobility,

with valor and virtue,
with perfection and learning, 380
and finally, seeing that among
angelic natures I was
the most illustrious, in short
the most perfect of all creatures,
I desired to be Narcissus's bride,
planning in my pride to be
seated with him on his throne,
his equal in greatness.
I judged it of no
small consequence 390
that my beauty was
the equal of his.
For which reason he, offended,
left me with great disdain,
angrily casting me
from his grace and his presence,
and leaving me (woe is me!)
no hope of ever again
enjoying the radiance
of his divine beauty. 400
I, seeing myself thus despised,
the pain of the affront,
changed love to hatred,
tenderness to spite,
affection to desire for revenge,
which, like a bloodied viper
exhaling noxious poison,
courses through my veins.
For when love
changes to hate, 410
more efficient than love
is the malice it engenders.
And fearful it would be
Human Nature's good
fortune to merit the
laurels I had lost,

I fabricated such a ruse,
fashioned a stratagem,
and caused the innocent nymph,
unaware of my deceit,   420
to alienate Narcissus
when ungrateful and careless
she offended him. And since he is
of a disposition so severe
that once offended
since the offense is infinite
in view of his divinity,
there is no way back
into his graces,
the debt being so great   430
that no one is able to
satisfy it.
I reduced the poor girl
to such misery that
however sadly she moans
at the sound of her chains,
her sighs are in vain,
her complaints useless,
since, like me, she cannot
eternally behold   440
the face of Narcissus.
Thus my injury
is avenged. Since
I cannot possess
the throne, it is not good
that another merits it,
nor that what I lost
should be attained
by a vulgar peasant girl
formed from coarse clay,   450
made from lowly matter.
So it is good to be watchful
so that never again will
Narcissus set eyes on her.

She is too much like him.
In fact, since she is made
in his image (Woe is me!
My heart explodes with envy.)
I fear that if he sees her,
and in her his own image,   460
his divinity will be obliged
to condescend to love her.
For the likeness
has such power
that there is no one
who does not desire it.
So I have always managed
with care and diligence
to blot out this likeness,
by making her commit   470
such sins that he himself,
loosening the reins of Aquarius,
destroyed the world by water
in punishment for the offense.   (Gen 6:13, 17)
But since it is his custom,
mercifully to mix in
with the means of justice
the prospect of clemency,
after the shipwreck by means
of the first floating plank   480
he sought to save her life,
which she conserves to this day.
Along with his wrath
he always remembers
his mercy, and uses
it more generously.
With hardly time to catch
her breath after her escape,
the proud one with haughty self-homage
planned to scale the heavens.   490
In her ignorance believing
the celestial spheres attainable

through corporal labor
and material tasks,
she built a tall tower,   (Gen 11:4–9)
when it would have been better
to weave immaterial ladders
by doing penance for her sins.
For her crazy ambition
the proportionate pain was   500
discord and division,
through scrambling of speech.
A just punishment for
those fool enough to think
themselves experts in things
beyond all understanding.
Thus divided, I kept
them in factions,
so that some worshiped the sun,
or the course of the stars.   510
Others bowed down before
beasts or worshiped stones,
and fountains, and rivers,
and groves, and forests.
There remained no creature
too unclean or obscene
that their blindness omitted,
their ignorance excluded.
Delighting even in adoring
their own inclinations,   520
they forgot the true
worship due to their God.
So that through love of stone   (Ps 113:4–8; 134:15–18,
                                      Vulgate)

statues, blind and unknowing,
they were themselves into stone
nearly transformed.

Scene iv

Despite these derelictions
sparks never were lacking
to remind them of the
nobility of their origin.   530
They tried to return
to their original dignity
and with tears and sighs
attempted to appease God.
Look at Abel, who   (Gen 4:4)
gathering his sheaves of grain
laid them on the coals
to make God an offering.

*(The second float opens up and as it turns at an upper level, there
we see ABEL lighting the fire and then hiding, as he sings:)*

ABEL
Powerful God   (Gen 4:2–4)   540
of immense mercy,
accept from my hand
this humble offering!

ECHO
Listen to holy Enoch   (Gen 4:17, 26)
the first one who began
to invoke God by name
with new invocations.

*(In the same way ENOCH, on his knees, his hands raised in
prayer, as he sings:)*

ENOCH
Powerful Creator
of heaven and earth
my tongue confesses
you alone as God!   550

ECHO
See Abraham, that monster   (Gen 22:2–18)
of faith and obedience
who did not hesitate to kill
his son, much as he loved him,
because of God's command.
Nor did he doubt the promise
that the number of his children
would equal the stars.
See how God's kindness
in fair return,   560
spares the victim
but accepts the sacrifice.

(ABRAHAM *passes by as he is commonly painted, and the angel* sings:)

ANGEL
Do not extend your hand
to wound the child.
It is enough to see
how much you fear the Lord!   (Gen 22:13)

ECHO
See Moses the leader chosen
by God to govern the people,
who seeing their idol worship
and God's plan to punish them,   570
interposed his authority
and boldly prayed:

(MOSES *with the tablets of the Law, passes by and sings:*)

MOSES
Oh, pardon the people,   (Exod 32:32)
Lord, with your mercy,
or erase me from
the book of life eternal!

ECHO
But why weary you?
Listen to the prophets
and patriarchs in chorus
as with sweet and gentle voices   580
they ask God for a remedy,
to relieve their suffering.

CHOIR I
Open, clear heavens
your high gates,
and let the heavy clouds
rain down the Just One.   (Isa 45:8)

ECHO
Listen to another,
mysterious petition
seemingly opposed
saying in a different voice: 590

CHOIR II
Let the parched mouths
of the earth open
to let spring forth as fruit
of the earth her savior!

ECHO
Since some pray that
he descends from heaven,
and that he be born
of the earth, it would
seem to indicate that
the savior must have both natures.   600
But (Woe is me!) I know by
certain signs that Narcissus,
is Son of God, and
born of a true Woman:
sufficient reasons

to fear that he is this
very Savior. And because,
returning to the allegory again,
I say again that I fear
that Narcissus, who disdains   610
my nobility and my worth,
loves this shepherdess.
Frequently his taste
observes no convention,
disdaining brocade
for coarse woolen cloth.
And so to prevent (How sad!)
beyond the injury done
my being and my beauty,
a greater hurt from coming   620
my way, we need to consult
to see if we can prevent
him seeing her. Is it not possible
at least to put something
in the turgid waters
of her sin,
so that his image will
be blotted out?
What do you think?

PRIDE
What can I think, since I   630
am your idea? Since the first
moment of your being I have been
your inseparable companion,
so much so that for consenting
to my arrogant proposals,
you are in disgrace with Narcissus.
Though he and all his band despise
your talents and your nobility,
you already know when
the rest abandon you,   640
I alone remain at your side,
always your Pride.

DRAMA

SELF-LOVE
You engendered me
the instant you planned
to set your supreme seat
above the highest heaven,   (Isa 14:13)
and become equal of God
Most High, to counter
those indistinct visions
that seemed to inform you,   650
that one although inferior
to you in nature,
in merit would
be more exalted.
Seeing yourself then
the target of the offense
caused such resentment,
engendered such pain,
that your tenderness was transformed
into mortal hatred,   660
your loving devotion changed
to raging fury.
Since I am your Self-Love,
why do you doubt that I
think you perfect, and
that when you suffer,
all the world suffers?
May this vile shepherdess suffer!
May Narcissus suffer and die,
if their dying will erase,
the injury done us!   670

ECHO
Since you agree, let us go
to that mountain's sublime
height where he is hiding
with wild beasts for company,
so forgetful of himself
that he has not eaten

111

in forty days. And with a
stratagem I will
learn if he is divine.
Such fortitude would   680
indicate as much, but later
when hunger torments him,
it will reveal him
as no more than human,
brought low by hunger.   (Matt 4:1–4)
It is then I intend to arrive,
alluring and full of love.
Who doubts that temptation,
will be stronger if it touches
him in the form of a woman?   690
Thus you both will be
witnesses of all
that happens.

PRIDE AND SELF-LOVE
We shall do it because
our strength lies in your company.

ACT 2

Scene v

*(A mountain and at its peak DIVINE NARCISSUS, as a hand-
some shepherd with some animals. As ECHO climbs the mountain,
NARCISSUS says from the summit:)*

NARCISSUS
On this high mountain whose
proud face is kissed by heaven,
animals oblivious to my misfortunes,
in their innocence are my companions,   (Mark 1:13)
and songbirds
with their sweet music

greet my beauty,
more brilliant than the sun, purer than the dawn.
I do not receive food
of a material nature
for my abstinence compensates
for a shameless bite freely consumed.

(*ECHO arrives at the summit and sings as recitative:*)

ECHO
Most beautiful Narcissus,
to these human valleys
from the summit of your glory
you bring heavenly things.   710

Listen to my troubles,
unworthy to be heard,
but even if you do I hardly hope
for help in my troubles.
I am Echo, the richest
shepherd girl of these valleys.
Even in misfortune
call me beautiful.
But since you so severely
censured my beauty,   720
what once I sang as lovely
I now weep as ugly.

Since you know best of all
how your eyes' magnetic
power pulls all
wills to your own,
it can be no surprise to see me
come in search of you
since all the world adores
your celestial perfection.   730

And thus I come to tell you
since my nobility and
endowments fail to soften
your hard heart,
perhaps something in you
looks with interest on
my bounty available
for your pleasure.
I plan to pay you, so
there will be no mismatch   740
between what is offered
and the person begging to offer.

Since selfishness
at every age
motivates those
love's arrows have
pierced, behold a view
of all that the eye can see
from this exalted mountain,
a vision that puts Atlas to shame.   750

See these flocks
that flood the valleys,
grazing in fertile meadows,
as though set among emeralds.

See the milk's
snowy curds, whose
whiteness shames
the jasmine
born of the dawn.

See the ruddy spears of grain
as they grow in the fields   760
like straw-colored silk
billowing in the wind.

See the mountains
rich with minerals,
heavy with gold,
rubies, and diamonds.

See how in the proud sea
in sea shells congealing,
the dawn's tears transform
into oriental pearls.   770

See the fertile gardens
where fruit-bearing trees
of different species
yield wonderful fruit.

See the green pines
crowning the mountains
as they try like the giants
of old to assault the heavens.

Listen to the harmonies
of the songbirds   780
in choirs distinct
forming sweet descants.

See from one pole to the other
kingdoms expand,
their borders divided
by the arms of the oceans.
See the sailing ships
as with ambitious prows
they plow the sea's
crystalline reflection of the sky.   790

See how diverse are
the animals in these caves.
Some come out ferociously,
others flee like cowards.

Beautiful Narcissus, all this
is subject to my will,
all these are my possessions,
my bridal gifts.

All will be yours
if you set severity aside
in your gracious heart
and come and adore me.

800

NARCISSUS
Hateful Nymph, your own
ambition deceives you.
My beauty alone is
worthy to be worshiped.

(Deut 6:13)

Get out of my sight. Go
to the ends of the earth
to continual suffering,
to suffering without end.

810

ECHO
Very well, I'm going, but be advised
that from this point on
my hatred is declared.
I must procure
your death to see
if my implacable pain
will die when you die,
will end when your end comes.

ACT 3

(Landscape with wood and meadow; and in the background a fountain.)

Scene vi

(The mountain disappears and HUMAN NATURE emerges.)

HUMAN NATURE
Spent from my search for Narcissus,
permitting no pause in my rambling,   820
nor respite for my weary feet,
for many days now I have
examined the stony ground
finding no more than a trace.
I have arrived at this woods hoping here
to find news of my lost love.
All signs I consult
confirm that flowering meadows
of such delight spring from
the sweet kiss of his feet.   830

Oh, how many days have I examined
the forest, flower by flower, plant by plant,
as I wasted away in anguish,
my heart constricted with pain
and my feet, exhausted, stumbling on
through time become centuries, through woodland
    become world.

Let the ages be my witness
to regions I have traveled.
to sighs uttered,
to tears in torrents shed,   (Jer 9:1)   840
to labors, shackles, prisons
suffered on many occasions.

Once as I sought him, the guards
of the city came upon me. Insolent,
not only did they take
my cloak, but inflicted a thousand wounds,
these sentries of the high walls,
holding me fast, certain of my evil ways.　　　　(Song 5:7)

O nymphs living in this flowery
and pleasant meadow, earnestly I entreat you,　　　850
should you perchance encounter
the one my soul desires, tell him
of my passion, of the yearning
with which love has made sick my soul.　　　(Song 5:9)

If you want me to show you my Beloved,
I will paint him in ruddy splendor
on snowy jasmine.
Around his neck fall curls of gold.
Loving are his eyes, like the eyes of the dove　(Song 5:11–13)
who dwells on the banks of rushing waters.　　　860

His breath exhales the fragrance of myrrh.
Round about his hands are
hyacinths, for festive dress,　　　　(Song 5:13–14)
or to show his grievous pains,
since the hyacinth is luminous with *AIs*
it boasts as many rings as it does cries.[3]

Two pillars of marble, above bases of
gold, support his beautiful form.
Delightful in many ways is he,
and most gentle. Ivory, his white throat　　　870
is all appealing and desirable.
Such is, O nymphs, my divine Lover!　　　(Song 5:9–16)

One among ten thousand is he,　　　　(Song 5:10)
as the graceful pomegranate shines
in the flowery meadow

planted among trees more common,
so no other shepherd equals him.
He stands out among all the others.

Tell me where is he whom my soul adores   (Song 1:6)
or where does he pasture his lambs,   880
or where at the noonday does
he rest his eyes, so that I do not start
aimlessly wandering among the flocks,
in my search for him.   (Songs 2:7)

Yet, to my joy, I see fulfilled
the mysterious weeks of Daniel.   (Dan 9:24–7)
It is my desire to obtain
the joyous, loving promises
Isaiah offers me
in all his holy prophecies.   890

Already that child, lovely and beautiful,
has been born, that tender Son,
on whose soft hair glory, on whose
shoulders governance shall rest:
Marvelous, God of Power, Counselor,
King, and Father of ages to come.   (Isa 9:5)

Already on Jesse's mysterious branch
buds the beautiful flower
on whose crown will rest
the divine spirit, which unites   900
wisdom, counsel, intelligence,
fortitude, piety, reverence, and knowledge.   (Isa 11:1–3)

Already the fruit of David's line   (Luke 20:41)
has his father's throne. The wolf
and lamb are joined, bound together
the kid with the wild leopard.
The bear and the calf together rest,
and the lion, like the bull, grazes in the pasture. (Isa 11:6–7)

119

The newborn prince calmly plays
in the hollow with the poisonous asp.   1000[4]
To the cave of the noxious basilisk,
the beautiful boy arrives,
binds him, and enters safely,
unharmed by his impure breath.[5]   (Isa 11:8–9)

The sign Ahaz refused to request
and God granted without his asking
is now visible. God has made
a marvel, miraculous far exceeding
the expectations of nature:
A virgin gives birth and remains a virgin. (Isa 7:10–14) 1010

Kept was the promise made to Abraham,
repeated to Isaac, that
from his stock and noble line
God would bless all people.
Those born to all nations,
should share in his blessings.   (Gen 22:18)

The scepter of Judah (though seeming lost),
according to Jacob's prophesy
foretold the arrival of the hope
and joy of the world,   1020
the Lord's long sought salvation,
which he in prophetic vision foresaw.   (Gen 49:10, 18)

All I need now is to see the greater
sacrifice consummated.
Oh, if only it would happen,
so that my love would merit seeing
the sweet face of my beloved!
Then no matter how exhausted, follow him I would,
since he said who follows him will find him.   (Jer 29:12–13)

O my divine beloved! Who will enjoy
approaching your generous spirit,   1030
more fragrant than rare wine,
than the most precious ointment!
Your name is like oil poured out,
for this the nymphs have loved you.   (Song 1:1–5)

Following your fragrance, I run quickly.
Oh, how right that all adore you!
But you are not expecting
me colored by the sun's hot rays.
See, though I am black, I am beautiful,
since your marvelous image I resemble.   (Song 1:5)   1040

But over there a beautiful shepherdess I see!
Who could this beautiful pilgrim be?
Does desire deceive me?
Did I once see her divine light?
I will draw near her
to see if I can confirm this.

Scene vii

(GRACE enters, as a shepherdess, singing. The two approach.)

GRACE
Rejoice, world! Rejoice,
Human Nature,
because these steps you take
draw you nearer to Grace.   1050
Happy the soul
who merits receiving me in her dwelling!
A thousand times blessed
the one who sees me up close.
The sun is close
at the break of day.

Happy the soul
who merits receiving me in her dwelling!

*(MUSIC repeats the final verse, as HUMAN NATURE reaches
her.)*

HUMAN NATURE
Beautiful shepherdess, who astounds,
sweet siren, who enchants
no less with your beauty
than with your voice beyond compare!
Since you direct your voice to me
and demand that I rejoice
at some happy news,
according to your harmonies:

HUMAN NATURE AND GRACE
Rejoice, world! Rejoice,
Human Nature,
because these steps you take
draw you nearer to Grace.
Happy the soul,
who merits receiving me in her dwelling!

HUMAN NATURE
What is this? And you, who are you?
Tell me. Because though
it seems that long ago
I saw your face,
the details remain so clouded
that I do not recognize you.

GRACE
This does not surprise me since only
briefly was I with you. Then you were
careless and did not know my worth,
until you lost sight of me.

1060

1070

1080

122

HUMAN NATURE
Well, then, tell me, Who are you?

GRACE
Do you not recall a lady
in that beautiful garden
where you were created
at your father's command?
It was my pleasure to accompany you,
assisting you, until
that disgrace,
which left him angry,
left you an outcast,
left me apart from you
in punishment for your crime
until now.

HUMAN NATURE
Oh, happy she
who once more beholds your face,
divine Grace, for you are
the soul's greatest gift!
Embrace me!

GRACE
No, not yet!
You still need
one great quality
before I can embrace you.

HUMAN NATURE
If it be a question of my diligence...

GRACE
It is not in your hands, although
you can apply your diligence
to be well disposed to attain it.
Human effort is not strong enough

1090

1100

123

to merit it, although
with tears you can beg   1110
to attain it as the gracious gift
it is. For this is not justice, but grace.

HUMAN NATURE
How do I prepare for it?

GRACE
How? By following in my footsteps
and arriving at that fountain
whose crystal clear waters
have been free of impurities,
forever clean, forever intact.
From its first instant
forever unsullied flowing.   1120
This is the sealed fountain
according to the Song of Songs
from which issues paradise,
from which flow life-giving waters.   (Song 4:12)
The mysterious tiny stream that Mordecai
dreamed, whose flow
increased to such abundance,
forming a great river,
which in its turn was transformed   1130
by light and sun, flooding
the fields with its force.   (Esth 10:5–6, Vulgate)

HUMAN NATURE
I know this spring was Esther
and in Esther was prefigured
the divine image
of the one who is full of grace.
O divine Fountain, O wellspring
of life-giving waters!
From your life's first instant
you were spared   1140
the primal poison

of the transcendental fault
infesting all other rivers.
You reflect the clear image
of Narcissus's beauty.
In you alone is his beauty
portrayed with perfection,
his likeness delivered intact!

GRACE
Happy Nature,
now so near   1150
to attaining your relief!
Come to the sacred spring
of whose crystal currents
I have been the keeper.
Yesterday its flow
began immaculate
by singular privilege.
Let us wait for Narcissus,
hidden among these branches.
I am sure he will be drawn here   1160
to cool the burning thirst
that consumes him.
Try your best to have
your face reflected in the water,
so that when he comes,
seeing in you his own likeness
he will fall in love with you.

HUMAN NATURE
Before I do so, let me greet
her through whom
my yearning will be stilled.   1170

GRACE
A worthy request that is, and so
I will help you to invoke her.

SOR JUANA INÉS DE LA CRUZ

(GRACE sings:)

O fountain ever crystal
clear and lovely,
linger, linger!
Let my ruin be restored
by your waves as they rush,
clear, clean, lustrous, life-giving.

HUMAN NATURE
Let not your clear stream
skip by so swiftly,   1180
but tarry, tarry!
Wait for my tears
to flow in your current,
holy, pure, sparkling, and bright.

GRACE
Fount of perfections,
of all creatures the best,
replete, replete
with merits and gifts,
untouched by stain,
risk, shadow, or sin!   1190

HUMAN NATURE
The venomous serpent
dares not come into your sight.
Faraway, faraway
from your lovely spring
his venom loses its sting.
You flow clean, safe, and free.

GRACE
No wild or wily beast,
can approach your waters.
Such are they, such are they
and such is their nature that   1200

along with their sweetness they bestow
strength, health, pleasure, and good fortune.

HUMAN NATURE
Reflect my image
if Narcissus stops by
clearly, clearly,
so that when he sees it
he feels the effects of love,
its yearning, desire, tears, and devotion.

GRACE
Now on the flowery bank,
where its liquid silver   1210
reflects the carnations set
in emerald fields,
we sit awaiting his approach.
I do not doubt
that whatever Nature
pulls him this way
is united to Grace.

HUMAN NATURE
If I can prepare to receive Grace
as much as my human
strength permits,
I obey what you command.   1220

Scene viii

(The two arrive at the fountain. HUMAN NATURE places her-
self among the branches, as does GRACE, so that it seems that they are
looking at each other. NARCISSUS enters from another direction, with
a sling, dressed as a shepherd, and he sings the last verse of each stanza
and speaks the rest.)

SOR JUANA INÉS DE LA CRUZ

NARCISSUS
Little lost lamb,
who forgot your Master,
where have you wandered?
See how when estranged from me   (Matt 18; Luke 15)
(Sings)
a stranger to your own life you become.   (Jer 2:13)

You drink from
exhausted cisterns   (Jeremiah. 2:11)
to quench your foolish thirst,   (Mic 7:16)
and with deaf ears
(Sings)
drift away from the waters of life.   1230

Remember my favors.
Know that my love will always
watch over you with care,   (Deut 32:6)
free you from your offense,
(Sings)
and invest my life in your defense.   (John 10:17–18)

Covered with frost and snow   (Song 5:3)
I continue to follow
your foolish steps, knowing,
ungrateful one, that you are not touched
(Sings)
by seeing that for you ninety-nine I left behind.
          (Matt 28; Luke 15)   1240
See how my beauty
by all is loved
by all pursued,
no creature excepting,
(Sings)
but only you did I destine for delight!

Along paths of horror
I follow your steps

128

wounding my feet
on the painful thorns   (Deut 32:9–11)
(Sings)
produced in this unfriendly forest.   1250

Pursue you I must.
Though it cost me my life
in pursuit I remain.
I may not leave you,
(Sings)
before giving up my life to find you.

Foolish one, of erring reason
is this the way you respond to me?
Am I not the One who created you?   (Deut 32:6–7)
Why do you not respond to me?
(Sings)
And why (as if you could) do you hide from me?   1260

Ask your forebears
about my favors:
the abundant rivers,
the pastures and green grasses   (Ps 22:1–2, Vulgate)
(Sings)
in which my love sustains you.

In a field of thistles,
in uninhabited land
when I found you alone, at risk
of being ravished by the wolf
(Sings)
I protected you, daughter, light of my eyes!   1270

I took you to the greenness
of meadows most pleasant
where I nourished you
with the sweetness of honey,

(Sings)
and oil pressed from hard rock.   (Deut 32:13)

I sustained you with
a delicious food made
from the marrow
of finest wheat
(Sings)
and with wine from fragrant grapes.   (Deut 32:14)   1280

You became fat and frisky,
full of pride and conceit
at your own splendor,
vain and haughty
(Sings)
you forgot my sovereign beauty.

You sought out other shepherds
unknown to your parents
unacknowledged and
unhonored by your forebears   (Deut 32:15–17)
(Sings)
and incited my fury.   1290

I broke away enraged.
I will hide my face
(at whose glare the golden
chariot of the sun stands still)
(Sings)
from this ungrateful, perverse, unfaithful flock.

I will let my fury
consume the fields,
and the grazing grass.
My rage can level
(Sings)
even the highest mountains.   1300

DRAMA

Swiftly my arrows
will seek them out. Hunger will
cut the thread of life.
Birds of prey and
(Sings)
wild beasts will devour them.

They will taste the venom
of slithering snakes.
Different deaths
my rage will exact:
(Sings)
The blade without, terror within.   (Deut 32:20–25)   1310
Sovereign am I,
none is stronger.
Life and death I deal.
I wound and I heal.
(Sings)
See, not one escapes my hand.   (Deut 32:39)

But a burning thirst
afflicts and fatigues me.
It is good that the path
leads to this clear fountain,
(Sings)
where I will try to temper its heat.   1320

Since for your sake I have suffered
the hunger to possess you,
it is a small thing to show you
how to win my devotion
(Sings)
and how much I am ablaze with thirst for you.

ACT 4

Scene ix

(The same landscape, but with a fountain center stage. Everything above has to be said on the way to the fountain. When he arrives at it, he looks in it and says:)

NARCISSUS
Here I am at last. What is this I see?
What sovereign beauty
affronts with its pure light
the sapphire blue of heaven?
Shining as it turns, the sun   1330
all along its shining path
as it travels from east to west
does not scatter in signs and stars
so much light, so many sparks
as does this one fountain.

Heaven and earth conspire
to surround her with a fiery glow,
the heavens with its lantern,
the meadow with its flowers.
Everything in the heavenly spheres   1340
serves as her adornment.
But no, such a beauty
without equal, surpasses all
the diligence of earth
or heaven to fashion.

Pink of pomegranate seeds
paints her cheeks.
Her two lips parted
as a rosy ribbon embellish
her delicate voice that   1350
puts choirs to shame
and exhales wisdom

and the scent of carnations.
Her mouth pours forth milk and honey.
Her lips distill honeycombs.   (Song 4:3, 11)

The pearls in their shallow shell
like a flock of sheep
driven together
descend like snowflakes.   (Song 4:2)
Her body with its graceful motion   1360
sways like the palm tree.   (Song 7:7)
Her eyes, which reveal
a glowing soul,
shine brilliant as the sun,
gentle as the dove.   (Song 5:12)

Smooth the delicate figure,
offered to view,
appears as heaps of wheat,
among lilies of the valley.   (Song 7:2)
Her neck, a graceful column   (Song 7:4)   1370
of sculpted marble.
No thing can equal
the radiance of her beauty,
as unique as the sun,
lovely as the moon.

A glance from her eyes
has inflamed my heart,
a lock of her hair
has pierced my breast.   (Song 4:9)

Open the crystal seal   1380
of this clear cool center,
so that my love can enter!
See, frost crowns my golden hair,
my curls are laden
with pearls of dew.   (Song 5:2)

Come, my spouse, to your beloved.
Break this clear veil,
show me your lovely face,
let your voice resound in my ears!   (Song 2:14)

Come, from matchless Lebanon!   1390
As soon as you come
I will crown the gold
of your precious hair
with a fragrant crown from
Amana, Hermon, and Senir.   (Song 4:8)

Scene x

*(He remains as if suspended leaning over the fountain. Enter
ECHO, as if she has been lying in wait for him.)*

ECHO
What is this my eyes behold?
Either I am suffering delusions because of my troubles
or I see Narcissus at this fountain,
whose clear currents
have escaped the course of my fury.   1400
Would I were so lucky as to put
poison in its crystal waters
to bring an end to all my troubles!
By drinking my poison there
he would suffer the anguish I suffer.
I need to hurry, since I think that now as he bends
over the water he is quenching
his thirst.

(She arrives at the fountain and then draws back.)

But what do I see?
Confused, I lose courage and draw back.
He is contemplating   1410

his own likeness and seeing
Human Nature.
O fatal destiny of my star!
How I feared that if he saw her clearly,
he would fall in love with her,
and finally it has happened! Oh, pain! Oh, rage!
I curse heaven that has so wronged me!
So fierce my pain, not even
leaving me breath to complain,
such anguish I feel as if there were   1420
a snake, a dagger at my throat.
If I want to articulate my voice, I cannot
and with half a voice remain,
raw rage leaving me
only a final syllable.
Holy scripture, which defames me,
on occasion calls me mute
(because although formally
I cannot be so, I am by means
of efficient cause, rendering mute   1430
those I have possessed with my fury.
It spoke metaphorically
as when we say "the happy meadow"
meaning it causes happiness,
or of a fountain, when we say it laughs.)
Narcissus also from time to time
renders me mute,
by publishing his divine Being,
and rebuking me he cuts off my voice.   (Mark 1:24–26)
Little wonder now that he would also want   1440
the ferocity of my longing
when I see him to strike me speechless.
But, oh! my throat is tied in a knot;
pain renders me mute.
Where is my Pride? Why does she not appear?
Why does she not alleviate my hurt?
And my Self-Love, why does he not stir up

or inspire my arguments?
I am struck dumb! Woe is me!

Scene xi

(She gestures as though she wants to speak but cannot. Enter as if frightened PRIDE and SELF-LOVE.)

SELF-LOVE
What confusion
causes Echo's sad lament?   1450
And though it is nothing new to see what she feels,
this appears to be some new trouble
depriving her of her senses.

PRIDE
Like a statue of her self, struck dumb,
even breathing causes her pain.
Her affliction is suffocating her,
though she signals silently, moaning and weeping.

SELF-LOVE
We are here to console her in her distress,
though it may serve to augment her affliction.

PRIDE
Let's find out what offends her,   1460
although it may cause greater grief.

SELF-LOVE
Since to have her Self-Love with her,
is clearly more punishing.

PRIDE
Since in view of her Pride, who doubts
that her torment will now be greater?

SELF-LOVE
Look, I think carried away by her fury
she is going to throw herself off the mountain.
Let's restrain her!

PRIDE
I want to pursue her,
though I am the one precipitating this.

(They get to her and seize her. She struggles as if she wants to throw herself down the mountain.)

PRIDE
Stop, lovely Echo! Where are you going? Wait!　　　1470
Tell us what has led you to this!
Why do you intend to cast yourself down?
Doesn't it inspire you to see your Pride?
How could I want to see you downcast,
since I have always worked to see you exalted?

SELF-LOVE
Doesn't seeing your Self-Love encourage you?
How can I bear that you hurt yourself,
if it means for having loved you
so much, we are reduced to this state?

(They say all this while holding fast to her and from this position she responds to them.)

PRIDE
Halt! I've got you! I have…　　　1480

ECHO
I have…

SELF-LOVE
Recount your anguish and pain.

ECHO
…pain.

PRIDE
Tell us the cause of your rage.

ECHO
…rage.

(From backstage MUSIC on a sad note, repeats the echoes.)

SELF-LOVE
Because you are so wise
tell us, what has happened,
or what you are feeling?

ECHO
I have pain, rage…

SELF-LOVE
So what do you want us to see?   1490

ECHO
To see…

PRIDE
Why or what has caused that…?

ECHO
…that…

SELF-LOVE
Is there news of Narcissus?

ECHO
…Narcissus…

PRIDE
Tell us, what made you

stop here, by chance
or is it only...?

ECHO
To see that Narcissus...

PRIDE
Don't despair! Ah...   1500

ECHO
Ah...

SELF-LOVE
even could he stop from being...

ECHO
...being...

PRIDE
Not even this clay, so fragile

ECHO
...fragile...

SELF-LOVE
can rival your charms,
nor oblige your Lover.
But whom is he looking for?

ECHO
...a being, fragile...

SELF-LOVE
Can it be that she is the one he loves?   1510

ECHO
...loves.

PRIDE
Is this an insult?

ECHO
...an insult.

SELF-LOVE
She is the cause of this affront to me.

ECHO
...to me.

PRIDE
My rage pours forth
fueled by my insane fury;
such a worthless, low-class...

ECHO
...loves, an insult to me...

PRIDE
Let us sing her words, which though cut off   1520
express her suffering in pieces,
so that we may learn
fully of the injury, still unknown.

SELF-LOVE
It is better to listen to her,
as she repeats them in the rhythm of her lament.

(ECHO says with furious broken cadences:)

I have pain, rage
to see that Narcissus
a being fragile loves,
an insult to me.

(MUSIC repeats the entire stanza.)

SELF-LOVE
Let us hide her in the hollow trunk   1530
of this dead tree, so that hoarse moan
of her tearful lament
does not reach the ears of Narcissus.
There sadly we both must accompany her,
since we cannot be separated from her.

Scene xii

(They exit, carrying her away. NARCISSUS rises from the fountain.)

NARCISSUS
Woodlands, whom have you seen
the long years of your life,
who yearns as I yearn,
who loves as I love?

Whom have you seen, in the centuries'   1540
incessant course of endless days,
whom witnessed, my woodlands,
who died of the disease I die of?

I see what I desire,
but am unable to enjoy it,
and in the longing to attain it,
I suffer mortal anguish.

I know that she adores me
and returns my love
because she smiles, if I smile,   1550
and when I weep, she weeps.

I cannot deceive myself.
Well I know,
it is my own likeness

causing me this pain.
I am in love with her
and though it kill me,
it is easier for me to leave
this life than to cease caring.

(He says the following as he arrives at ECHO's hiding place. She responds to him from where she is.)

NARCISSUS
Intolerable is the torment...   1560

ECHO
...torment.

NARCISSUS
...of the pain I suffer...

ECHO
...I suffer.

NARCISSUS
...with a severity intolerable.

ECHO
...intolerable.

NARCISSUS
Because there is in me a terrible grief
and in the pain I'm dying of
from not attaining what I love.

ECHO AND NARCISSUS
Torment I suffer intolerable.

NARCISSUS
Oh, how sad it will be when...   1570

ECHO
...when...

NARCISSUS
...disfigured will be my beauty.

ECHO
...my beauty.

NARCISSUS
Of all, the most perfect!

ECHO
...perfect...

NARCISSUS
My pain without equal
has made me subject to suffering,
since it has violated my being.

ECHO AND NARCISSUS
When my beauty most perfect...

NARCISSUS
How has love...   1580

ECHO
...love...

NARCISSUS
...the power to subject me thus...

ECHO
...thus...

NARCISSUS
...and to wrench me from the immortal!

ECHO
...mortal.

NARCISSUS
For love I suffer this sickness
and feel its terrible grief
for the one who was immortal...

ECHO AND NARCISSUS
...love thus made mortal.

NARCISSUS
How can such fierceness subject...   1590

ECHO
...subject...

NARCISSUS
...to such pain that is inhuman...

ECHO
...human...

NARCISSUS
...my divine nature, which is impassible?

ECHO
...passible.

NARCISSUS
Moreover, without a doubt
love's strength is invincible,
since it has made my beauty...

ECHO AND NARCISSUS
...subject, human, passible.

MUSIC AND NARCISSUS
Torment I suffer intolerable   1600

when my beauty most perfect
love thus made mortal,
subject, human, passible.

NARCISSUS
Boldly Love...

ECHO
...Love...

NARCISSUS
...wanted to show that he could,...

ECHO
...could...

NARCISSUS
...and me with his arrows wound.

ECHO
...wound.

NARCISSUS
Who else could lead me   1610
to where I now so painfully live
except him, and his swift shafts?

ECHO AND NARCISSUS
Love could wound?

NARCISSUS
He set his sights on me.

ECHO
...me.

NARCISSUS
And he showed,...

ECHO
He showed…

NARCISSUS
…even flaunted his might,…

ECHO
…his might.

NARCISSUS
…by lowering the scale   1620
of my sovereign divinity
to make it equal to humanity.

ECHO AND NARCISSUS
He showed his might.

NARCISSUS
My soul is sad and loving.   (Matt 26:38)

ECHO
…loving.

NARCISSUS
And without regard for me, now…

ECHO
…now…

NARCISSUS
I go to look for my likeness.

ECHO
…my likeness.

NARCISSUS
Who would not be touched   1630
by the mystery of my sighs?
Who not astounded to see me…

ECHO AND NARCISSUS
...loving now my likeness.

NARCISSUS
...meek and loving from heaven,...

ECHO
...from heaven...

NARCISSUS
...from my throne I came,...

ECHO
...I came...

NARCISSUS
...unaware I came to die.

ECHO
...to die.

NARCISSUS
No one can measure   1640
how great my tender affection.
Forgetful of my majesty,

ECHO AND NARCISSUS
from heaven I came to die.

MUSIC AND NARCISSUS
Love could wound me.
He showed his might.
Loving now my likeness,
from heaven I came to die.

NARCISSUS
It seems that from this hollow tree I hear an echo...

ECHO
...echo.

NARCISSUS
...who with sad voice and lamenting...

ECHO
...lamenting...

NARCISSUS
...thus to my words responds...   1650

ECHO
...responds...

NARCISSUS
Who are you, O voice? Oh, where
are you concealed, hidden from me?
Answer me, afflicted one?

ECHO AND NARCISSUS
Echo lamenting responds.

NARCISSUS
Well, since from what you have been seeing...

ECHO
...seeing...

NARCISSUS
What is it that your love...

ECHO
...that your love...

NARCISSUS
...hopes, your spite desires...   1660

ECHO
…desires…

NARCISSUS
…since without recognizing your error
guided by your Self-Love
you only walk in error?

ECHO AND NARCISSUS
Seeing that your love desires.

NARCISSUS
If you see that I always have to love…

ECHO
…to love…

NARCISSUS
…even though it be a being…

ECHO
…a being…

NARCISSUS
…that although you judge inferior   1670

ECHO
…inferior…

NARCISSUS
is the object of my love.
Just what your pride disdains,
my own goodness teaches me

ECHO AND NARCISSUS
To love a being inferior!

NARCISSUS
Love I must, and so…

SOR JUANA INÉS DE LA CRUZ

ECHO
…so…

NARCISSUS
from you my beauty I will hide,   1680

ECHO
I will hide…

NARCISSUS
And remain concealed from your eyes.

ECHO
…from your eyes.

NARCISSUS
Since there can never be a match
between your pride and the humility
which my beauty desires.   (Job 22:29; Matt 23:12)

ECHO AND NARCISSUS
So I will hide from your eyes.

ECHO AND MUSIC
Echo complaining responds,
seeing that your love desires
to love a being inferior,   1690
so I will hide from your eyes.

(Narcissus goes to the fountain.)

NARCISSUS
Now suffering has crushed me. Now, now I arrive at
my destined death for my beloved's sake.
Scant is the material of one life
for the form of a fire so great.
Now I give license to death. Now I give over   (John 10:18)
my soul, to be separated from my body,
although both soul and body remain

150

rooted in my divinity, later to be reunited.
I thirst. The love that has consumed me,   (John 19:28) 1700
and all the pain I am suffering,
have still not been able to fill my heart.
Father, why in such a fearful hour
do you forsake me? Now it is finished.

(Matt 27:46; John 19:30)

Into your hands I commend my Spirit!

(Luke 23:46)

ACT 5

Scene xiii

(Sounds of an earthquake. NARCISSUS fall behind the curtain. Enter ECHO, PRIDE, and SELF-LOVE terrified.)

ECHO
An eclipse!

PRIDE
An earthquake!

SELF-LOVE
Stupefying!

ECHO
Horrifying!

PRIDE
Terrifying!

ECHO
The sun's light extinguished
in the middle of its course.

SOR JUANA INÉS DE LA CRUZ

SELF-LOVE
The air is full of spirits! 1710

PRIDE
The moon has put on mourning!

ECHO
The earth, contradicting
its characteristic firmness,
shudders with dread,
and opens its secret center,
collapsing mountains,
to reveal the tombs of the dead. (Matt 27:45–53)

PRIDE
Rocks, moved to compassion
their hard faces break open,
and crack into pieces, showing 1720
even the insensate capable
of sentiment.

ECHO
And the most
astonishing thing I have discovered
is that this eclipse was not caused
by the natural concourse
of sun and moon, when
both luminaries are together
in a perpendicular line
and the interposition of the one
does not allow us to see the other, 1730
and so the sun appears darkened,
not because it is, but
because its pure brilliance
cannot be seen. But now,
following separate paths,
they are distant from each other.
No heavenly body moves in front

to obscure its light.
Rather, ill-fated and faded   1740
it shuts down its brilliance
as if it were an ember.

SELF-LOVE
And perhaps since having
observed this, in all the uproar
where all the universe
is at the service of the rabble
I seem to hear
some great astrologer's voice breaking
through the astonished multitude.

VOICE FROM BACKSTAGE
Either the author of the universe is suffering,   1750
or the machinery of the world is perishing![6]

SELF-LOVE
Oh, the power of love! Oh, the power
of a loving impulse,
to cross the line of death,
to break the wall of hell!
The surrender to love
leads to an even greater triumph!
But wait, another distinct voice
I hear among the multitude.

VOICE FROM BACKSTAGE
This man was truly just!   (Luke 23:47–48)   1760

PRIDE
Another voice no less clear,
or the same, with the arrogance
of faith, and in wonder
confesses with many others.

VOICE FROM BACKSTAGE
Without doubt this man was the Son of God!   (Matt 27:54)

SOR JUANA INÉS DE LA CRUZ

ECHO
Oh, woe is me! Already his death
is beginning to bear the fruit
of that mysterious seed
which hidden in the earth's depth
appeared dead, and later   1770
produced so many sheaves of grain!   (John 12:23–25)
Oh, never prophecy
was heard, through impure lips,
that for all to live
one must die!   (John 11:50)
Oh, never when, deceived and blind,
would I have sought his death
by so many different paths,
judging my offense
to be avenged with his death,   1780
had I known that all my diligence
would only result in providing
the means for his loving pride
to work the greatest benefit of all
by dying for his image!
But although the savage serpent envy
ripped my heart
to shreds, now at least
I have the consolation (as if
I had any room for consolation)   1790
of achieving that in the world
he is not present to the eyes
of that vulgar girl. Given her coarse
nature, and her ungrateful
demeanor, it will not take long,
since she cannot see him, for her to forget him.

SELF-LOVE
Very well said. I have no doubt
when her eyes can see him no longer
she will forget the greatest
benefit she owes him   1800

154

and return to the path
of her past sins.
Habitual insults
are difficult to forget,
with no one to erase
them from her mind
with contrary material,
with different memories.

PRIDE
So now our task will be
to see that she forgets   1810
his benefits.
If after receiving so many
she offends him again, I have no doubt
it will be for her greater pain
and our greater glory.

ECHO
Well said. But here she comes
with a pious parade
of nymphs and shepherds
weeping as misfortune
what is her great good luck.   1820
Let us wait here hidden,
to see where these ill-fated
pronouncements are leading.

Scene xiv

*(They go over to one side. Enter HUMAN NATURE weeping,
and all the NYMPHS and SHEPHERDS and MUSIC, sadly.)*

HUMAN NATURE
Nymphs who live
in this wild land,
some in clear waters,

others in green trees.
Shepherds, who roam
these happy meadows,
you keep the flocks
in rustic simplicity.   1830
Early death
has closed the divine eyes
of my beautiful Narcissus,
the glory of your refuge.
Respond, respond, to my anguish!
Bewail, lament his death!

MUSIC
Bewail, lament his death!

HUMAN NATURE
Through his love, came his death.
What fate had not
within its power
his own love conquered.   1840
Seeing his reflection
he fell in love unto death.
A mere copy of his image
had such a great effect.
Respond, respond to my anguish.
Bewail, lament his death!

MUSIC
Bewail, lament his death!

HUMAN NATURE
All the universe regrets   1850
his untimely end.
Boulders crack apart.
Mountains melt with compassion.
The moon puts on mourning.
North and South Poles shudder.
The sun hides its light.

The sky grows dark.
Respond, respond to my anguish.
Bewail, lament his death!

MUSIC
Bewail, lament his death!   1860

HUMAN NATURE
Air is cloaked in clouds.
Earth shudders.
Fire flames up in agitation.
Water seethes and churns.
With open mouths
the dark graves
now reveal
that even the dead can feel.
Respond, respond to my anguish.   (Matt 27:52)
Bewail, lament his death!   1870

MUSIC
Bewail, lament his death!

HUMAN NATURE
In the temple the reverent
veil is rent,
revealing now
the abrogation of the Law.   (Matt 27:51)
All the universe,
grieving his beauty,
goes hooded in mourning,
begging in black.
Respond, respond to my anguish.   1880
Bewail, lament his death!

MUSIC
Bewail, lament his death!

SOR JUANA INÉS DE LA CRUZ

HUMAN NATURE
Oh, you who are
passing by, look at me
and see if there is a pain
to equal my pain!   (Jer 1:12)
Alone and abandoned
I am, with none
by my side but pain,
my constant companion.
Respond, respond to my anguish.   1890
Bewail, lament his death!

MUSIC
Bewail, lament his death!

HUMAN NATURE
From force of weeping
my face is swollen,
my eyes are blinded
from tears shed.   (Job 16:16)
Within my breast,
my heart seems like
melting wax touched
by the burning flame.   (Ps 21:15, Vulgate) 1900
Respond, respond to my anguish.
Bewail, lament his death!

MUSIC
Bewail, lament his death!

HUMAN NATURE
See how his love crosses
death's border!   (Song 8:6)
Seeking his image
he goes into the abyss.
Yes, only to see her
in the waves of Lethe
he breaks the locks   1910

of rebellious diamonds.
Respond, respond to my anguish.
Bewail, lament his death!

MUSIC
Bewail, lament his death!

HUMAN NATURE
Woe is me! For my sake
his beauty suffers!   (Gal 2:20)
From my sad eyes run
two fountains of tears.   (Jer 9:1)
Look for his lovely body,
because my love   1920
wants to anoint him
with oils, sweet smelling and precious.   (Mark 16:1)
Respond, respond to my anguish.
Bewail, lament his death!

MUSIC
Bewail, lament his death!

HUMAN NATURE
Look for my life in this
image of death,
since to give life to me
was the goal of his death.   1930

(They search for him.)

But alas, unhappy me!
The body has disappeared!
Stolen away, no doubt.
Oh, who could have seen it?

(Enter GRACE.)

GRACE
Beautiful Nymph, why

this tender weeping?
What do you seek in this place?
What is the sorrow you feel?

HUMAN NATURE
I am searching for my beloved Master,
who is missing. I do not know   1940
where the harsh fates
have hidden him from my sight.   (John 20:11–13)

GRACE
Your Narcissus lives.
Do not weeps, do not mourn,
do not seek among the dead

the one who lives forever!   (Mark 16:6; Luke 24:5)

Scene xv

*(From behind HUMAN NATURE, enter NARCISSUS, with
other SHEPHERDS, as the Resurrected One. HUMAN NATURE
turns to look at him.)*

NARCISSUS
Why are you weeping, shepherdess?
These pearls that you shed
soften my heart,
touch my soul.   1950

HUMAN NATURE
I am mourning my Narcissus,
Lord. If you have him
tell me where he is, so
that I can go and take him away.   (John 20:13–15)

NARCISSUS
How, my bride,
do you not know me,

if my divine beauty
is like no other?

HUMAN NATURE
Oh, adored husband,
allow me joyfully
to kiss your feet! 1960

NARCISSUS
You may not touch me,
because I am going with my Father
to his heavenly throne. (John 20:14–17)

HUMAN NATURE
So, you are leaving me alone?
Oh, Lord, do not leave me;
the Serpent, my enemy
will return to deceive me!

Scene xvi

(Enter ECHO, PRIDE, and SELF-LOVE.)

ECHO
It is clear, that although
you showered her with many gifts, 1970
no doubt after you leave her
she will again become my prey.

PRIDE
Since she is of such a vulgar condition
if she does not see you
she will forget your affection,
and set aside your gifts.

SELF-LOVE
And I will put such snares
in her way and on her path

that she will not be free
not to be my prisoner. 1980

ECHO
I will put such blemishes
on her much esteemed beauty
disfiguring her again,
so once again she will offend you.

GRACE
Not so. I will be
at her side, defending her;
since I will be with her,
it will be hard for you to control her.

ECHO
What will it matter when it is so easy
for her to go astray, fragile as she is,
and by losing you, she must
once again become ugly? 1990

NARCISSUS
No matter, to counter your cunning
I will give her
help in danger,
and a shield for her defense.

ECHO
What good is help or shield
if as before she offends you,
with an infinite offense,
which she could never repay?
Since for one offense already 2000
you needed to die,
it is clearly not fitting
each time that she sins
for you to die
again for her.

DRAMA

NARCISSUS
For this fragility
my immense love
has anticipated remedies
so that if she falls   2010
she can pick herself up.

PRIDE
What remedy could there be
to restore her to your grace?

NARCISSUS
What remedy? Penance
and the other sacraments
that I have bound to my church
as medicine for the soul.

ECHO
Even should these be sufficient
she would not use them,
careless as she is. In your absence   2020
she will forget your love
for want of your presence.

NARCISSUS
Neither will this be lacking,
for my immense wisdom
has prepared, first
for my bitter death to be
a memorial of my love,   (Luke 22:19; 1 Cor 11:24–25)
so even when we are apart,
together we remain.

ECHO
To see how this could be   2030
is beyond my comprehension.

NARCISSUS
Well, to increase your suffering
since your torment
will be greater if you know,
and as a demonstration
of my kindness unequalled,
let Grace arrive, and summarize,
in the same metaphor
we have been using up to now,
my story!   2040

GRACE
It is right
that I obey you. And so
listen to me.

ECHO
Already my suffering
awaits you, to my sorrow.

GRACE
Well, it happened thus:
Once the beauty
of sovereign Narcissus
possessed all happiness
in his own glory,
since in himself he contained
all possible goodness   2050

as king of all loveliness,
archive of all perfection,
sphere of miracles,
center of marvels.
Heaven's crystal spheres,
chronicled his glory.
The course of their rotations,
were their feathered pens.
The shining firmament

164

announced his works   (Ps 18:2, Vulgate) 2060
and radiance of the morning stars   (Job 38:7)
sang his praises.
Fire acclaimed him with flame,
the sea with frothy crests,
the earth with lips of roses
and the wind with echoing song.

The brilliant sun boasted
to be a spark of his beauty,
and in his light the sparkling
stars went begging.   2070
Concave mirrors of
his divine radiance,
were the burnished surfaces
of the eleven sapphire spheres.
A mere sketch of his light
was the exquisite craft
of the order of the planets,
of the concert of the zodiac.
To imitate his beauty
with ornamented attire   2080
the fields decked themselves with flowers,
the mountains adorned themselves with cliffs.
The wild beasts in their caves,
the birds in their nests
lovingly determined
to adore his divinity.
In the sea's dark womb,
fish rendered him worship.

The ocean for its offering
erected altars of glass.   2090
All worshiped him
with fond devotion,
from the lowliest grass
to the tallest pine.
He revealed himself an ocean

of infinite perfection,
source of all beauty,
flowing like rivers.
In short, all things inanimate,
rational and animate, 2100
found their being when he thought them, (Col 1:16–17)
and lost it when he forgot them.
This, then, was the marvel of Loveliness
who regaled himself with roses,
who fed among lilies (Song 2:16)
in the flowering fields,
who seeing in humanity
the fleeting beauty
of his splendor
fell in love with his own image. (Gen 1:26) 2110
His own likeness
induced his love,
since for God, only God
can be a worthy object.
He rushed out to meet her,
but the more his affection
lovingly sought
the object of his desire,
the envious ones
in order to impede his noble 2120
devotion, audaciously interposed
the waters of her sins.
And seeing it nearly impossible
to attain his designs
(even for God in the world
there is no love without danger)
he determined to die
at this exacting task,
to demonstrate that risk is
the test of excellence. 2130
He humbled himself, wrote Paul,
and (if one may say so)
was consumed, tenderly

melting in the sweet fire of love.   (Phil 12:7)
Undignified anguish,
as lover he embraced,
dying finally of love,
a voluntary victim.
He gave his life to witness   (John 15:13)
his love but did not want   2140
such a glorious gift
to remain unacknowledged.
Thus he arranged to leave
a reminder and a sign
in memory of his death,
as a pledge of his affection.
This disposition was born
of his infinite knowledge,
which does not show itself as loving
without boasting of what it understands.   2150

He wanted to remain
as a white flower,
so that his absence would
not be cause for apathy.

No wonder it flourishes today,
since in times past in his writings
he called it flower of the fields,
and lily of the valley.   (Song 2:1)
Its white dress is a veil
over his loving designs,   2160
a disguise to the gross
cognition of the senses.
He wanted to remain hidden
in ermine white
to assist as a lover,
vigilant and zealous.   (Exod 21:3–5)
Who, as the soul's spouse,
is jealous of her wanderings,
spying on her from windows,

lying in wait around corners.   (Song 1:9)   2170
Generous as he is,
he stayed to grant new favors,
but did not want to give a gift
that was not beneficial.
He showed his love
with loving extravagance.
He did everything he could,
the one who could do anything he wanted.
                                        (Ps 65:3, Vulgate)
As food for our souls he remains,
generous and kind,
nourishment for the just,   2180
poison for the guilty.

*(The float with the fountain appears. Next to it a chalice with a
host on top of it.)*

See from the clear fountain's
crystalline edge has come
the beautiful white flower
of which the lover says:

NARCISSUS
This is my body and my blood
martyred so many times
for you. Repeat this
to commemorate my death.
        (Luke 22:19; Matt 26:26–27; 1 Cor 11:23–26)   2190

HUMAN NATURE
At such a token of love,
of affection beyond measure,
my soul dissolves,
my heart moved with
tenderness, sheds tears of joy.

ECHO
Ah me! Woe is me! What I have seen
renders me mute. I live alone
with suffering, dead to all relief.

SELF-LOVE
I, self-absorbed, raging, and blind
poisonous and dangerous as a snake,   2200
I give myself over to death.

PRIDE
I, who am the cause of your
destruction, a second time
I bury myself in the abyss.

GRACE
And I, now the obstacles
have been removed, and seeing
your fault undone,
which for so long has separated us,
happy Nature,
I admit you to my embrace.   2210
Come, since I want to celebrate
an eternity of peace with you!
Fear not, come into my arms!

HUMAN NATURE
With all my soul I accept!
But I come fearfully
out of appropriate reverence,
since to approach such a sacrament,
a mystery so divine,
it is only right that love
arrives arrayed in fear.   2220

(The two embrace.)

GRACE
Well now, is your happiness complete?

SOR JUANA INÉS DE LA CRUZ

HUMAN NATURE
The only thing lacking
is to give the thanks we owe;
The only thing lacking
is to give the thanks we owe;
and so in melodious harmony
let us sing his praises,
all together with me:

(They sing.)

Sing, my tongue, the deep mystery
of the glorious body,
which for a price worthy
of the world, he gave us as royal
fruit, high born, of the most pure Womb!   2230
Let us venerate this great sacrament,
where the new mystery replaces the old,
where faith supplies the effects
to replace the defects of the senses.
Glory, honor, benediction, and praise,
majesty and virtue to the Father and the Son,
be given; and to the Love that from both proceeds,
equal praise let us render![7]

Section 3

Devotional Works

Devotional Exercises for the Nine Days before the Feast of the Most Pure Incarnation[1] of the Son of God, Jesus Christ, Our Lord

Dedication

Supreme Empress of the Angels, sovereign Queen of Heaven, Lady ruling all creation: As I dedicate this work at your royal and sacred feet, you know well that it is not only a voluntary offering, but is also what I owe you as restitution for belonging to you before belonging to myself. Not only because of the sacredness of the matter at hand, but because you, Princess Immaculate, inspired some souls devoted to you to order me to prepare this. As a result nothing in it is truly my own except the crude manner and the awkward style in which it is written. For this I ask pardon of your maternal clemency, not so much for the simplemindedness of my reasoning, as for the tepid and insubstantial nature of these meditations, and for having had the audacity to take your exalted mysteries and the holy testament of your Son into my unclean mouth and write of them with my humble pen (Ps 49:16). So I entreat you, O Mediator and Gate of God's mercy! Turn your eyes away from these faults of mine. Look rather at the fruits these *Exercises* can inspire in my neighbors if you perfect them by increasing the fervor of their hearts devoted to you so that they complete them in a spirit greater than mine, with greater benefit to their souls, honor to you, and glory to your precious Son, with whom you reign for all eternity.

Introduction

The Venerable Mother María de Jesus recounts the ineffable favors with which his divine Majesty showered his chosen, beloved mother the nine days before the loving, and never sufficiently appreciated,[2] Incarnation of the eternal word in the pure womb of most holy Mary, conceived without stain of original sin, to provide and adorn her with the greatness she needed when he elevated her to the inconceivable position of his mother.[3] One of these favors was to show her the creation of the universe and to require all creatures to swear allegiance and obedience to her as their queen. Then raising her up to heaven three times, the third time in body and soul, he clothed and adorned her with glory and greatness beyond compare, summing up in her apparel the honor and glory unequaled of being his mother.[4] This was known to all the heavenly court, except for our great lady herself, from whom this mystery would be hidden until the happy hour when St. Gabriel announced it (Luke 1:26–38).

I, therefore, seeing this, and considering that we (for whom this incomparable benefit resulted to our advantage) think it only right that we anticipate the celebration of this feast with some devotional exercises to rectify in some measure the dull neglect with which we generally attend to such holy mysteries and such inestimable benefits, have arranged them in the following order to provide a norm through which the prayer of many may be united, so that under the protection and sponsorship of the good and the just, divine Mercy will hear and tolerate the prayers of evildoers and sinners, such as myself. Having been given, with the help of his Sovereign Majesty, this lukewarm foundation, there will surely be those who, filled with the spirit and virtue that such holy material demands, will expand it and furnish it with the dignity that it deserves. All that I ask of those who use these exercises is that they pay me for this slight work by remembering me in their prayers, so that their debt to me render me a creditor in the eyes of the Lord.

To continue with my subject, I say that I have arranged these exercises to be as mild as possible so that all types of people (even those in poor health or busy) can do them. This does not prevent those with more spirit and strength from adding whatever they wish for their greater profit and to the honor of the Lord. On the other hand, those who cannot do even these exercises can change them at will. Since they are written principally for my reverend priests and nuns, there are certain things that would be nearly impossible for some, such as reading the psalms in Latin if they do not know how to read it; or disciplines, acts of obedience, and similar things, which are an ordinary part of the life of vowed religious but not so for other people. But, as I say, the goal is that in the course of these exercises some service be done for the Lord, as a token of gratitude for the singular benefit of his becoming flesh for love of us, and that thanks be given to God for having selected such a mother. Whatever will be done in devotion and reverence to her will be pleasing to his Majesty, although that which is most pleasing is the prayer of many united in one method and formula in the manner that our Holy Mother Church recites the Divine Office, with the same prayers, psalms, and supplications, et cetera. And with that, let us proceed to the first exercise.

The First Day

(Which would be the sixteenth of March)

Meditation

In the beginning God created the heavens and the earth, and on the first day God created the beautiful first fruit of all creatures, saying: "Let there be light" (Gen 1:3). He divided the light from the darkness, and he named it day, because he saw that it was good. This was the first creature he made, and the first to render obedience to his most pure mother, Queen of Light, without the darkness of sin, the most radiant light of all. If light is the servant of

Mary most holy, and it cannot suffer darkness, so that God separated it and made it of its nature incompatible with darkness, how could it be possible for the Queen of Light and all creation to ever suffer the deep darkness of original sin? Let us rejoice greatly at this privilege of hers without parallel and congratulate her on her luminous and pure conception, saying:

Offering

Queen of Light, more beautiful than material light, since you illumine the heavens with your splendor, illumine our souls with your gifts. Because you are the nearest to the faultless, inaccessible Light of the divine Essence, send us a ray of this divine light to enlighten our understanding, so that freed from the darkness of human ignorance we may contemplate heavenly things. You are our Mother. Your apostle[5] commands us to walk in the light so we may be children of the light (1 John 1:7). Grant, most tender Mother, that our works, made in the light of your influence, shine before your divine eyes and those of your Son and our Lord, so that by possessing the light of his grace in this world, we may enjoy the light of his glory in heaven.

Exercises

On this first day when you see the first ray of light, bless its Author, who created such a beautiful creature, and thank him with all your heart, not only for having created it for our benefit, but also for having made it a servant of the one who is his Mother and our advocate. Attend Mass with all possible devotion. Those who are able should fast and in thanksgiving say the hymn *Benedecite omnia opera Domini Domino* [All you works of the Lord, bless the Lord—Dan 3:57–90]. At the verse *Benedecite lux et tenebrae Domino* [Light and darkness bless the Lord], understand that it is not only the just, who are like the light, who are called to praise the Lord, but also sinners who are like the darkness. Let each one of you recognize yourself as a sinner and repent for having added to original sin, darkness upon darkness, sin upon sin. Bow down and reflect on the vileness of dust from which you come. Resolve to reform and so that the most pure light of Mary reaches you, recite a Hail Mary and a Magnificat (Luke 1:46–55) nine times, prostrate to the ground. During this entire day in which we celebrate the light, strive to avoid even the shadow of sin: abstain from impatience and gossip; suffer patiently that which is most naturally repugnant to you. If it is a day for communal discipline, that suffices. If not, you may engage in a particular penitential practice for this day.[6]

Those who do not read Latin should pray the Hail Mary nine times bowed down to the ground. You should fast if you are able, but if you are not, make an act of contrition so that the Lord will give you light to be able to serve him, just as he gives you material light to sustain your life. So that on this first day the first and foundation of all virtues, humility, will match the first of all sins, which is pride, make acts of humility and abstain from acts of pride, so that the first and most capital vice will be banished.

The Second Day

Meditation

On the second day the Lord said: "Let the earth appear in the middle of the waters, and he divided the waters that were above the firmament, and the waters that were below the heavens." He did this, and he called the firmament heaven (Gen 1:7). This was the second work of his infinite power and immense wisdom. During this mysterious time he placed this lovely mechanism at the virginal feet of his Mother, for she alone among all the daughters of Adam was like the heavens created between crystalline currents of grace, with no participation in anything but grace, no separation from it through the stain of sin. No, she was totally pure, totally clean between these life-giving waters. There is nothing purer and cleaner than water, for although many foul things are thrown into it, water alone casts them out and purifies itself. Not only does it purify itself, but it has the particular quality of washing and cleaning that which is thrown into it. Likewise our great queen, was not only most pure and holy, but also is the means of our purification and sanctification. If we look at the properties of the heavens, what is more like it in its marvelous constancy? What more stable? She whom neither the common lot of original sin caused to fall, nor the struggle against temptations caused to tremble. Amid the currents and tempests of human misery, amid the squalls and storms of the sorrowful passion and death of her most holy Son and our most beloved Savior, amid the waves of incredulity and doubt of the disciples, between the reef of the treachery of Judas and the shoals of so many timid souls, she always maintained her resolve, not only firm but also as beautiful as the firmament.

According to mathematicians, the firmament has this excellent quality beyond those of other celestial spheres: not only is it ornamented with innumerable stars, all those we see with the exception of the seven planets, but those stars contained in this sphere are fixed, without movement.[7] The other heavenly spheres rotate. This one is the exception. In addition to being beautiful and luminous it has this other quality, that is, that of being fixed, which the other spheres do not enjoy. Similarly most holy Mary was not only pure in her luminous and pure conception, but also later was adorned by the Lord with innumerable virtues, which sparkle like stars, and decorate her, the most beautiful firmament. Not only did she have all of the virtues, but they were all fixed, immovable, all well ordered and in admirable concert. If in the rest of the children of Adam we observe some virtues, they are unstable, not fixed. Today we have them; tomorrow we lose them. Today we have one virtue, tomorrow another. Today it shines. Tomorrow it is obscured. Let us rejoice in this her prerogative and say to her:

Offering

Lady, honor and crown of our humanity, divine firmament containing the stars of the fixed virtues, grant their beneficent influence on those devoted to you, so that under your influence we hasten to acquire them. Communicate this light, which you share with the Sun of Justice, to our souls. Fix in our souls your virtues, the love of your precious Son, and your sweet and tender devotion to your blessed spouse, my lord and advocate, St. Joseph. Make firm and deep rooted the holy intentions that your Son, our Lord inspires in us, so that by carrying them out with perseverance in this life we will merit the perpetuity of your loving company, where for all eternity we will enjoy the sight of your greatness and praise the Lord for creating you for our benefit.

Exercises

Today you will do the same things as the previous day, except for the canticle, which today will be the psalm *Laudate Dominum de Coelis* [Praise the Lord from the highest heavens—Ps 148]. Invite all the celestial spheres to praise the Lord with the harmony of their revolutions, the concert of their movements, and the variety of their influences, for having created them to be the carpet beneath the feet of his Mother. Praise him for exchanging his starry majesty and his bright throne for the abbreviated, more worthy, and more beautiful firmament of the Virgin's womb. Consider this benefit of the divine Word with attention, because however limited your intelligence, if you reflect on this slowly, you have material for centuries of meditation. At the end of each day say the gospel passage: *In principio erat Verbum* [In the beginning was the Word—John 1:1–14], and when you reach the *Verbum caro factum est* [The Word was made flesh], kneel down to kiss the ground and thank the Lord for becoming human and our brother.[8] O gracious gift! Who could know you sufficiently to know how to thank you! Those who do not read Latin, pray the *Corona*,[9] begging our great queen to deign to accept our prayers. Be filled with the desire to be before her eyes as bright and sumptuous as the stars in the firmament. In order to be even more agreeable to her, you should abstain especially from the sin of avarice, which is the second vice. Strive for the corresponding virtue, which is generosity, and give alms according to your means. O Lady, may we participate in your generosity!

The Third Day

On the third day God said: "Let the waters below the heavens come together in one place, and let dry earth appear" (Gen 1:9). And so it happened, and God named this heavy sphere earth, and the gathering of the waters, sea. God saw that it was good and said: "Let the earth produce green plants that have seeds and trees which bear fruit each according to their species" (Gen 1:11). And so it happened, and the third day was made. On this day these two marvelous creatures appeared in their places: earth and sea. On this day they pledged obedience to their queen, and all the elements bowed down before her virginal feet. No wonder, since the highest and most exalted heavens wanted to kiss her feet! The assembled waters rejoiced to be symbols of the exalted virtues and merits of most holy Mary, the *mare magnum* [great sea] of all grandeur, and that their name was (if we add a letter) the same as that of our most exalted Queen and Lady, since its name is *mar* [sea] and that of the great Lady, Mary. Thus the Lord wished to indicate by the short name of the sea, *mar*, and the long name of Mary that the sea in all its greatness, with its great swelling waves, its many sunken caverns, its hidden minerals, its variegated monsters, with the wonder of the ebb and flow of its tides, and finally with the terrifying vastness of its body, when compared to the sea of Mary's exalted virtues, is puny, narrow, and unworthy of representing her virtues even symbolically.

The earth in astonishment venerates this heavenly fruit, and marvels that it could be her own, well knowing that she had become sterile through sin, that she was capable of only producing the thorns and thistles of sinners. She is astounded to see this pure and fresh rose of Jericho, this beautiful lily of the valley, all innocent and clean, made fertile with the dew of grace and set deep in its currents. Instead of being afflicted by the thorns of sin, innumerable angelic spirits like satellites surround her. Earth sees herself the envy of the heavenly gardens, which, though they have pure angelic substances springing forth eternally from them, have never produced a rose with beauty to equal this one of royal purple. Earth rejoices because as the center of the universe she can represent most holy Mary as the center of all virtues.[10] She rejoices in being called the common mother of all living things, as our most sweet mother Mary is called with more justification.[11] She kisses those holy feet, and the heavens envy her glorious expectation. She revels in being the symbol of Mary's admirable humility when she calls herself *dust*. Grieving, she received the beautiful and holy body of the Lord and won back through this good fortune the curse under which the serpent had humiliated her.

Ladies and gentlemen, let us love humility very much. If she who was totally heaven, and heaven more truly than the heavens themselves, called herself dust, what do we, who are dust, do in confessing the same?[12] The nine days will pass. Let us at least retain this love of humility. See, ladies and gentlemen, our queen, who is the compendium of virtues, the archive of merit, the treasury of all holiness, who never praised herself, never boasted, only spontaneously demonstrated her humility. She did not do it out of mortification, like those who call themselves dust and worms, but by way of merit, giving her humility as the reason for her exaltation. "Because he saw (she says) the humility of his servant, and for this reason all generations will call me blessed" (Luke 1:48). This is the virtue most prized by Mary most holy and is the one that should be most appreciated by all who are devoted to her. His Majesty had all the virtues, and to a superlative degree, but this one is Mary's prize. Ladies and gentlemen, whoever is not humble strives in vain to be devoted to our Lady. There is no love of her without humility, for how could it be that she, who is humility itself, would be served by pride? No, brothers and sisters, whoever is not humble or does not at least attempt to be so, should take leave of our Lady. Let us be humble because we are servants of Mary, and because we cannot be so without her intercession, let us say to her:

Offering

Our Lady, loving Mother, ocean of perfections, Mother of the living! Since it is only through your intercession that we live the life of grace, acquire for us from your precious Son your virtue of humility, and remove from our hearts every thought of pride, self-love, vanity, and the desire for honors in this world. Grant that here, in imitation of you and out of respect for you, we humble ourselves, so that in heaven in your company, enjoying your honors and privileges eternally, we will praise the Lord who gave them to you and who honored us by assuming our nature in your most pure womb.

Exercises

Today you will do the same prayers as yesterday. In addition, because you have called upon the most sweet name of Mary, pay attention to how mysterious it is and pray her Divine Office of five psalms. You should also say Psalm 95: *Cantate Domino canticum novum* [Sing the Lord a new song], requesting that our Lady, who is the star of the sea, liberate the seafarers from its dangers. Ask our Lady as Lady of the earth to quiet the earthquakes, which a few years ago threatened us with such terror. This we entreat also of our advocate the most glorious St. Joseph, on whose feast day the most dreadful one we have seen occurred.[13]

Those who do not read Latin, should pray the *Camándula*,[14] the *Dios te salve* [Hail Mary], *Hija de Dios Padre* [Daughter of God the Father], and so forth, and give thanks to the Lord for creating the earth that sustains us. Remember that we are made of the earth and will return to it. With this in mind pay special attention to refraining from any immodest thought, which is the sin of lust, and whose contrary virtue is chastity. Fast in order to help develop this virtue, and flee those objects that can arouse the contrary vice. Wear a hair shirt if possible.

The Fourth Day

Meditation

And God said: "Let there be two great lights to illumine the firmament, and divide the day and the night, and let them be signs of the time of the days, and the years, and let them illumine the Earth." The greater light shall preside over the day, and the smaller one over the night. And he made the stars and put them in the firmament, so that they shed light over the earth and he divided the light from the darkness. And so it was, and God saw that it was good (Gen 1:14–18). And thus the fourth day was made. These two beautiful creatures, the sun and the moon, which preside over all the celestial bodies and are sovereign over the republic of the other luminaries, came forth this day from the perfect exemplar of the eternal Idea to enlighten the universe and to reveal the light of the Lord. On that mysterious day they acknowledged their divine queen, shown in times past in visions and symbols as clothed by the sun, shod by the moon, and crowned by the stars. Now with astonishment they beheld the perfect original of the portrait in the Apocalypse (Rev 12:1). The sun saw that she was the more singular and exceptional than all its brilliance. The moon saw that she was more beautiful than its shining simplicity. The sun would have clothed her as before but found her illuminated by the sun of justice. The moon would have served as her footstool but saw her feet elevated not only over the empyrean, but also above all the angelic choirs. The stars would have crowned her but found her already crowned by the rays of the holy Trinity. What a sight it would have been to see the way these luminous yet insensate creatures rendered their queen homage! What a sight to behold our great Lady's supreme wisdom, through which she knew with perfect intuition all the natures and qualities of these luminous bodies: their influences, rotations, motions, retrogradations, eclipses, conjunctions, the waning and waxing of the moon and all the effects that can be produced in sublunary bodies, the generation of rain, hail, ice, and the terrifying flash of thunderbolts! She knew with absolute clarity and understanding all the causes of these marvelous effects that for so many centuries have held in abeyance and fatigued the understanding of the most scrupulous of men without their arriving at a perfect knowledge of them. With greater reverence than when it followed the command of Joshua (Josh 10:12–14), the sun halts its luminous chariot before the authority of the sovereign empress of the angels! Let us rejoice in her greatness and power, in her admirable infused wisdom! The pure angelic intelligences are struck dumb with wonder and enchanted with her perfection as they behold her. That we may acquire from her most precious Son, our Lord, this gift of wisdom, let us say to her with tender and warm affection:

Offering

O Queen of Wisdom, more learned and wise than the queen of Sheba (1 Kings 10:1–13; 2 Chron 9:1–12), since you enjoyed the instruction of the true Solomon, from his Majesty acquire for us true wisdom, which is virtue, and the intelligence of heavenly things in order to inflame us with love of you and of your Son. For nine months your most pure womb was the chamber and sanctuary of Eternal Wisdom. Illumine our souls, most gracious teacher, and liberate us from all error, the deceptions of the devil, and the cunning of his sophistical arguments. Grant us knowledge of your Son, our Lord, and of your merits, so that we may become truly devoted to you, serving you here on earth as we ought, and hoping through divine mercy and your intercession to enjoy your presence in heaven.

Exercises

If the day is a Friday when you would normally say the Stations of the Cross, use them as the exercise. Afterwards say the Magnificat nine times to our Lady. If it is not the day for the Stations, you should scourge yourselves and say Psalm 103: *Benedic, anima mea, Domino* [Praise the Lord, O my soul—Ps 103:1, Vulgate]. Those who do not know Latin, pray the Creed nine times, making lively and fervent acts of faith as you profess it. Consider especially the manner in which God created the universe. Bow down to the ground when you pray the sacred words: He was conceived by the work and grace of the Holy Spirit and born of the Holy Virgin Mary. Give thanks to the Lord for becoming human for love of us. Take time to ponder the indescribable nature of this great gift. Do not say it from habit, skimming over it quickly, but reflect and consider: If the king came to our homes and called us brothers and sisters, if he suffered much travail for our sakes, going as far as to give his life for us, how amazed, how astonished, and how thankful would we be. How much more thankful ought we to be when the King of kings, the Lord of lords, does this very thing? Unless you have hearts harder, colder, and more insensitive than stones, it is impossible to consider this with due deliberation and not desire to change your life. Today you should abstain from the fourth vice, which is anger. Try to exercise patience by enduring everything that offends you and that you find loathsome. If you have quarreled with others, settle your differences with them. Seek their friendship without paying attention to the small points of honor of this world or whether you are right and they do not seek amends with you or want to humiliate you. Because if you are in the right, so much more will it be for God's sake that you will be doing it. You will confound and edify others all the more. How much more important is this fruit than all the honors and riches that the entire world has to offer! The less obligatory an action, the greater are its merits. Those who do so imitate God, who humiliated and abased himself without needing to. With this in mind, resolve to pardon forever all your enemies, past, present, and future, for the love of God and for the honor of his holy Mother.

The Fifth Day

Meditation

"On the fifth day God said: 'Let the sea produce different fish, and the air bring forth birds that fly beneath the firmament.' God created whales and all the different species of fish in the waters, and all the birds of the air, each according to its species. God said that it was good. He blessed them and said to them: 'Be fruitful and multiply and fill the sea; and the birds should multiply over all the earth and thus the fifth day was made'" (Gen 1: 20–23). Since on the third day God gave a vegetative soul to the plants, on the fifth day he brought into being fish and birds that possess sentient souls, thus step by step increasing the exquisite works of his immense wisdom. God gave his Queen these even more noble creatures. The fish with rhetorical silence did her homage by

185

praising her as the Star of the Sea. The birds saluted their new Dawn with harmonious song, surrendering as they swooped down before the Royal Eagle who soared up to the throne of the holy Trinity. They bow before the dove of creamy white, whose ruby beak brought back to the world the olive branch of peace (Gen 8:8–11). They bow before the industrious bee that formed in its womb the honeycomb of Samson (Judg 14:8).[15] How appropriate that the fish and the birds are servants of Mary most holy! The fish because they dwell in the purity of the waters, as Mary dwells in the purity of grace. The birds because they soar to the stars and against the natural gravity of their bodies, rising up and searching the heights, as does holy Mary, the bird of purity who (although born on the earth) always inhabited the heights of heaven with soaring flights of contemplation and the outstretched wings of her fervor. Her advance in virtue was never in steps but flight so rapid as to be imperceptible, even to the seraphim. Mary was a bird so light that with one bound she arrived above all the choirs of angels. Like the heron she soared to hunt the eternal Word and brought it to earth so that we could satiate ourselves with his flesh and blood. Like the true phoenix that rose from the dead ashes of Adam, she rose beautiful and exquisite from the blazing fires of grace to become privileged like no other. Let us render her obedience like the birds and say with sincere affection:

Offering

Ave, ave, Reina de las aves! Hail, Hail, Queen of birds! Hail, bird crowned and soaring above all creatures! *Ave gratia plena!* (Luke 1:28), as the archangel St. Gabriel saluted you with this name, and so we invoke you with the same! Teach us, divine bird, so that our affections take flight. Teach us like the eagle who teaches her chicks by flying above them. Inspire the flight of our contemplation so that we may drink in the rays of the sun of justice and protect us beneath your wings from the infernal serpent. Grant that in the secure nest of your fervent devotion and under the sovereign refuge of your maternal vigilance, we may pass through the perils and troubles of this life to fly to the heights of glory in your company. There we will enjoy the clear light of the

Lord, the beatific vision, which we hope to possess in your company for all eternity.

Exercises

Say the Magnificat (Luke 1:46–55) and an Ave Maria [Hail Mary] with attention. Read the gospel: *Missus est angelus Gabriel* [the Angel Gabriel was sent—Luke 1:26–38], genuflecting at the words *Ave gratia plena* [Hail, full of grace] as a sign of gratitude for the gift of a pure creature whom the Lord elevated to the dignity of his Mother, filling her with grace. We ask our Celestial Princess to enfold us in the grace that abounds in her majesty. Say the psalm *Cantate Domino canticum novum, quia mirabilia fecit* [Sing the Lord a new song, because he has done wondrous things—Ps 97, Vulgate].

Those who do not read Latin should pray the fifteen mysteries of the Rosary, and since it is the day when the Lord created the birds, greet Mary, the bird most pure, full of grace. Today abstain from the vice of gluttony with special care, not only fasting but omitting the foods that are most to your taste and contenting yourselves with satiating the desire of your soul with this celestial bird. In place of the vile material food from which we abstain for love of her, beseech her to inflame our souls with the influence of grace and to beg effective help for us from her most precious Son, so that we resolve to do his will on earth in order to enjoy his presence in heaven.

The Sixth Day

Meditation

"God said: 'Let the earth produce animals and different species of beasts.' And it was so and God saw that it was good and said: 'Let us make humankind in our image and likeness to rule over the fish of the sea, and the birds of the sky and the animals of the earth.' And God created humankind in his image and likeness, male and female, he created them, and blessed them, saying: 'Be fruitful and multiply and fill the earth, take possession of it and dominate over the fish of the sea and the birds of the sky and over all the animals that move over the earth;' And God said: 'See I give you all the plants to be your nourishment, and also for the nourishment of the fish, birds and animals.' And so it was. And God saw that all the things that he had made were very good. And thus the sixth day was made, and the heavens and the earth were complete with all their ornaments. God completed his works and on the seventh day he rested from all the things he had made" (Gen 1:24—2:2).[16]

God finished his creations ad extra and perfected them when he formed humans in his likeness as rulers over the entire world. The creatures created on this day (the animals of the earth and humans) rendered obedience to the one who the Lord predestined and distinguished as Mother of his Son as an act of justice rather than grace. When Adam was created in original justice and grace, it was his nature to be ruler over all that was created on the earth, and so all the lesser creatures rendered him obedience. When he sinned and transgressed against God he was rejected by his inferiors. The elements and the rest of the creatures rebelled against him. Therefore, if Mary most holy was preserved from this original poison, in justice she would be owed all the privileges due her because of being conceived in grace. Therefore, as a matter of original justice all creatures would be subject to her, because she did not participate in that sin which caused their rebellion against Adam and all of his children. This benefit is not to be considered as a new gift but a manifestation of the benefit that her Son and our Lord gave to her by preserving her from original sin. And all the homage rendered her by the creatures of the earth resulted from the grace of her conception, like the grace of the original creation of Adam, and is a testimony to her being immaculately conceived. She alone was the one in whom the image and likeness of God, erased by the sin of our first father, the perfection of all the universe, was restored. Holy scripture calls Adam "the perfection and ornament of all creation"[17] (Gen 2:1) either because the final creature is the crown of the entire work or because the rest of the creatures were created for his sake. All the other creatures were left imperfect through the sin of Adam. Divine Omnipotence is to be credited not only with restoring human nature, by redeeming it, but by making use of human nature, by predestining and preserving in his eternal mind a pure creature adorned with sanctifying grace from the first instant of her being. Through her the image and likeness of God was restored, perfecting the rest of his work and restoring it to its rightful order. For this reason it is not only human beings who are in Mary's debt but all the other creatures as well because she gives them perfection and nobility. They all owe her their service for this, if for no other reason. On this day, therefore, all the brute beasts render her obedience.

On this day also the Lord made her our Lady, sovereign over all,[18] although at that time they had no sense or knowledge of the benefit which God did for them by giving them such a ruler, sovereign, mother and refuge. Let us, then, who are so blessed in our time when the Lord had given us the knowledge of such deep secrets and admirable signs of his omnipotence, make up for the lack of attention in ages past to the mysteries operating in the world. Let us lift up our spirits to the Lord in recognition of so many graces and offer him sacrifice of praise. Let us swear obedience to our great queen, kiss the holy hand of our sovereign empress, acclaim her as our legitimate ruler, our mother, and our advocate. Let us make haste to do it so that we will not be less than the irrational creatures who have already sworn fealty to her as their lady. Let us repeat: Long live the queen of all humanity, the honor of nature, the crown of the human race, the restorer of our honor lost through Adam, the glory of Jerusalem, the joy of Israel, the supreme honor of our Christian people, the restorer of the image of God in nature, the ultimate perfection of all creation. Let us cast ourselves with prostrate hearts and burning affection before her royal feet as we say to her:

Offering

Our Lady and Queen, our honor, our consolation, and our goodness, Mother of our God and Savior, door of heaven, means of our redemption, we regret our tardiness in rendering you the obedience you deserve and in recognizing that we are unworthy of being your servants. However, trusting in your maternal clemency, we dare to put ourselves at your divine feet, pledging ourselves to you as our true and legitimate queen, absolute sovereign, our particular advocate, and our unique refuge and help. We render you homage by becoming your perpetual servants and slaves and by welcoming with all possible fervor everything that results in your honor and the glory of your Son, as well as the spread of sincere devotion to you. We offer our lives in defense of your privileges, and we swear by the holy gospels of your Son to keep and to observe especially the privileges of your Immaculate Conception. We vow to defend it to the fullest extent possible, even to the point of spilling our blood in defense of this doctrine, and we hope, our Lady and our supreme good, to merit dying in your service. We entreat you as our queen to keep us beneath your protection and defend us from our spiritual and temporal enemies, especially our adversary the devil (the angel who rebelled against your Son and our King), whose proud neck you, our Lady, crushed. As such, we give you dominion over all our concerns to reign and govern according to your holy will, so that, by obeying your will, we your servants will merit seeing you in your kingdom, where you live and reign with the blessed Trinity, for all eternity.

Exercises

Today you should pray the Magnificat nine times and the canticle of Habakkuk, *Domine, audivi auditionem tuam, et timui* [Lord, I heard your pronouncement and I feared—Hab 3:2], and then the litany to the blessed Virgin and *Alma Redemptoris mater* [Soul of the mother of the Redeemer], the verse *Angelus Domini* [the angel of the Lord], and the prayer *Gratiam tuam* [Your grace].[19] Those who do not read Latin should say fifty Our Fathers, with *requiem aeternam* [eternal rest] at the end, or without it, if you do not know it, for the souls of the dead who were devoted to the Virgin, offering up the prayers to her Majesty so that she applies them to whomever she wants. Entreat her through her intercession to restore in us the image of her Son and our God. So much did God love human beings, so much hunger to be like them, that seeing it was not enough to create them in his image and likeness to ensure that ungrateful and ignorant humankind would not erase his image with sin, he looked for another means to establish the likeness, a means even more beautiful and precious than before. And so it was that his Majesty took on the image and likeness of a sinner. Since he knew that all things love their equal, and since he so desired that we love him, he did not spare himself the effort of becoming like us so that we would love him. Oh, what a great gift! Oh, what design! Oh, the beauty of divine Love! How poorly we respond to you! How long will this blindness, this gross insensitivity of ours endure? What more can God do in order to lovingly solicit our friendship! Thus says this same Lord when speaking of his vineyard: "What could I have done for you that I did not do?" (Isa 5:4) What ingratitude! There are no words to express, nor mind capable of conceiving, how monstrous this ingratitude is! If the being of God, infinite, immaterial, invisible, exceeds the power of our primitive understanding, we cannot know how to meditate appropriately on the infinite perfections of his immutable, immense, and unchanging being. However, to reflect on the holy humanity of Christ, on his passion and incarnation, and to acknowledge all that we owe him, how difficult can that be? Come, gentlemen! Let us be inspired at least to some effort! At the ringing of the noon bells and the call to prayer, let us make an act of love and thanksgiving, as we say: "Blessed are you Lord, who for love of us became human. And blessed is the womb of our Lady, in which you became flesh."

Today it is especially appropriate to abstain from envy, because if we need to love the image of God and if this image is in other people, it is clear that we need to love them, and loving them and envying them are in no way compatible. Let us consider how if an image of the Lord made of wood or bronze moves us to veneration and reverence, how much more the living image and likeness which is that of our neighbors? Do you dare to wish evil to a child of God and of the Virgin, and a brother or sister of Christ? Furthermore, all of us are, although not naturally, sons and daughters of God and Mary and brothers and sisters of Christ our Lord. They are images made in the likeness of God, and Christ is the image of God made in the likeness of humankind. Behold this mutual loving relationship! So how can you hate and desire evil for someone whom God loves and desires the good? I believe that with God's help you would not commit the sin of envy, which is so foreign to human nature and which is only truly proper to the devil, whose sins all have their origin in hate. Even more so, this sin is so vile that it dishonors the one who commits it, and so dangerous that it brings forth its own evil from the good of another. To flee this very wicked sin, strive today for the opposite virtue, which is charity, by visiting and consoling someone who is sick, doing that person a favor or giving alms. Considering that by attending to these wounds you are assisting Christ, as the same Lord revealed to the venerable Mother María de la Antigua,[20] or even without this revelation of hers, as the law of charity instructs us.

The Seventh Day

Meditation

On the seventh day, as the holy book of Genesis says, God rested from all his works. But in this mysterious description of creation, God did not rest from granting favors to his dear chosen Mother.[21] He added favor upon favor and honor upon honor because he wanted everyone to know that Mary's privileges were not limited to being like Adam in paradise, a king of lesser creatures, but that the immense sea of her merits broke the bounds of nature. Their waves surged not only to heaven, but once there inundated the pure angelic substances. He raised her up in spirit to the eternal city so that the celestial citizens could render obedience to that queen whose rights and privileges, ages before, had made them take up intellectual weapons against that rebellious spirit who with his schism and strife brought discord into the tranquil kingdom, into the peaceful and well-governed republic of the stars. The Celestial Princess was raised up to them and adorned by the angels with innumerable mysterious jewels and secret signs, indicating the dignity of the Mother of the Most High. They swore allegiance to her as queen of all the eternal princes, and as the one who enjoyed the unutterable favors of the blessed Trinity. Although in the divine court there is no precedence in rank or seniority of one angelic choir to the others, to me it seems that for the purpose of the method of these remaining three days we will divide them into three hierarchies according to the three prerogatives that were communicated to her by the three divine Persons: power, wisdom, and love.[22]

Today, then, we celebrate the power Mary enjoys over all creation and especially over the angelic choirs. The first level, according to the glorious St. Gregory, is divided into another three: angels, archangels, and virtues.[23] To the angels belongs the safekeeping and care of humankind, to the archangels the proclamation of great mysteries and enterprises, and to the virtues the working of miracles. In the first choir they honor God as Spirit, in the second, they manifest God as light, and in the third they operate as virtues. These three sovereign choirs of pure intelligence render obedience to their solicitous, mysterious, miraculous queen.[24] In her greatness as Mother of God they recognize the communication she enjoys with this same Lord, which inspires the angels, illuminates the archangels, and operates in the virtues. They recognize from the perspective of their perfections the excessive profit they gain through her in their ministries: she keeps and shelters humankind with more care and love than the angels; she participates in the divine secrets and proclaims them better than the archangels; she performs greater marvels and miracles than the virtues. Her majesty alone represents the incomprehensible mystery of the most blessed Trinity with a perfection greater than the three sovereign choirs of angels.

Oh, gentlemen, the contemplation of the greatness of our queen can fill us with wonder and amazement! Considering that the little that I understand of her greatness leaves me stunned and astonished, how much more amazing would be the knowledge of what she is in herself, a greatness that exceeds even the comprehension of the angelic substances! When I think of this, I do not know how I have the heart not to spend every instant of my life in the service of the Lord, who created her for his glory and for our benefit. My dear ladies and gentlemen, even if we did not owe God any more than the benefit of having created her, would we not want to spend our entire lives in his service? At least I, the most ungrateful creature ever created by his Omnipotence, must say that there is not one day when I awake and thank him for the gifts I have received that I do not thank him especially for having created his Mother and for having created me under the law of grace, where I enjoy her protection. I believe firmly that all of you, men and women, already do this with great devotion, but should there be one among you who has not yet done so, I pray that you do so now, and remember me in this sweet act.

Returning now to our original purpose, let us bow down in worship to our Queen, petitioning the angels, archangels, and virtues, especially our guardian angels, to make up for our ignorance and tepidness by rendering obedience for us. Let us say in their company:

Offering

O Lady of the angels, O Queen of archangels, O Empress of virtues! We rejoice exceedingly in your greatness and power over these three exalted choirs. We also rejoice in seeing our human nature in your person lifted above that of the angels. We rejoice that not only do you have dominion over creatures equal or inferior to you in nature, but also that you reign over the pure angelic substances, who, though by nature superior to you, are only worthy to be servants of your purity, which far exceeds their own. Because of your exalted dignity, we who are of the dust of the earth by nature entreat you that we become like angels in our thoughts so that we may be worthy of contemplating your perfection. We beseech you to command these three choirs, sovereign spirits, especially our guardian angels, to guide and accompany us to the height of perfection, so that here and in eternity we may rejoice and praise you in their company forever. Amen.

Exercises

Let us pray the following today in their name: Nine times the Magnificat; the psalm *Confitebor tibi, Domine, in toto corde me, quoniam audisti verba oris mei. In conspectu angelorum psallam tibi* [I will praise you, Lord, with all my heart, because you have heard the words of my mouth. In the sight of the angels I will sing to you—Ps 137]; the three antiphons *Ave, Regina coelorum* [Hail, Queen of Heaven], *Alma Redemptoris mater* [Mother of the Redeemer], and *Salve, Regina,* [Hail, holy queen];[25] the hymn *Tibi, Christe, splendor patris* [To you, Christ, splendor of the Father],[26] with the prayer *Deus, qui inter caeteros angelos, ad annuntiandum* [O God, who from among various angels to announce…];[27] and so forth.

Those who do not read Latin, will say:[28]

Hail, Queen of Heaven,
and of the angels, queen!
Hail, root of Jesse,
light's clear gate!
Rejoice, Virgin most glorious,
most beautiful of all.
Hail, most exalted one,
pray Christ for us.
So that I may sing your praises
give dignity to my tongue,
and against your enemies
give me your virtue and strength.
And you, powerful Lord,
grant us your mother
as our advocate to defend
us in our weakness,
so that with the help
of her maternal clemency
we may raise our heads
above our iniquities.

Today you should visit altars with the Blessed Sacrament and venerate that holy and sovereign Lord sacramentally present there in the bread, which is the bread of the angels. Consider with reverence how many thousands of sovereign spirits are there enraptured at this presence. Entreat them to make up for our tepidness and to offer up our prayers to the Lord. We should ask our guardian angels, especially, to teach us to venerate the Lord and guide us to perfection, as we say: "In the presence of the angels I praise you, Lord: I adore you in your temple and confess your name."[29] Try to avoid the seventh sin, sloth, source of all the sins of omission and impediment to all good works. It is in opposition to and contradiction of all God's positive commandments, causing lethargy of soul, torpor of mind, failure of will, slumber of the heart, and death of all the good movements of our spirit. Try to do everything possible to expel it with its opposite, which is diligence, because the Lord condemns those who are negligent in doing his works. Let us imitate today all the holy angels, who neither cease nor tire of praising the Lord and beseech them to attain the Lord's help so that we may be diligent in his holy service.

The Eighth Day

Meditation

The second hierarchy, according to the same St. Gregory, is divided into three other choirs, which are powers, principalities, and dominations. The powers restrain and subject the demons. The principalities direct the heads of nations. The dominations direct the offices of the angels. In the powers God is present as salvation. In the principalities God reigns as preeminent. In the dominations God dominates in majesty. Today these sovereign choirs will render obedience to their powerful, supreme, and dominant queen and ruler, recognizing in her majesty a power greater than subjecting demons: crushing the dragon's proud head. The principalities recognize the power with which she governs and directs the nations. For this reason Holy Church applies these words of wisdom, as related to her person: "Through me the kings rule, and through me princes govern, and the powerful distribute justice" (Prov 8:15–16). The dominations recognize in her a greater wisdom through which she enlightens and distributes the offices of the angels. Let us give our triple allegiance to these three choirs, praying that they rule, govern, and enlighten. Let us entreat these three sovereign choirs to make good our defects, and let them celebrate her glory and the obedience we owe her with the offering of our hearts.

Offering

O Lady, more powerful than the powers! O Princess, who rules the principalities! O Lady, who dominates the heavenly dominations! We delight and rejoice in the depths of our being at your exaltation and greatness, and we celebrate the joy you experience to see yourself sworn as queen of these lofty princes and of these monarchs most high. With profound humility, and sincere joy, we entreat you to assist us. With heartfelt charity and love we swear to you the obedience we owe, and we ask that these three choirs render you homage in our name. And you, most elevated and high queen, we implore you to assist us with your maternal protection. Subject and check with your power our perverse inheritance as well as your rebellious, treacherous vassal, the devil. Command the principalities to rule and govern the heads of your Christian people, especially our most Catholic king. Command the dominations to illuminate the offices of the lesser angels, so that all the creatures with one voice praise the Lord, who created you for his glory and for our good. With you as our model, help, and example we will serve you in this life and rejoice in your company in life eternal where you reign forever. Amen.

Exercises

You should pray the Magnificat nine times, and the psalm *Qui habitat* [Who lives—Ps 40], and the antiphon *Ave Regina coelorum* [Hail, queen of heaven],[30] the gospel *Missus est angelus* [The angel was sent—Luke 1:26–38], the hymn *Placare, Christe, Servulis* [Have pity, Christ, on your servants],[31] and the prayer *Deus, qui ineffabili providentia* [God, whose ineffable providence].

Those who read Latin, pray the third decade of the joyful mysteries of the Rosary, which commemorates the Incarnation. Today you should try not only to abstain from mortal sin but also from venial ones, imitating angelic purity, which is free from all sin. Abstain especially from lying today, even in the most minor way or by chance, because any kind of lie is intrinsically bad and born of the devil. It is not good during these days that in our hearts, where we are endeavoring to have the holy angels influence us with holy thoughts of love, and love of the eternal truth, which is God, we consent to bad angels engendering abominable evils in the form of lies. Let us undertake sincerely to uproot from our hearts this base vice, which not only stains the soul but also discredits reputations. I don't know what kind of enjoyment the liar could obtain, given the confusion and the shame of being discovered that accompany every step. This is a vice so evil and vile that those who do it are not united among themselves, as happens with other sins, but detest each other, since each one fears being deceived by the other. Even the world holds a poor opinion of those known to be liars. If the world, which is all deceitfulness and falsehood, detests lying, how much more must God detest it, who is the highest truth. How much greater the guilt of the liar when it is so easy to free oneself from this plague! Doing so requires no action but only omission. Thus it is easier, more advantageous, more honest, and more delightful to tell the truth. I will never tire, gentlemen, of persuading you of this, which of itself contains its own persuasion. Who cannot see that this fiendish, bleary-eyed and base sin has so many enamored that there are persons who, without any need to do so, lie merely from habit, to the great detriment of their reputations as well as of their souls. They pay no attention to lies in small matters, as though they do not know that for venial sins there are rigorous punishments awaiting them in purgatory. Let us flee, then, all possible forms of lying and ask the holy spirits we honor this day, and their queen and our mother, to grant us the gift of not only speaking but of knowing and loving the eternal truth that is God, in whom we will delight for all eternity.

The Ninth Day

Meditation

The third hierarchy according to this same holy doctor [St. Gregory] is divided into three choirs: thrones, cherubim, and seraphim. The thrones consider the justice of God, the cherubim the power of God, and the seraphim the goodness of God. In the first choir God resides as justice; in the second God is known as truth; in the third God is loved as *caritas*. These elevated spirits, these beautiful creatures, admirable examples and extraordinary manifestations of divine omnipotence, humble themselves and prostrate themselves at the feet of a pure human creature. What tongue is sufficient to praise, what mind sufficient to comprehend the merit of this miraculous Lady who possesses such greatness? Certainly even the angels are not equal to the task. Since we do not know how exalted the privileges of these spirits, how elevated their greatness, how sublime the thrones they occupy, how pure and perfect their nature, how much glory they enjoy, neither can we understand to the smallest degree the merit of their great queen and our Lady. Oh, what a privilege we enjoy by her being of our nature! Who would doubt that if the angels were capable of envy, they would envy this good fortune? I, for myself, know that if it were possible to exchange the miseries of my human nature with the privileges and perfections of angelic nature, thereby losing the relation we have of family ties with Mary most holy, I would not accept them, even if I could, in view of this, and in consideration of the fact that I cherish and appreciate with all my heart being of her lineage. I say, therefore, that today thrones, cherubim, and seraphim do her homage. The thrones are entranced to see the perfection of the seat of the justice of God; the cherubim are in astonishment at her incomparable virtue; the seraphim at her burning love. Finally, all see in Mary the summation of incomparable advantages, all her privileges, honors, and perfections. Let us render homage again to this great lady and entreat these three choirs to do her homage in our name, so that their sovereignty will supplant the defects of our baseness and ignorance.

Offering

O Lady, whose throne is above the thrones! O Lady, full of wisdom greater than the cherubim's! O Lady, inflamed with love greater than the seraphim! In the company of these three choirs we render you obedience as your most indebted servants. We entreat you in your magnanimity, remember, divine Esther, your afflicted people and your oppressed lineage. Liberate us, sovereign Judith, from the dominion of the devil. Reward our works according to your justice. Enlighten our understanding with your wisdom so that we may contemplate your greatness. Inflame our hearts with your love, so that filled with the fervor of your sweet devotion, illuminated with your light, and aided by your maternal protection, we will know in this life the means of serving you and of fulfilling the will of your most holy Son, so that we merit entering the glory where we will enjoy your company forever by passing through the portal of your intercession. Amen.

Exercises

Pray the Magnificat (Luke 1:46–55), the hymn *Christe sanctorum decus, angelorum* [Christ, glory of the holy angels],[32] *Confitemini Domino, quoniam bonus* [Give thanks to the Lord for he is good—Ps 135], the antiphon *Angeli, Archangeli*,[33] or the prayer *Deus qui miro ordine Angelorum*.[34] And because this is the ninth day of the novena and the eve of the feast of the Annunciation, you will engage in ascetic practices. As for fasting, those able will do it even without this devotional exercise because it is Lent. Make arrangements for a good confession today in order to be worthy to receive communion tomorrow, since it is on that day that we commemorate the great mystery of the Incarnation which was brought about for our benefit. Let us ask the Lord with tender hearts and burning love, just as he deigned on that day to lodge his immense Majesty in the virginal womb of his most pure Mother, after adorning her with many virtues, that he purify and adorn our souls, so that we deserve to be the dwelling of his body in the sacrament of the Eucharist. Let us implore our great Lady and teacher to instruct us on how to prepare ourselves to receive the immense majesty of the Lord, just as she was prepared to receive the Eternal Word, without ever having expected this benefit but only that of always conceiving him in her soul. Our Lady, lend us the rich jewels of the royal fortress of your pure soul to adorn the lowly hovels of our hearts so that they become decent dwellings for such a visit. Endow us with the treasures of your virtues so that we may give lodging to and entertain that Lord, who delights in the children of humankind. Let us strive for this through her merits and those of the Incarnation and passion of the Lord. Today it is clear that we need to abstain from all vices, since we detest all of them forever in confession.

Those who do not read Latin should pray the *Crown of Flowers*: "Blessed be God, because he made you his Mother," engage in ascetic practices, and omit the conference on spiritual matters, since it is the eve of communion. Abide in the grace of the Lord. Amen.

Day of the Incarnation

Meditation

Today's subject would be more appropriate matter for the most learned eulogist, the most eloquent orator, the most elegant rhetorician, than for the feeble instrument of my discourse. But what eloquence, what elegance, or what learning would suffice to elucidate (although all the sovereign angelic choirs may try to explain it) the greatest of the gifts, the crown of all graces, the highest privilege God could make and concede to a pure creature: to elevate her to the incomprehensible dignity and grandeur of becoming his mother? How believable do they seem, how easy to imagine, and how apt do the great gifts we have considered during these nine days appear to us now! If she were to become the mother of the Word, no wonder she was blessed and honored with all the privileges that we know and the infinite number of which we are ignorant! Well, it was fitting and necessary that it occur to one of such great purity, that only God's is greater. After God there is no holiness, no virtue, no purity, no merit, no perfection like Mary's. Therefore, after God, there is no grandeur, no power, no privilege, no exaltation, no grace, no glory like that of Mary most holy. Therefore, although the ineffable graces of these days are in themselves so admirable, they are not admirable when compared with the dignity of God. Oh, may that same Lord help me, who enclosed himself in this phrase: Mother of God! Mother of God? No wonder she is the queen of the world! Mother of God?

201

Of course all people must render her homage! Mother of God? No wonder the elements become her vassals! Mother of God? For this reason the heavens bow down before her! Mother of God? It is only just that the angels swear her allegiance as their queen! All this is appropriate, all is included, all is embraced, all is merited in the one who is Mother of God! For this purpose God created her, for this he preserved her *ab aeterno* [from eternity], for this he adorned her with so many gifts, for this he granted her so many perfections, for this he animated her with so many helpers, for this he enlightened her mind, for this he exalted her with such graces and favors. What greatness, what excellence, or what prerogatives can be conceived that our great Lady does not have? Oh, how many are there? To what supreme degree of perfection do they need to be? Only God, who created her, can understand them, and only our Lady could allude to them when she said that his Majesty had done great things for her (Luke 1:49). Our devotion to her is such that we believe all are possible.

But look, gentlemen, God did many favors for his sacred mother, graciously, and as the theologians say, without considering her merits, such as preserving her from original sin. By so doing he preserved her from all movements of nature inclined to evil through sin, so that all her actions were balanced by reason without resistance from the inferior part. He infused her soul with intelligence before setting limits on intelligence as he did for all other living creatures. However, the remainder of her privileges were given out of justice to her high merits, supreme fidelity, burning love, and the extreme courtesy with which she responded to the divine benefits, rendering herself worthy to conceive in her womb the eternal Word because of having first conceived it in her soul. And that is the reason the glorious St. Augustine said that it was more blessed to conceive the faith of Christ than the flesh of Christ.[35] Also St. Bonaventure in the eleventh chapter of his commentary on St. Luke says: *Beatus venter qui te portavit* [Blessed be the womb that bore thee]. It was not so blessed for Mary to hold Christ in her womb as it was to hold him most perfectly in her soul. His conception in her soul preceded his bodily one. Her own conception was more ancient, since it was from the first instant of her being. Thus she was made ready and worthy to be the natural

mother of Christ, who this blessed day became incarnate in her
virginal womb for the love and good of humankind. He assumed
our nature, clothing himself in the semblance of a sinner. Oh, what
wonder, what tenderness consideration of this mystery evokes!
What heart does not dissolve, and whose eyes are not wet with
tears when they repeat: "The Word became flesh and dwelt among
us?" (John 1:14). What nation, however great, enjoys such familiarity with its gods as our God grants to us? O mystery of the
Incarnation! O Incarnation of the Word! O union most happy for
us, that of God and humankind! O wedding celebrated by the
eternal king of his only begotten Son with human nature! When
will we be able to understand you? When will be able to reciprocate such a favor? When will we be able to make use of this benefit? O Mother and Virgin, whose womb was three times
privileged: to conceive without sin, to sustain the divine burden
without trouble, and to give birth without pain! As St.
Bonaventure says, you were the subject of three miracles: uniting
the infinite with the finite, nourishing the one who created you,
and containing what is limitless.[36] O Mother and Virgin, in your
pure and holy womb occurred those three admirable works, those
three incomprehensible combinations: the reciprocal union of
God and humanity, motherhood and virginity, faith and human
knowledge. In the virginal bridal chamber of your pure womb is
enclosed the one who cannot be contained by the wondrous mechanism of the heavens! Teach us to meditate and be grateful for this
favor, so that thankful for this great benefit that was done for love
of us, with tender and loving voices, we can say with that woman
of the Bible, Elizabeth:

Offering

O Mother of the Eternal Word, and so merciful, that you
deign to be the mother of humankind! Blessed be your name and
your most pure womb that was found deserving to be the taberna-
cle of divinity for nine months! Blessed be your holy breasts,
which fed the one who maintains and sustains the entire universe
with the sweet nectar of your most pure blood! We rejoice to see
you already in your most exalted position as Mother of God. We

congratulate you on the dignity to which you have risen and through which you have exalted us so that we have become related to your Son and our Lord. It is through you that we see ourselves, as entitled to be part of the royal house of the Lord, who treats us as and calls us his kin. O my Lady, grant that we know how to attain the dignity you have achieved and are grateful for, as we ought to be! Grant that we recognize the flesh and most pure blood that today you gave to the Eternal Word, as the same flesh and blood that was the price of our redemption on the cross, so that we can see the part you played in that redemption! How can we repay you, my Lady, all that we owe you? You see our poverty and our ignorance. Enrich us with your treasures and with your wisdom illumine us, so that we may be able to repay you in some small measure or reimburse you a small part of what we owe you. Beseech your Son and our Savior that just as today you receive him in your womb most pure, we do the same through the sacrament in our unworthy breasts. Let us thus receive and conceive him perpetually in our souls, so that we may attain the promise of eternal bliss that your Majesty made to those who hear the word of God and keep it. You possess this word of God with such an abundant excess of glory greater than that of the other blessed souls, which can only be measured by the Lord, with whom you reign in all eternity. Amen.

Exercises

Today we will pray the Magnificat (Luke 1:46–55) nine times; the hymn *Ave, maris stella* [Hail, star of the sea];[37] the Canticle of Zachary: *Benedictus Dominus Deus Israel* [Blessed be the Lord God of Israel—Luke 1:68–79]; the gospel text *Missus est angelus Gabriel* [The angel Gabriel was sent—Luke 1:29–38]; and the prayer *Deus, qui de beatae Mariae Virginis utero* [God, who in the womb of the blessed Virgin Mary].[38] The priests who pray at home can pray the Holy Office, at least vespers, on their knees out of reverence for this great mystery.

Those who do not know Latin should pray the fifteen decades of the Rosary; if that is too much for them, a third of that, the joyous mysteries. Pray the Hail Marys with great devotion, considering how much was included in that mysterious greeting to our Lady by the holy angel, Gabriel. At the end pray the following:

> God, who from the womb
> of the lovely Virgin Mary
> caused your Eternal Word
> to take on human nature
> as Gabriel proclaimed,
> grant those who confess
> her ever Virgin
> and truly Mother of God,
> that her intercession
> help and protect us
> through the Word and Love
> who live and reign with you.[39]

For the time remaining, give thanks to God for the holy communion that he has allowed you to receive. Use a devotional book to help you, as there are many that treat of this material. For the greater glory of God offer with all your being not only the exercises of these days, but also the works of your life past, present, and future, for all intentions that were for the greater pleasure of his Majesty and for the advantage of souls. Try not only to refrain from sin on this day but to resolve with all your heart never to sin again for the rest of your life. And if we do sin because of our weakness, we should not lose heart or diminish our love for this mystery. We should ask our great Lady to grant us the graces to raise ourselves up. Let us try at least to retain some benefit from these exercises for the rest of our lives, by abstaining forever from one of the vices and acquiring a virtue, as well as cultivating the most lively affection for the holy mystery of the Incarnation. Through the mystery of the Incarnation and the love with which he carried it out for love of us, and through the intercession of his holy Mother, let the Lord be so kind as to give us his grace in this life and his glory in the next. Amen.

Offerings for the Rosary of the Fifteen Mysteries to Be Prayed on the Feast of the Sorrows of Our Lady, the Virgin Mary

First Offering

When Mary arrived fatigued and weeping, she saw the inhuman executioners take the cross off the shoulders of the Lord. She saw how in haste they tore off his garments, pulling with them pieces of his torn flesh and leaving his virginal body, once again naked, exposed to the view of the multitude.

Offering

O Mother most holy, you are the most afflicted and shamed of all women because of the insults suffered by your beloved Son and our beloved Redeemer! We offer you these ten Hail Marys and one Our Father for the incomparable pain that pierced your tender soul and for the blush of unspeakable shame that suffused your holy face when your virginal eyes saw naked in such a public and dishonorable place the One who was the clear mirror of all chastity and purity. For his sake we implore you to intercede with his Majesty so that the insults and wounds of our sins and the nakedness of our merits will be covered over and replaced by the dishonor suffered by our Savior and by your tears. With these as our adornment may we appear with all modesty before the tribunal of his justice, and through your intercession be taken up to eternal joy, where you reign forever.[1]

Second Offering

When She Saw Him Crucified

O most holy Mother, become center and target of all sorrows! We offer you these ten Hail Marys and one Our Father for the shuddering of your maternal heart as it was pierced at the sight of your precious Son, our Lord's delicate and tormented body, nailed with three nails to the hard wood of the cross. Through him, my Lady, we beseech you, pierce our thoughts. Nail them with the holy fear of your Son, so that they do not increase to offend his Majesty. Thus secured by the nails of his commandments to the narrow cross of our obligations, may we merit eternal liberty and freedom in your company in heaven, where you reign eternally. Amen.

Third Offering

When They Lifted Him up on the Cross

O Mother most afflicted, mother submerged and drowning in the immense sea of torments of your precious Son! We offer these ten Hail Marys and one Our Father for the pain that passed through your tender heart when you saw the holy body of your precious Son so heedlessly and hurriedly raised up on the cross. You saw the living streams of blood pouring from his feet and hands, new wounds torn open by the weight of his body and by the pitiless jerking of the cross. You saw his other wounds created anew by the instruments with which they raised the cross. We beseech you to intercede with his Majesty to give us an intimate appreciation of his pains and of yours. In compensation for that ignominious exaltation may he be truly exalted through the adoration in our souls and in our hearts made pure and loyal, so that in the days to come we merit being lifted up into his glory, and in your company, where you live and reign forever, etc.

Fourth Offering

At the Words Christ Said

O Mother most afflicted and thus become the consolation of all those in distress, we humbly offer you these ten Hail Marys and one Our Father for the most deeply felt pain that went through your loving heart when you heard your precious Son, the refuge of all people, reproach his Eternal Father for having abandoned him (Matt 27:46; Mark 15:33–41; Luke 23:44–49; John 19:28–30) and commend you, my Lady, to his disciple (John 19:26–27). With profound humility and resignation you accepted this exchange, so unequal, the exchange of God for a man. For this sorrow, my Lady, we beseech you, look not upon our sins, but accept us as your children. Assist and protect us in the abandonment of the hour of our death so that through your intercession we will pass through death's dark door to freedom and the joys of life eternal with you forever. Amen.

Fifth Offering

Gall and Vinegar

O Mother bereft of consolation and afflicted by the incomparable torment our Savior and your Son, we humbly offer you these ten Hail Marys and one Our Father for the bitterness that shrouded your most holy soul at the sight of the torture that they inflicted on your dear Son. Instead of giving him relief and refreshment from his burning thirst, they gave him wine mixed with gall, whose bitter sting was more deeply felt in your maternal heart than on his delicate tongue (Matt 27:48; Mark 14:36; Luke 23:36). In view of this pain we entreat you to give us the will to endure the bitter humiliations of this life with patience and to nourish our souls with the sweet food of grace, so that thus fortified we will direct our steps along the path to eternal glory, where you live and reign forever. Amen.

Sixth Offering

When She Saw Him Die

O Mary, sea of grace and virtues, and now an immense sea of sorrows where pain and suffering flow in like rushing rivers! We offer you these ten Hail Marys and one Our Father for the unspeakable sorrow that penetrated your anguished soul like a vicious knife when you saw that head incline as he committed his sacred soul to his Eternal Father as it left his tormented body (John 19:30). Your own soul would have doubtless been severed from your holy body had it not been miraculously maintained in life by the Lord of life—this pain leaving you beside yourself and transfixed. You would have needed the strengths of many lives to be able to bear it without accompanying him into death had not the Lord protected you from the experience of even greater pain. Because of this pain, our Lady and our Mother, we entreat you to give us the strength and courage to die to the things of this world and to live only in the Lord, so that when we arrive at the necessary and feared hour of death, prepared and comforted through your intercession, we will have the courage and the permission to pass through that narrow gate where we hope, due to your son's mercy and your protection, to move on to a better life, where you live and reign forever, etc.

Seventh Offering

When She Remained Alone at the Foot of the Cross

O Mother, alone and forsaken! Humbly we offer these ten Hail Marys and one Our Father for the abandonment and poverty in which you found yourself at the foot of the cross. You saw hanging the One on whom all that is depends for its being and could find no way to take him down, no shroud to enfold him, no tomb for his burial.[2] You saw him hung like a criminal, exposed to the inclemency of the weather, an ignominious spectacle to the eyes of the passersby. Allow us, my Lady, to participate intimately in your loneliness, poverty, and abandonment. We beseech you, do not cast aside our company, wretched though it may be. Accept our crude and tepid compassion. Inspire in our souls an intense awareness of your sorrows, so that as you joined us in the afflictions of this life, we merit joining you in eternal joy, where you reign forever, etc.

Eighth Offering

When He Was Pierced by the Lance

O most sorrowful of mothers! O woman of sorrows, intended in all things to be a copy of your suffering Son! We offer you these ten Hail Marys and one Our Father for the unimaginable pain and cruelty you saw inflicted on your dead Son, as his most loving heart was pierced with a hard and pitiless lance (John 19:34). Your own maternal heart felt his wound so deeply that it is called by extension, yours (Luke 2:34–35). For this sorrow, my Lady, we beg you to intercede for us with your precious Son. Make us partakers of the fruits of his open side, which are the sacraments of the Holy Church, through which we are restored to the grace, lost through our sins. May we persevere in this grace, through your intercession, so as to merit eternal glory, where you live and reign forever, etc.

Ninth Offering

When They Lowered Him from the Cross and Put Him in the Arms of His Most Holy Mother

O Mother drowned and debilitated in the flood of your own tears, consumed by your own suffering, we humbly offer you these ten Hail Marys and one Our Father for the pain you felt when you received the inert and disfigured body of your holy Son in your virginal arms. Oh, how different and how other was that Son, reflection of all beauty, as you took him in your arms to nurse him, your whole soul filled with bliss! How different a dwelling those arms of the cross than your arms! How unrecognizable the body now returned to you! O most tender Mother, what would have been your thoughts at that moment? We beseech you to lend us your vision and instill in us your kindness, so that we see and examine honestly those divine wounds suffered for love of us. Help us respond as we ought to both his and your gifts so that we may serve him in this life and merit accompanying you in the next, where you live and reign forever, etc.

Tenth Offering

When They Buried Him

O Mother alive only to torment and dead to all consolation! We humbly offer you these ten Hail Marys and one Our Father for the pain you felt as they took the broken body of your beloved Son from your arms to place in the grave, depriving your weeping eyes of even the presence in death of the one who had been their light. How different his final resting place from the first! Instead of your pure, maternal womb, the cold, hard stones receive him. Woeful, the stone sealing the tomb falls with more weight on your wounded soul than on his dead body. Most clement Mother, we ask you to cleanse our hearts of the impurity of our sins. Subdue and soften them in consideration of your suffering, so that they will not be like the cold tomb, but rather like your pure and tender womb, as we receive your Son in the Eucharist, our present food of grace, and future food for eternal life in glory, where you live and reign forever, etc.

Eleventh Offering

When They Returned to the Place of the Last Supper

O most lonely Mother, weeping over the best Son, widow of the best spouse, and orphan of the best Father![3] We offer you in humility these ten Hail Marys and one Our Father for those dolorous steps you took through the bitter streets as you retraced those you took as you followed your beloved Son. You contemplated and adored each of his footsteps and washed the traces of his precious blood with your bitter tears. The sight of these places brings ever more vividly to your suffering soul what you saw the sweet Lamb suffer at the place where he knelt down, where he fell, where he was dragged down, where they gave the cross to Simon the Cyrenian for help (Mark 15:21; Matt 27:32; Luke 23:26), and where his tender, penetrating gaze pierced your holy soul. As you contemplate all his afflictions in your heart, your own sufferings become a substitute for his.[4] Grant us a true knowledge of his suffering, direct all our steps to your greater service, to the honor and glory of your Son, and for the benefit of our souls, so that by following your steps through the bitter street of mortification on the path of this life we will arrive at the peace and tranquility of the Last Supper of glory, where you reign forever, etc.

Twelfth Offering

For What She Felt for Those Who Die without Baptism

O sorrowful mother, not only for a Son dead to temporal life, but grieving even more for the infinite number of those dead to eternal life! Oh, how monstrous and atrocious, how unbelievable your suffering at their fate! Our Lady and our Good, was not the suffering of your Son enough? Were the daggers of your Son's humiliation and torture, which stabbed your heart, too few to satiate your capacity for suffering? Were you thirsting for more pain as you turned your eyes on the most sorrowful object there is, turned your generous and royal heart toward the sight of the innumerable multitude of those without knowledge of his goodness and redemption, and without the life-giving waters of baptism, who will be fodder for eternal death? O Lady, you whose wisdom understands fully the extent of this harm, what a dagger's thrust to your heart was this, given your burning love for all people, and given your acceptance of the torture of your only begotten Son for their salvation! How did you feel to see wasted the fruit of his blood and the salvation of the unenlightened pagans in the darkness! For this, my Lady, we offer you these ten Hail Marys and one Our Father and beseech you to intercede with his Majesty to give the light of the gospel to the peoples in the darkness of paganism so that his name will be praised and known, and all peoples will live in his service, possess the glory for which they were created, in your company eternally. Amen.

Thirteenth Offering

What Our Lady Felt about Heresies

O Mother, martyr to the three most noble but most inhuman scourges: your indelible memory, your infused wisdom, and your ardent love, through which you are aware of, ponder, and feel all the pain of all those who have ever been born. Your suffering grows by degrees as you see the perdition not only of the blind pagans, ignorant of redemption, but also the loss of those already on the road to life, already on the path of light, who turn back and defame the baptism they have received with heretical teachings, splitting like ungrateful serpents the womb of Holy Mother Church in which grace is conceived. Not only do they tear the seamless garment of your Son, but they bring discord to the harmony of the members of his mystical body, Holy Church, by falsely interpreting holy scripture. Sorrow for you, my Lady, more intense for being lost from the flock branded, marked, stained no less with the blood of its shepherd. For this reason, my Lady, we offer you these ten Hail Marys and one Our Father, beseeching you to intercede with your Son to return these erring sheep to his flock, delivering them from the mouth of the eternal wolf, so that reconciled here with the church militant they will all enjoy the church triumphant, where you live and reign forever. Amen.

Fourteenth Offering

Of Christians Condemned

O Mother of the Son of God, you so much wanted to be our mother that this costs you more than to be the mother of your Only Begotten One! How can we repay you, our Protection and our Good, for what you have suffered for us and the pain you felt when your most lucid understanding perceived that not only will the infernal caverns be filled with those who sin against faith, but also with those who sin against love. There many believers die in a state of mortal sin and are lost forever. Does not this pain exceed all the others in infinite degree? Honoring this pain, we offer you these ten Hail Marys and one Our Father, entreating you as a merciful mother to enlighten those in such a miserable state and provide them the aid of your most Holy Son, so that they will escape this peril. Do not permit especially those who are near to death to be trapped in such an unfortunate circumstance, but allow them time to repent and do penance so that they merit being cleansed of their sins and go to the heavenly glory where you live forever. Amen.

Fifteenth Offering

What She Felt Seeing the Sins of the Just

O Mother tireless in suffering! O valiant woman! O most holy soul! Whence comes your capacity for such immense pain? Where can you turn your eyes, when, instead of coming to your aid, we afflict them with more suffering? Who would not think that the virtues of the just would be a relief from the anguish that the ingratitude of the wicked causes you? But since this was not a time of comfort for you, our Lady and our Refuge, you saw only what is painful, contemplating the faults and sins with which even those predestined to heaven offend your Son. You experienced the denial of St. Peter (Matt 26:59–75; Mark 14:66–72; Luke 22:54–62; John 18:15–18, 25–27) and the cowardice of the disci-

DEVOTIONAL WORKS

ples (Matt 26:56; Mark 14:50). You felt their faults all the more than more serious sins of others because the ingratitude of children is more keenly felt than that of slaves. This was even more the case because (although you are the compendium and queen of all virtues) with your profound humility when you turned to look upon yourself, it appeared to you that you also were ungrateful toward your Son. You reproached yourself as a sinner and as an ungrateful creature, accusing yourself all the more pointedly and severely because of your more intimate connection to the Lord. O Queen of humility! Who can know how to ponder the pain that these judgments caused you? In recognition of this we offer you humbly these ten Hail Marys and one Our Father. We beg to attain a fervent love of your Son, so that we do not offend him even in the smallest things (which never are truly small since they offend him). Grant us also a perfect humility so we recognize our defects, so that by doing penance for them in this life, we enjoy his love forever in life eternal, etc.

Section 4

Theological Works

CRITIQUE OF A SERMON OF ONE OF THE GREATEST PREACHERS, WHICH MOTHER JUANA CALLED *Response* BECAUSE OF THE ELEGANT EXPLANATIONS WITH WHICH SHE RESPONDED TO THE ELOQUENCE OF HIS ARGUMENTS

Muy Señor mío, My dear Sir: When amid the pleasantries of a conversation you were so kind as to recognize in me a certain acuity of mind, there was born in you the desire to see in writing some of the arguments that came to me spontaneously at that time, especially those concerning the sermons of an excellent preacher. Sometimes I praised his fundamental arguments, sometimes I disagreed, but always I admired his unsurpassed ingenuity. There is not as much to admire in the beauty of a structure built on a solid foundation as there is to admire in one built on a weak foundation, which still has the capacity to dazzle with its brilliance, as do some of the propositions of this subtle mind. Such is his finesse and his sharp wit that even as one disagrees, one is enamored with the beauty of his oration, astonished by its sweetness, bewitched by its charm, and exalted, surprised, and enchanted by the whole.

We spoke of these things, and it pleased you (as I have said) to see this in written form. Now I have done it so that you may know that I obey you in the most difficult matters, not only with my mind concerning such an arduous task as that of taking issue with the propositions of such a great individual, but also in that part of my character that finds loathsome anything which might appear to impugn anyone. Although this latter objection is modified to some degree, because in any case you alone will be witness to it and because the authority of your command will render honest the mistakes resulting from my obedience, which to other eyes might appear due to disproportionate pride, especially coming from a member of a sex so discredited in matters of learning as is commonly accepted by all the world.

And so that you see how purified of all passion my opinion is, I propose first of all three reasons that contribute to my special love and reverence for this illustrious man. The first is a most cordial and filial affection for his holy religion, of which I am no less a daughter than he a son. The second is the great affection I have always considered due to the marvel of creative genius, and this to such a degree that if God granted me a choice of talents, I would elect no others than his. The third is that I have a secret sympathy for his noble nation. These reasons joined to the general one of hating controversy would have been more than enough to silence me, had I not your command to the contrary. However, all of them do not suffice to cause human reason, a free power that assents or dissents necessarily according to that which it judges to be or not to be the truth, to yield to the sweet flattery of desire.

Given this distinction, I say that I am not here engaging in a rebuttal but simply relating my opinion. In so doing, I am far from believing of myself what said preacher thinks of himself when he claims that no one can improve on his arguments, a claim deriving more from his nation than from his profession and his understanding.[1] Of course I think and believe that anyone could improve on my arguments to an infinite degree.

I cannot refrain from repeating that in whatever may appear to be impudence on my part, he himself opened the way, being the first to tread paths untouched, leaving through his example ventures less bold easier, in light of his greater daring. If he then felt strength enough in his pen to improve on three writers, imminently learned and canonized in one of his sermons (which will be the only subject of this essay), how much more likely now that there will be those who attempt to surpass his pen, which is not yet canonized, albeit very learned? If there is a modern orator with the talent of Cicero who dares to take on Augustine, Thomas Aquinas, and John Chrysostom, how much more likely now that there will be those who dare to respond to such a Cicero as he? Since one man has dared do battle with the genius of three more than men, how much more likely is it now that there will be those emboldened to face up to one man, even one as great as this one, especially when supported and accompanied by those three giants, as my intent here is to defend the arguments of the three holy fathers. I expressed myself poorly. My purpose is to defend my position with the arguments of the three holy fathers.[2] Now I think I've found the right words.

And so I begin. In my response I will use the method of the preacher of the sermon in question, that is, the sermon for the ceremony on Holy Thursday commemorating Jesus' washing the feet of his disciples. This is how he proceeds: he speaks of the benefits of Christ's love, which Christ demonstrated at the end of his life: in *finem dilexit eos* [In the end he loved them—John 13:1]. And he proposes to treat the position of the three holy fathers [Augustine, Thomas Aquinas, and John Chrysostom] with the following boundless audacity: "The style that I will be maintaining in this discourse will be as follows. First, I will give an account of the views of each of these saints, and then I will give my own position, with one difference; namely, that there is none of the benefits of the love of Christ that these same saints hold to which I will not add one that is better. Furthermore, I maintain that to the demonstrations of the love of Christ that I hold the greatest, there is not another one to be found to equal it."[3] These are his exact words, this is his proposal, and that is what motivates my response.

The first opinion he considers is Augustine's, who held that the greatest demonstration of Christ's love was his death, based on the text: *Maiorem hac dilectionem nemo habet, ut animam suam ponat quis pro amicis suis* [No one has greater love than he who gives his life for his friends—John 15:13]. This preacher, however, says that Christ's absenting himself was a greater demonstration of Christ's love than his dying. He argues as follows: Because Christ loved us more than his life, he gave up his life for us. Therefore, it is a greater demonstration of love to be absent than to die. He supports this view by citing the text of the Magdalene, who wept at the tomb and not at the foot of the cross. On the cross she saw Christ dead. At the tomb she found him absent, which caused her greater pain than his death. Another proof of his against Augustine's position is that Christ did not demonstrate any emotion on the cross when he died, bowed his head, and gave up his spirit. *Inclinato capite emisit spiritum*.[4] He did, however, show emotion in the Garden because the hour had come for him to leave them. *Factus in agonia*. He went into agony. This was because absence is more deeply felt than death (Luke 22:43). He also uses the argument that Christ could have been resurrected in the very second in which he died and could have given himself in the Eucharist after the resurrection because the former was the remedy for death and the latter the remedy for absence. However, Christ delayed the remedy for death until the third day, whereas the remedy for absence, not only did he not delay it, but he anticipated the remedy by making himself available in the Eucharist the day before he died. Therefore Christ felt absence more strongly than death.

Another argument: He says that Christ died once and absented himself once. However, to death he only gave one remedy, resurrecting once, but for his absence he looked for an infinite number of remedies by becoming present in the Eucharist. Thus he gave one remedy for death—the resurrection—but for one absence he was multiplied into infinite presences. Therefore, Christ considers absence to be more painful than death. Furthermore, he says that even though the sacrament of the Eucharist, in as far as it is a sacrament, is presence; in as far as it is a sacrifice, it is death. Christ, by dying every time as sacrifice when he made himself present in the sacrament, felt absence so much more than death that he paid no attention to the fact that each presence cost him a death. Because he felt absence so much more profoundly than death, he subjected himself to a perpetuity of deaths in order not to suffer an instant of absence. Therefore, absenting himself was a greater demonstration of Christ's love than his dying.

This is substantially his line of reasoning, and these are his arguments, although in order not to go on at length I have abbre-

222

viated them in my own rough style, whereby they lose no little of their energy and liveliness. It will be necessary for me to do the same in regard to his other points. Your Grace can read them at leisure in the author's own words in the text in question. The above are nothing more than summaries of his position in order to give clarity to my response, which is the following:

I hold, with St. Augustine, that the greatest demonstration of Christ's love was his death. The proof is as follows: What we most value are our life and our honor, and Christ gave up both in his ignominious death. As God he had already given us demonstrations of love worthy of his omnipotence, such as creating us and maintaining us in existence, but in as far as he was human, he had nothing greater to give than his life. This can be proven not only with the text "Greater love..." [*Maiorem hac dilectionem*—John 15:13], etc., which could be understood to apply to loves other than Christ's, but with many other texts, such as where Christ says that he is the Good Shepherd: *Ego sum pastor bonus. Bonus pastor animam suam dat pro ovibus suis* [I am the Good Shepherd. The good shepherd gives his life for his sheep—John 10:11]. Since Christ is the only one who knows which is the greatest gift of his love, it is clear that had there been a greater one he would have said so. Therefore, since he does not furnish any proof greater than his willingness to die, his death was the greatest demonstration of his love. Furthermore, the greatness of a demonstration of love is measured from two perspectives. The first (*a quo*) concerns the one who demonstrates love; the second (*ad quem*) the one who receives the demonstration of love. The first measures the greatness of a demonstration of love based on the cost to the lover, the second based on the benefit that accrues to the beloved.

Many demonstrations of love have one of these perspectives but lack the other. Consider the example of Jacob's fourteen years of servitude (Gen 29). Oh, what labors! In freezing cold! Under blazing sun! It was a great demonstration of love on Jacob's part. Let's see how these labors benefited Rachel, which is the *ad quem* perspective. Not at all. Her beauty would have gotten her a husband without all these efforts. This demonstration of love was great only from the first perspective. An example of the second case is Esther, who was elevated to the royal throne in place of Queen Vashti (Esth 2). Certainly a great good fortune! A stroke of luck! A great benefit for Esther! But let us examine it from the *a quo* perspective. What did it cost Ahasuerus? Nothing. He had only to desire it. This demonstration of love only has the *ad quem* perspective. Therefore, the greatest of all demonstrations of love has to cost the lover and profit the beloved. So I ask, what demonstration of love could have cost Christ more than his death? What was more beneficial for us than the redemption that resulted from his death? From both perspectives, then, his death was the greatest demonstration of his love.

The Word became flesh and for love of us overcame the immense distance between God and humanity. He died and overcame the bounds of death. Clearly he perceived his death as overcoming the greater distance, since when he reminded us of his love and entrusted his memory to us, he did not remind us of his incarnation but did emphasize his death. *Hoc est Corpus meum, quod pro vobis tradetur; hoc facite in meam commemorationem* [This is my body which will be given up for you. Do this in memory of me—1 Cor 11:24]. Could not Christ have said to us: This is my body, which for love of you I assumed and became human? No, the incarnation was not painful for him, and therefore did not instantly result in our redemption. Christ wanted to accord us his effort and our profit, which are the two characteristics of a perfect demonstration of love. Both are contained in his death, which is the greatest demonstration of his love.

The incarnation was a greater marvel, but it was not as great a demonstration of love because, though it was wonderful for God to become human, it cost him more to die. Becoming human, as Christ, he lost nothing of his divinity, but when he died, he ceased being Christ when in death the sundering soul and body dissolved the unit that had been Christ. Therefore, his death was the greatest demonstration of his love. The Lord himself intended it thus. This can be demonstrated by a syllogism. All those who choose means to any end hold the means in less esteem than the end to which they are directed. The incarnation was the means for his death, since Christ became human in order to die for humanity. Therefore, the greater demonstration of love was to die rather than to become incarnate, even though it is a greater marvel to become incarnate than to die. Therefore, death was the greatest gift of love in the estimation of Christ himself, his Majesty being the only one who could measure it. For this reason when he died he said *Consummatum est* [It is finished—John 19:30], because his dying was the consummation of his love.

According to the author, Christ paid for each presence in the Eucharist by dying. I maintain that he did so because he wanted his presence in the Eucharist to commemorate his death: *Quotiescumque feceritis, in mei memoriam facietis* [Whenever you do this, do this in memory of me].[5] The gift that the lover desires be imprinted in the memory of the beloved is the one he holds to be the greatest. Christ says: "Remember that I died"; he does not say: "Remember that I created you, that I became incarnate, that I became present in the Eucharist." Therefore, the greatest gift is his death.

This truth is confirmed in the following: That demonstration of love which the lover displays and reaffirms most is the one he holds as the greatest. Christ reaffirmed his death and nothing else. Therefore, this was the greatest. Though he had infinite benefits at his disposal, he only granted us his death. Therefore, this is the greatest.

Furthermore, Christ's other gifts can be referred to but not represented. Death can be referred to, recommended, and represented. Therefore, not only is his death the greatest gift, but it is the summation of them all. I prove it thus: Christ through his death repeats for us the benefits of creation, because with his death he restores it to its original grace. Christ through his death reiterates the gift of preservation, not only because he preserves temporal life, dying in order that we may live, but because he gives us his flesh and blood for sustenance. Christ through his death recapitulates for us the benefits of the incarnation, because whereas in the incarnation he is united with the most pure flesh of his mother, in his death he becomes united to us all, shedding his blood for all. Only apparently is the Eucharist not represented in his death because the Eucharist itself is the representation of his death. And this proves that the greatest demonstration of love is his death.

Indeed, the greatness of the Eucharist comes from it being a representation of his death.

Truly, up to this point we have not responded directly to the author but rather defended the opinion of Augustine that the greatest demonstration of Christ's love was his death. Let us turn now to consider the arguments of the author, because we have already considered their foundation. Of course we concede that Christ loved humanity more than his life since he gave up his life for it, but we deny the premise that Christ absented himself. Even if he did, we also deny that absence causes a greater sorrow than death.

Let us go to the first point, which is to prove that Christ did not absent himself. As far as I am concerned, the author's own argument proves this. He says that Christ felt his absence so much and his death so little that he postponed the remedy for death, the resurrection, until the third day and anticipated the remedy for the grief his absence would cause in the sacrament of the Eucharist at the Last Supper. Why then did he sweat in the Garden? *Factus est sudor eius?* (Luke 22:44). Why did he suffer anguish unto death? *Factus in agonia* (Luke 22:43). Why would he suffer absence to this extent if he were already present in the Eucharist at the Last Supper? And if he remedied his absence before it occurred, in what sense was it absence, if it had already been remedied? Of course, one who is already assured of remaining does not experience the agony of separation. Therefore, taking all this into consideration, we can infer that absenting himself not only cannot be counted as the greatest demonstration of Christ's love, but it is not a demonstration of his love at all because he never did it. The author says that Christ left us because it was good for us. *Expedit vobis ut ego vadam* [It is good for you that I go—John 16:7]. It is true that he left us but false that he absented himself. Let us not waste time on this. We already know the infinity of his presences.

Now that we have proven that Christ did not absent himself, the example of the Magdalene's weeping does not support the conclusion that he did. It would only do so if you, like the author, presume the absence of Christ, which I deny. My argument is that the death of Christ was the greatest demonstration of love, not his presumed absence, which I totally deny. There is no basis of comparison between that which has being and that which does not have being. However, because I propose to prove that absence is not a greater grief than death and consequently not the greatest demonstration of Christ's love, but rather the contrary, I will need to respond to the example of the Magdalene. I maintain that the Magdalene's weeping at the tomb and not at the foot of the cross does not allow us to infer that absence is a greater grief than death. Rather, the contrary is true.

My proof runs thus: When one is struck by a great sorrow, the vital spirits rush to help the agony of the heart in crisis. This withdrawal of the spirits causes a general embargo and suspension of all action and movements until the pain has moderated. At that time the heart, revived from its collapse, emits those same spirits that had congregated through tears to comfort it. Tears, then, are a sign that there is no longer the necessity for as much solace as there was initially. This is the natural reason that the heart's pain is less when tears are shed than when they are not, because when the heart does not allow the exhalation of the spirits into tears it does so because in its extreme anguish it needs all the vital spirits for consolation and comfort. Tears can also result from an occasion of joy. Therefore, tears of themselves are not an indication of very great pain, because they commonly serve to express grief or joy indifferently.

Christ designated two men with the title of friends. One was Lazarus: *Lazarus amicus noster dormit* [Our friend Lazarus is sleeping—John 11:11]. The other was Judas: *Amice, ad quid venisti?* [Friend, why have you come?—Matt 26:50]. Both suffered misfortune: Lazarus died temporal death; Judas died a temporal and eternal death. It is clear that this latter would be the more deeply felt by Christ. We see that he wept over Lazarus, *lacrymatus est Iesus* [Jesus wept—John 11:35], and that he did not weep for Judas, because in his case the greater pain blocked tears, and in the other, the lesser pain permitted them.

The Queen of sorrows, in order also to be Queen of merits, finds her way to the sorrowful spectacle of the death of her Only Begotten, and whereas the daughters of Zion, who hardly know him, weep, the Mother whose heart is pierced does not. *Stantem video, flentem non video* [She was seen standing there, not weeping].[6] This was because whereas the lesser grief allows tears, the greater grief inhibits them.

The example of Magdalene provides yet another proof. There is no doubt she loved Christ very much. Our Lord testifies to it: *Remittuntur ei peccata multa, quia dilexit multum* [She loves much whose many sins have been forgiven—Luke 7:47]. This love is so meritorious as to be perfect, and perfect love is to love God above all things. Of course Magdalene loved Christ more than Lazarus her brother. How then could she weep at the death of her brother—*ut vidit eam Iesus flentem* [Jesus saw that they were weeping—John 11:33] and not weep at the death of her Master? It is because she experienced less pain at her brother Lazarus's death than at the death of her Master. Therefore this is evidence that greater suffering inhibits tears, and lesser suffering allows it.[7]

Another proof: What suffering is there in absence, if not the lack of seeing the beloved? This is what is most characteristic of death. Other absences are of limited duration, but the absence of the beloved through in death is perpetual. Therefore the pain of the beloved's death is greater than the pain of other absences, because it is a greater absence.

Another point is this: The one who is absent suffers not seeing the beloved, without suffering any other harm, and without any other harm done to the beloved. When we see someone die, we suffer both the absence and the death of the beloved. Similarly, when we die ourselves, we suffer our own death as well as the absence of the beloved. Therefore, death causes a greater suffering than absence because absence is only absence, whereas death is death and absence. Thus, if death is understood to include absence as well as the pain of dying, suffering at death is greater than the pain of suffering absence.

Let us proceed to the second opinion, which is that of St. Thomas. The Angelic Doctor says that the greatest demonstration of Christ's love was to remain with us in the sacrament of the Eucharist when he left to go to his Father in glory. (Notice how this fits into the much debated absence of the foregoing discussion.) Let us come to the case at hand.

The most subtle mind of the author in question maintains that the greatest demonstration of Christ's love was not his presence in the Eucharist as such, but rather his remaining there without the use of his senses. His support here is the passage in which Absalom chances death rather than endure the pain of exile and returns from Geshur to the royal court even though he has not been fully restored into the good graces of David (2 Sam 14:32–33). At this point in the sermon Your Grace will note the elegance of this argument. First, I want to test the structure of this syllogism, then to consider the position of the saint and the response of the author.

St. Thomas says that becoming present in the sacrament of the Eucharist was the greatest demonstration of Christ's love. The author replies that, no, it was rather his remaining without the use of his senses in the Eucharist. What form of argument is this? The saint proposes the genus; the author responds with the species. Therefore, the argument is not valid. If the saint had spoken of one of the infinite species of gifts of Christ's love that are contained in this rich treasury of divine Love under the accidents of bread, the point would be valid. But if all of the infinite gifts of divine Love contained in the Eucharist are intended by the saint, how can the author maintain that only one of those many gifts is a greater gift than the gift of Christ's presence in the Eucharist as a whole? If someone were to maintain that the most noble category were substance, and another would retort that, no, the most noble category is the human being and bring many elegant arguments in support of it—as does the author—would we not be right in maintaining that they are insufficient because the argument is sophistical and deficient in its form since human being is a species of the genus, substance, and is subsumed under it? Of course we would. This in my assessment is the case, unless I am mistaken. This is of course possible, but I assure you it is not a mistake due to passion. Your Grace is aware that I remain subject to his correction in this, as I am in everything.

It appears to me that once the basic premise is removed on which the proof is built, the entire structure of the proof collapses. The more elaborate the structure, the closer it is to the edge of collapse due to its weak foundation.

I think I have satisfied everything touching the defense of St. Thomas, whose position embraces and comprehends all the demonstrations of love in the Eucharist. However, if I had to argue from species to species with the author I would say that of all the species of demonstration of love that Christ effected in the Eucharist, the greatest was not to be deprived of the use of his senses but to be present to the rebuff of insults.

To deprive oneself of the use of one's senses is only to abstain from the delights of love, which is a negative torment. But to make oneself present to offenses is not only to seek the positive offense of jealousy but—which is even more—to suffer outrage to one's honor. The latter is as much a demonstration of love when compared to the former as the distance between a love wronged and a love that is spurned. In the same measure as the pain of a pleasure denied is a far cry from an offense tolerated, so is the privation of the senses a far cry from standing up to insults. Not to see what gives pleasure is painful, but it is more painful to see what causes displeasure.

Joseph's brothers sold him into Egypt and deprived Jacob of the delight of the sight of him. Ruben dared to violate the bed of his father. Both great crimes! But let us see the punishments Jacob provided for them. He deprived Ruben of his rights as firstborn and, signaling his reasons, he cursed him and wished he had never raised him: *Effusus es sicut aqua, non crescas; qui ascendisti cubile patris tui, et maculasti stratum eius* [You spilled yourself out like water. You shall not increase, you who climbed into the bed of your father and stained his couch—Gen 49:4]. A well-deserved punishment for his offense! But let us see what punishment he assigned to the rest of them for having sold Joseph into slavery? None at all. He does not even mention it.

How is that possible? Such an enormous crime remained unpunished? To sell one's brother, and a brother like Joseph, the delight and consolation of Jacob, and later the refuge of them all? This he forgot and punished Ruben? Yes, because selling Joseph only deprived Jacob of the delight of his love, but Ruben had both offended his love and his honor. It is less painful to be deprived of the benefits of love than to suffer harm to love and honor. Therefore, for Christ the latter is greater than the former. I say this only in passing, as an argument from species to species, which can be made to the author, not to the saint.

Let us go to the third position, that of St. John Chrysostom. The saint says the greatest demonstration of Christ's love was to wash the feet of his disciples. The author maintains that it was not his washing their feet but the motivation for washing them that was the greatest demonstration of his love.

Here we have another argument, not very different from the last one. There it was of genus and species; here it is of cause and effect. God help me! Would it have entered the mind of the divine Chrysostom that Christ effected such a thing without a cause, and a very great cause, at that? Clearly such a thing cannot be imagined. Rather, not only one cause but many causes are manifest in such an extraordinary effect, that is, the self-humbling of his immense Majesty at the feet of his disciples. This is the effect. Given its great power, Chrysostom wants us to infer the greatness of the causes without his specifically mentioning them. This is because there could be no more vivid expression of divine sovereignty in humble ministry than simply to say: "See how Christ loved us, since he humbled himself to wash our feet! See what he wished to teach us through his example, because he abased himself to wash our feet! See how eager he was for the conversion of Judas, because he washed his feet!" There are many more causes expressed in the gospel, and even more passed over in silence, as well as those Chrysostom includes when he says: He washed the feet of his disciples.

If the motive for the foot washing and its execution are related like cause and effect, and if the cause and effect are dependent on each other and here cannot be separated, where is this "greater" that the author finds between the washing itself and the cause of washing, if not the difference of being generative of the cause and of the effect generated? What demonstration of love is greater than the one that the saint recounts? The culmination of it all was that Christ abased himself at the feet of Judas, whose heart was the throne of Satan. This was the effect that the saint considered and expressed. To probe into the cause of this action would be to diminish it. This is the reason, or one of the reasons, that the saint includes it, narrating the effect with more mysterious deliberation than if he had stated the reason.

When the evangelist St. John wanted to give proofs of the love of the Eternal Father, he proves it with the effect: *Sic Deus dilexit mundum ut Filium suum Unigenitum daret* [God so loved the world that he gave it his only begotten Son—John 3:16]. Therefore, the effect is what proves the cause. In order to inflame our desire for eternal goods, he said that neither eyes have seen, nor ears heard, nor human heart comprehended the nature of eternal happiness (1 Cor 2:9). Well, in order to excite in us the desire for it, would it not have been better to paint heavenly glory? No, because it is more appropriate to pass over in silence that which of its nature exceeds expression. To say "heavenly glory cannot be expressed" expresses more of the nature of that glory than to say "this is what heavenly glory is like." For the same reason Chrysostom expresses the exterior work and suppresses the cause of it, omitting to express the inexpressible.

In order to clarify what has just been said and to give more support to the accuracy with which the saint spoke, let us investigate more closely what a *fineza* is.[8] Does it designate, perhaps, to have love? No, certainly not. Rather, it refers to the proofs of love. Those are called *finezas*. Those external demonstrative signs and actions that the lover practices, which have as their cause the motive of love, these are called *finezas*. Therefore, if the saint is speaking of *finezas* and external acts, it is extremely fitting that he brings forth the foot washing itself and not its cause, since the cause is love, and the saint is not speaking of love, but rather of the *fineza*, which is the exterior sign of love. Therefore, there is no point arguing about what the saint has presupposed and what others later will put forward as if it were something new.

We have already developed our response through the arguments of the three saints. Now we proceed to the most difficult part of our undertaking, which is the final opinion that the author formulates. Let us proceed to the Achilles' heel of his sermon. He asserted that he could reveal a demonstration of Christ's love which is the greatest of all, and which, as he said, "no one would be able to equal," which is "that Christ did not want a corresponding love from us for himself, but wanted it for us. Thus the greatest gift of love is to love without a corresponding love in return."

He supports it with the following words: *et vos debetis alter alterius lavare pedes* [you should wash each others feet—John 13:14]. From which he infers that Christ did not want a corresponding love from us or even that we love him at all, but that we love one another. This is the greatest demonstration of Christ's love, because it is a gift without any interest in love in return. To back up his assertion he does not bring to bear arguments from holy scripture because he says the greatest proof of this demonstration of love is that there are no proofs, because it is a demonstration of love without parallel.

If we look carefully, the proposition has two parts to which we need to respond. One is that Christ did not want our corresponding love. The other is that there is no proof of this demonstration of Christ's love. Therefore, there will be two responses. One will be to probe why what the author says is a demonstration of love is not one; rather, to the contrary, it is a demonstration of Christ's love that he wanted our love in return for his. The other response is to prove that holy scripture is full of examples proving Christ's desire for our love.

Let us proceed to the first argument, which is to prove that neither was what the author said a demonstration of love nor did Christ do it. The proof that Christ wants our corresponding love, and did not renounce it but rather requested it, is so easy because holy scripture is full of requests and precepts demanding that we love God. There we see that the first commandment is *Diliges dominum Deum tuum ex toto corde tuo, et ex tota anima tua, et ex tota mente tua* [You will love the Lord your God with your whole heart, your whole soul, and your whole mind—Deut 6:5]. How is it possible to think that Christ did not want our love in return when he commands it and recommends it with such force? It is clear that the author knew this better than I did, but he wanted to display his ingenuity rather than prove his point. Although the phrase *et vos debetis alter alterius lavare pedes* [you should wash each others feet—John 13:14] does not express Christ's request for us to love him, but rather the love which he commands us to have for our neighbor, this love of neighbor includes and envelops in itself the same love of God, although it is not expressed in this text with the same emphasis as love of neighbor that is commanded.

I prove it by logic. God commanded us to love our neighbor and wanted us to do it because he commanded it. There the unspoken presupposition is that we love God more than our neighbor because we love our neighbor out of obedience to God. When we do a favor for someone out of respect for someone else, we have greater esteem for the person requesting we do the favor than for the person for whom we do it.

When God wanted to destroy the people of Israel for their sin of idolatry, Moses intervened saying: "Oh, forgive them or erase me out of the book of life" (Exod 32:31–32). God forgave that ungrateful people because of Moses's intervention. I ask who was more obligated to God, Moses or the people? Clearly it was Moses, because God did it out of consideration for him. Christ wants us to love one another, but also that we love one another in him and through him. Therefore his love comes first. And if not, let us see how he considers those we love without regard for him. Christ commanded that we love our parents: *Honora patrem tuum* [Honor your parents—Exod 20:12]. He also commands us to love our neighbor: *Diliges proximum tuum, sicut te ipsum* [Love your neighbor as yourself—Matt 22:39]. Very well, but what is the nature of this love? To prefer his love to all others, not only illicit loves, not only depraved loves, but also legitimate and obligatory loves that he himself has commanded, such as between father and son, and between wife and husband. Of all the other loves his Majesty desires, he does not desire those that are not related to love of him; rather, he hates them and sets them apart. If this does not convince you, look at the admirable order in which the gospel goes about teaching the means to accomplish and practice that first commandment: *Diliges Dominum Deum tuum*, etc. His Majesty has commanded us to love our parents: *Honora patrem tuum*. So that we do not think that we may love our parents more than God, he says: *qui amat patrem, aut matrem plus quam me, non est me dignus* [He who loves father or mother more than me is not worthy of me—Matt 10:37]. Here it appears that God is content merely that we do not love our parents more than his Majesty. But no, there is more. Later, this obligation is further developed. Up to this point he has only commanded that we do not love our parents more than him, but later he commands us to hate them if they obstruct our serving him. *Si quis venit a me, et non odit patrem suum, et matrem, et uxorem, et filios, et fratres, et sorores, etc.* [If anyone comes to me and does not hate his father, mother, wife, children, brothers, sisters, etc.—Luke 14:26]. Here he commands us to hate all those close to us. What remains to us is our body, but, no, not even that. We should not spare even our bodily parts if they obstruct us in his service. *Si autem manus tua, vel pes tuus scandalizat te, abscide eum, et proiice abs te* [If your hand or your foot be a cause of scandal, cut it off and cast it away—Matt 18:8]. In truth, neither hand, nor foot, nor eye is exempt. Well then, life remains. Actually, it is not exempt either. *Qui non odit patrem suum, et matrem suam, et uxorem, et filios, et fratres, et sorores, adhunc autem et animam suam, non potest meus esse discipulus* [Whosoever does not hate his father, mother, wife, children, brothers, sisters and even his own life—Luke 14:26]. Good Lord! This commandment is so strict that it does not even exempt life itself! At least our being remains. What? Even our being is not exempt. We read: *Si quis vult post me venire, abneget semetipsum.* If someone wants to follow me, let him deny himself (Matt 16:24).[9] You see here how nothing is to be kept in reserve when it comes to his service. Then how can we possibly think that he does not want us to love him, if even the most legitimate loves are forbidden when they conflict with love of him? And it is not merely that he wants it, but he is ready to fight for it with blood and fire. *Ego veni ignem mittere in terram* [I have come to send fire upon the earth—Luke12:49]. And another text: *non veni mittere pacem in terram, sed gladium. Veni enim separe hominem adversus patrem suum, et filiam adversus matrem suam, et nurum adversus socrum suam; et inimici hominis, domestici eius* [I have not come to bring peace to the earth, but the sword. I have come to set a man against his father, daughter against her mother, daughter-in-law against mother-in-law, and a man's enemies will be his own servants—Matt 10:34–36]. I consider it very significant that Christ says he has come to separate daughter-in-law from mother-in-law and to make the servants enemies of their master. Why, Lord, would you find it necessary to set them against each other and make enemies of them? Aren't they already divided and already enemies of each other? To divide the father from son and daughter from mother, husband from wife, brother from brother, that is all well and good, because all these love one another; but the daughter-in-law and the mother-in-law, the servants from the master? This I do not understand. What daughter-in-law does not hate her mother-in-law? What servant is there that is not of necessity the enemy of his master? Then what necessity is there to set them against each other if they already are? This underscores the great difficulty of the commandment. Even the few exceptions of good servants and daughters-in-law loving their mothers-in-law—Eliezer, faithful servant of Abraham; Ruth, loving daughter-in-law of Naomi—are, nonetheless, included. Yes, even they are not free of this commandment because God is very jealous of what touches the primacy of his love. On nearly every page of holy scripture he tells us: *Ego sum Dominus Deus tuus fortis, zelotes* [I am the Lord, your God, mighty and jealous—Exod 20:5]. He demonstrates his love through his jealousy, such as when after having made various threats to the synagogue for its wickedness, the last and most terrible is *Auferam a te zelum meum* [My jealousy will depart from you—Ezek 16:42]. It is as if he is telling them, "Since after so many benefits you do not want to convert, nor reform after so many punishments, I carry out the greatest punishment of all." And what is it, Lord? What? *Auferam a te zelum meum*. My jealousy will depart from you, which is the sign that I am withdrawing my love.

God wanted to test the faith of the patriarch Abraham and commanded he sacrifice Isaac, his son. Now I ask you, Why is Isaac the one singled out? Was not Ishmael also his son? And if it were necessary to sacrifice a son, would it not have been enough for it to have been Ishmael? Or God might at least have said "Sacrifice one of your sons," without indicating which one, and have left the choice open to his father? Why then did he designate Isaac? Pay attention to the exact words: *Tolle filium tuum, quen diligis, Issac, et sacrifica mihi illum* [Take your son Isaac whom you love, and sacrifice him to me—Gen 22:2]. It is the beloved one, Isaac, who must be sacrificed. It appears that God is jealous that Abraham loves Isaac so much and wants to test which of Abraham's loves is greater, his love for him or his love for his son.

Furthermore, we know well that God knew what Abraham had to do and that Abraham loved him more than Isaac. Why then this test? He already knew, but he wanted us to know that he is such a jealous God that not only does he want to be loved above all things, but he wants this to be clear and known by everyone.

Therefore, he tested Abraham. From all this I judge that we can understand the great urgency with which Christ asks for our love and that when he commands we love one another, his Majesty himself has to be the medium of this love. Everyone knows that the means uniting two ends is united more closely and directly to them than they are to each other. Christ has established himself as means and union; therefore, when he commands that we love our neighbor, he wants us to love him.

Christ says furthermore that his commandment is that we love our neighbor as his Majesty loves us: *Hoc est praeceptum meum, ut diligatis invicem, sicut dilexi vos* [This is my commandment, that you love one another as I have loved you—John 15:12]. Here he only commands that we love one another. But in order to comply, what disposition do we need? Christ himself teaches us: *Qui diligit me, mandatum meum servabit* [The one who loves me will keep my commandments—John 14:15]. The evangelist St. John writes in his first epistle, chapter five: *Haec est enim charitas Dei, ut mandata eius custodiamus* [This is the love of God, that we keep his commandments—1 John 5:3]. Therefore, to comply with the command to love our neighbor we first need to love God. The author himself in another sermon refers to Christ's proclamation that he is the vine and we are the branches: *Ego sum vitis, vos palmites* (John 15:5). The branches are first united to the vine before they are united to each other. Therefore it is clear that Christ desires, Christ solicits, Christ commands that we love one another.

I believe I have elaborated to excess the obvious on a point so clear that in making it, it has been more difficult to decide what to omit than what to include. From what has been said above I judge that we may legitimately conclude that Christ did not demonstrate his love in the manner that the author assumes, that is, by not desiring our love in return.

If you were to ask me if there is a demonstration of Christ's love worthy of the name that he refrained from doing for us due to his immense love for us, I would answer, yes, there is. There are demonstrations of love caused by the limitations of our own nature. These Christ did not do, because they were not in conformity with his infinite perfection or proper to his immense Majesty, dignity, and sovereignty. *Verbi gratia*: The just demonstrate love for Christ in ways Christ did not do for them, such as by resisting temptation; by struggling with their nature, which, stained by sin, has a propensity to evil; by struggling with fear, the threat of being vanquished, and the uncertainty of victory or defeat. Christ was incapable of demonstrating love in any of these ways because he could not be tempted, much less fear the dangers of sin. Because although his Majesty was driven into the desert *ut tentaretur a diabolo* [in order to be tempted by the devil—Matt 4:1], the learned understand how to interpret this passage. The glorious doctor St. Gregory, when explicating this text, says that temptation occurs in three ways: by suggestion, by pleasure, or by consent.[10] In the first place, he says, Christ could only be tempted by the devil. We, because we are conceived in sin and are children of sin, having within us the seeds of sin, the *fomes peccati* that inclines us to sin, most often fall by consenting or by experiencing pleasure, or by both. But Christ, born of a virgin mother and through miraculous conception, was without sin. For that reason he could not feel in himself any contradiction or repugnance toward doing the good and consequently could only be tempted by suggestion, which is an extrinsic temptation. As extrinsic, it was very far from his mind, which could not be drawn to it or really need to struggle with it. And in as far as Christ did not have either the struggle or the risk to contend with, he was not able to demonstrate his love by resisting or fearing the danger of sin. About which the apostle [Paul] says: *adimpleo ea quae desunt passionum Christi, in carne mea pro corpore eius, quod est Ecclesia* [I add in my flesh to complete the sufferings of Christ on behalf of his body, which is the Church—Col 1:24]. Well, if the redemption was so abundant, *copiosa apud eum redemptio* (Ps 129:7), how could anything add or fill up the passion of Christ? Could the passion be lacking in something? What did St. Paul do that Christ did not do? This same apostle tells us: *Datus est mihi stimulus carnis mea angelus Satanae, qui me colaphizet* [God has given me a thorn in the flesh, an angel of Satan who beats me—2 Cor 12:7]. This was what was lacking in Christ's passion: struggle with temptation and fear of the dangers of sin. This is what St. Paul says completes the passion of Christ, and these are the demonstrations of love that we can do but Christ cannot.

Therefore, not desiring love in return would be a demonstration of human love because it would be disinterested, but in the case of Christ it would not be, because he has nothing to gain from our love. The proof is this: Human love is found through reciprocity. Something would be lacking if this were not the case, such as delight, utility, approval, etc. However, Christ lacks nothing, if we do not reciprocate his love. In himself he contains all delights, all riches, and all goods. Therefore, he would be denying himself nothing if he renounced our reciprocal love, because it would add nothing to him. To renounce something that is nothing would not be a demonstration of love. And as such it would not be a demonstration of love for Christ; for that reason Christ did not do it for us. In the book of Job, chapter 35, we can read of the sovereignty of God which has no need of us: *Porro si iuste egeris, quid donabis ei, aut quid de manu tua accipiet? Homini, qui similis tui est, nocebit impietas tua; et filium hominis adiuvabit iustitia tua* [Furthermore if you do justice what will you give him or what will he receive from your hand? Your wickedness will harm a man like you, and your justice may help the son of man—Job 35:7–8]. From this it is clear that we need to be loved in return because it benefits us, and for this reason would be a demonstration of love, and a very great one, to renounce this benefit. For Christ, however, there would be no resulting benefit from our love, so it would not be a demonstration of his love not to want it. Therefore, as I have already said, Christ did not do it for us. Rather, he did the opposite—he solicited our love without needing it—and this is the greatest demonstration of his love.

Christ's love is very different from ours. We want reciprocal love because it is a particular benefit to ourselves. Christ desires that same demonstration of love for the good of another, that is, ourselves. In my view the author was very close to this point, but he made a mistake and said the contrary. Because he saw Christ as disinterested, he persuaded himself that he did not want our love in return for his. And thus, the view of the author is that Christ did not want reciprocal love for his own but for our benefit. My view is that Christ wanted reciprocity for himself, but he wanted the benefits resulting from this reciprocity for our sakes.

Here we, the lovers, reciprocate for our own good. Christ returns our love for our own sake, not for his. Reciprocal love and the goal of reciprocal love are distinguished. Christ reserves reciprocal love for himself. The goal of reciprocity, which is the benefit resulting from it, he leaves to us. Here lovers want their love to benefit the beloved, but they want the benefit of the beloved's love for themselves. Christ wants both the love he has for us and the benefit of our love for him all for our sakes. Christ questioned Peter about his love for him, saying: *Petre, amas me?* [Peter, do you love me?—John 21:17]. Peter responded with ardent concern springing from his burning heart. Yes, he would give up his life from love. We see why this examination is so tricky for Christ. Without doubt he wanted Peter to do him a great service. Yes he did. And what was it? *Pasce oves meas* [Feed my sheep—John 21:17]. This is what Christ wanted: that Peter love him, but that resulting benefits be for the sheep. Christ could just as well have said to Peter, and it would seem more appropriate for him to have said: "Peter, do you love my sheep? Then feed my sheep." But he does not say that; rather, he says: *Peter do you love me? Then feed my sheep.* Therefore, he desires love for himself, and the benefit for us.

You might now respond by saying: If Christ did not need our love for his own benefit, but only for ours, and for our benefit Christ's love is sufficient, why would he solicit our love at all since without it he can still benefit us by loving us?

To respond to this objection we must remember that God gave us free will, the power to desire or not to desire to do good or evil. When we do not exercise it we suffer violence to ourselves, because it is a tribute that God has granted us and a deed of authentic liberty that he has awarded us. Well now, this liberty is the reason that it is not enough for God to desire to be ours, if we do not desire to be God's. Since becoming like God is our supreme good, and since this cannot occur without our desiring it, God solicits and commands us to love him, because loving him is our supreme good. The royal prophet David said that God is God and Lord because he does not need our goods: *Dixi Domino: Deus meus es tu, quoniam bonorum meorum non eges* [I have said to the Lord "You are my God, you have no need of my goods"—Ps 15:2, Vulgate]. Here it is clearly acknowledged that God does not need our goods. Later, speaking in the person of that very Lord, David says: "I have no need of your sacrifices or your holocausts. I do not receive your calves or your goats. Mine are all the birds of the sky and the beasts of the fields. Mine is the abundance of the fruits of the earth. Mine, the entire mechanism of the globe. Did you perhaps think that I fed myself on the flesh of bulls or that I drank the blood of goats" (Ps 49:8–13, Vulgate).[11] Well, most high Lord, we might respond, "If you need nothing because everything is yours; if you disdain our offerings and do not our accept sacrifices; if you are all powerful and infinitely rich, what can we do in your service, poor creatures that we are? Look upon our distress! Though we are obligated to you for your infinite benefits, there is nothing we can offer you who have everything." "Yes, you can," verse 14 of the same psalm seems to reply: *Immola Deo sacrificium laudis; et redde Altissimo vota tua. Et invoca me in die tribulationis; eruam te, et honorificabis me* [Give to God sacrifice of praise and keep the vows of the Most High. Call on me on the day of your distress. I will deliver you and you will honor me—Ps 50:14–15]. It is as if he were saying, "You, you want to give something in return for everything I have given to you? Then ask more of me, and this will be my payment. Call on me when you are in trouble, and I will liberate you. This confidence you have in me will resound to my honor." Oh, the beauty of divine Love that calls what is a benefit to us an honor for you! Oh, the wisdom of God! Oh, the generosity of God! And oh, what a demonstration of love worthy only of God! For this God wants our love for our good, not for his. The beauty of his gift of love is not, as the author maintains, that God does not desire our love in return, but that he desires this very thing for our sake.

We have already proven that Christ wants our love in return for his and that to want it is the greatest demonstration of his love. What is lacking at this point is the argument I promised, namely, that there is no lack of proof and examples from holy scripture, contrary to what the author maintains. He considers love desiring the benefits of love for another and not for self to be a demonstration of love so great as to be unparalleled and without equal. Let's see if I can find someone who has done this. Absalom killed his brother Amnon because he had raped Tamar. What did his father,

King David do? (2 Sam 13). He was so indignant that he obliged Absalom to go, fleeing death, to Geshur. The king remained so furious that even Joab, his prime minister, did not dare to speak about his pardon except by means of the woman Tecoa. Even after pardoning him, David did not want to see Absalom's face. What anger! What rage! Hardly had Absalom returned to the graces of his father when, proving himself a traitor and rebel to his father's love and crown, he had himself proclaimed king in Hebron. Not only did he try to wrest the kingdom from his father, but he tried to take away his father's life and his honor by publicly profaning his bed. What offenses! What ingratitude! What insults! What could we expect from an indignant, offended, and furious David against such an evil son, against such a treacherous vassal? Were the Eumenides enraged unleashed within his breast? As far as we can see there was little to hinder them, since the luck of battle was on David's side, and he could have avenged himself to his satisfaction. Let us hear the order that he gave to his general Joab: *Servate mihi puerum Absalom* [Spare the youth Absalom—2 Sam 18:15]. Jesus! How contrary is this order to what we would expect! But he does not stop here. Joab disobeyed the order and killed Absalom. And what did David do? What? He wept and turned the entire victory into lamentation. As if that were not enough, he said he would rather have died so that Absalom could live. *Fili mi Absalom, quis mihi det, ut ego moriar pro te!* [Absalom my son, oh, had it been given to me to die for you!—2 Sam 18:33]. What are you doing, David? You are mourning a son who was your enemy, a vassal who betrayed you? You want to leave this life to give him your life? And even though your love is already so great that you would pardon such despicable crimes against you, why, when he killed his brother Amnon, did you not demonstrate this tenderness but instead wanted to kill him? This is that very same Absalom. What? You were furious with him then over a lesser offense, that of killing his brother, than now for the greater offense of wanting to kill you! You were not even angry, but even more, you were tender? What? You showed greater feeling when Absalom was cruel to Amnon than when he was cruel to you? Were you more sensitive to the lack of love Absalom had for Amnon than to his lack of love for you? Yes, that is the case. Well then, from whom did David ask for love in return? It is clear that it was for Amnon and not for himself. Therefore we have proof and examples of someone who sought love owed to him in order for it to benefit another. So if it were a demonstration of Christ's love not to look for love in return, there are no lack of examples of this in scripture, contrary to what the author maintains. That was the second point to which I promised to respond.

With that it appears to me, that, although my arguments are unpolished, terse, and unlearned, I have obeyed Your Grace's order. The speed with which I have written this did not leave me time to polish my discourse because *festinans canis caecos parit catulos* [In haste the bitch gives birth to her blind pups].[12] I send it to you as an embryo, as the she-bear gives birth to her unformed cubs with this additional defect among the many others that your Grace will recognize. Some of them you will use your discretion to correct, others you will make good out of friendship. Furthermore, the subject with its difficulty already furnishes an excuse for not succeeding, since missing an inaccessible target is not as disgraceful as failing to hit a common one. For the pygmies it was a sufficient demonstration of bravery merely to dare to challenge Hercules. Considering the sublime genius of the author, even giants must appear as dwarfs. What then is a poor woman to do? Of course, it is true that a woman took the club from the hands of Alcides,[13] a deed considered one of the three impossibilities venerated in antiquity.[14] To speak within a more Christian framework: *quae stulta sunt mundi elegit Deus, ut confundat sapientes; et infirma mundi elegit Deut, ut confundat fortia; et ignobilia mundi et contemptibilia elegit Deus, et ea quae non sunt, ut ea quae sunt destrueret; ut non glorietur omnis caro in conspectu eius* [The foolish things of the world God has chosen to confuse the wise, and the weak things God has chosen to confound the strong. What is ignoble and contemptible God has chosen, and what is not, so that he might destroy what is, so that all flesh will not glory in his sight—1 Cor 1:27–29]. I believe it is true that if this paper has achieved some success, it is not the work of my understanding, but rather only that God desired to punish, through such a weak instrument, the pride of the author's assertion: *that there is no one who could maintain a demonstration of love equal* to his own. It seems that he believed his genius surpassed that of the three holy fathers, and that there was no one who could equal him. Judging that God had not stretched out his hand to Augustine, Chrysostom, and Thomas, he thought that God stopped at him so as not to create someone else who could respond to him. Had I achieved no more than daring to answer him, this would have been sufficient mortification for such a man as he, illustrious in so many ways. It is no light punishment for a man who believes no man would dare to respond to him to behold an ignorant woman, for whom this type of study is so alien and remote from her sex, doing so. But then, so was Judith and she took up arms, and Deborah, who became a judge. And if this seems imprudent, Your Grace by tearing up this paper will have meted out the punishment for my having made the mistake of writing it. Finally, although this paper is so private that I have only written it because Your Grace ordered me to do so and for your eyes alone, I subject it in everything to the correction of our Holy Mother the Catholic Church, and I detest and declare nullified and not said all that is at variance with her common opinion and that of the holy fathers. *Vale* [Farewell].

Your Grace might well have thought that having just closed this treatise, I had forgotten the other point about which you commanded me to write: What is, in my opinion, the greatest demonstration of divine Love? Your Grace heard me speak about this in the same conversation I mentioned above. However, I have not forgotten but done this intentionally, because this subject came up in a later conversation in which some arguments led to others that were not very much to the point. Here it is necessary to separate those that are and those that are not so as not to confuse one with the other. Let me explain. As we were speaking of the demonstration of love, I said that the greatest gifts of God's love, in my opinion, were negative benefits. That is, the benefits that he omits bestowing, knowing the difficulty we would have reciprocating. Now this manner of thinking is very different from that of the author, because he speaks of the demonstration of Christ's love, and specifically of those things done at the end of his life. The demonstration of love of which I am speaking is one God does as God, which is continual and everlasting. As a result, there would

be no reason to oppose it to those demonstrations of love proposed by the author. To do so would be mean-spirited and repre-
hensible. That is why I have decided to separate this discussion
and treat it as an independent argument, appending it here so that
Your Grace attains all he has requested of me, my only desire
being to obey him.

The greatest demonstrations of divine love, in my opinion,
are the benefits that God omits to do because of our ingratitude.
The proof is as follows. God is infinite kindness and supreme
good, and as such, in his nature relational and desirous of doing
good for his creatures. Furthermore, God has infinite love for us
and therefore is always ready to grant us infinite benefits. God is
all-powerful and can give us all the goods that he desires, without
it costing him any effort, and he desires to do so. Therefore, when
doing good things for us, God goes with the natural current of his
own goodness, of his own love, and of his own power without any
effort on his part. This is clear. Therefore, when God does not
grant us benefits, because we will use them to our own detriment,
God represses the torrents of his immense generosity, restrains the
sea of his infinite love, and holds back the flow of his absolute
power. Therefore, according to this line of reasoning, it takes
more effort for God not to grant us benefits than to grant us benefits. As a result, it is a greater demonstration of God's love to suspend them than to grant them, since God refrains the generosity
of his nature, so that we not be ungrateful, a characteristic
response of ours. God would rather appear stingy, so that we
would not be worse than we need be, by withholding his largess if
it would harm us. Since this is contrary to what is commonly
understood as being generous, God places our advantage above his
own reputation and his own nature.

The Redeemer preached his marvelous doctrine, and after
having worked many miracles and marvels in many places one
would think that when he arrived in his home country he would
have had a special place in the hearts of his neighbors and compatriots. However, he had hardly arrived, when instead of applaud-
ing him, they began to censure and accuse him of what they
considered his shortcomings, saying: *Nonne hic est fabri filius?*
Nonne mater eius dicitur Maria, et fratres eius, Iacobus, et Ioseph, et

Simon, et Iudas; et sorores eius, nonne omnes apud nos sunt? Unde ergo huic omnia ista? [Is this not the carpenter's son? Is not Mary his mother, and his brothers James, Joseph, Simon, and Judas? And his sisters, are they not among us? Where did all this come from?—Matt 13:55–56]. The evangelist continues: *Non fecit ibi virtutes multas propter incredulitatem illorum* [And he did not do many wondrous deeds there because of their lack of faith—Matt 13:58]. So that though Christ wanted to perform miracles in his home country, though he wanted to grant them benefits, they showed their wicked spirit by their malicious tongues and by the way they received his favors. Christ restrained himself from doing miracles so as not to give them the occasion to even greater wickedness, when according to the words of evangelist, "he did not perform many miracles because of their lack of faith." Christ also knew that they would complain about his not doing them, and that they would consider him mean and avaricious, and anticipating their reproaches he said to them: *Utique dicetis mihi hanc similitudinem: Medice, cura te ipsum; quanta audivimus facta in Capharnaum, fac et hic in patria tua* [You will quote me the proverb, "Physician heal yourself." And say "Do here in your home country what we have heard you have done in Capernaum"—Luke 4:23]. And in order to satisfy the anticipated slander he told them that in the times of Elijah there were many widows and only one was cured, and that there were many lepers in the time of Elisha and he only cured Naaman the leper, and that no prophet is accepted in his own country (Luke 4:25–28). They did not understand the comparison and, continuing in their wickedness, wanted to throw him off a cliff. They confirmed with this evil desire the reasons for Christ's not wanting to grant them positive benefits, but rather giving them the negative one of not giving them the occasion to commit a greater sin. This was the greatest demonstration of love that Christ could have done at the time for his thankless compatriots. He emphasized this by preferring the two cities that he himself had threatened for having been ungrateful for the miracles he worked in them when he said: *Vai tibi Corozain, vae tibi Bethsaida; qui si in Tyro et Sidone factae essent virtutes, quae factae sunt in vobis, olim in cilicio, et cinere poenitentiam egissent. Verumtamen dico vobis: Tyro et Sidoni remissius erit in die iudicii, quam vobis* [Matt 11:21–22]. "Woe to you, if in Tyre and Sidon they had seen the miracles that have been done for you, they would have converted! But I assure you that in the final judgment they will suffer less punishment than you."[15]

In so doing the Lord spared them this great burden by not granting them the benefits of his miracles, so that they were excused from the greater burden that would have resulted for them because of the miracles. *Gravius*—said the glorious St. Gregory—*inde iudicemur, cum enim augentur dona, rationes etiam crescunt donorum* [They will be more severely judged who have greater gifts. With increased gifts come increased responsibilities].[16] The greater the gift, the greater is the debt to be repaid. Therefore, it is beneficial not to grant benefits when we will use them badly.

God granted many particular benefits to Judas beyond the general ones, and when the time of his sacrilegious betrayal arrived, Christ lamented not his death but the harm done to his ungrateful disciple, saying: *Vai homini illi, per quem tradar ego, bonum erat ei, si natus non fuisset* [Woe to the man through whom I am delivered up. It would have been better had he never been born—Matt 26:24]. This indicates that he repented the benefit of having created him, because it would have been better for him never to have been born than to have been born to become so wicked. This becomes even more clear when we see that God, when offended by the many evils of human beings, determined to end the world by water. Using human expressions, the text says that he said: *Delebo, inquit, hominem, quem creavi a facie terrae, ab homine usque ad animantia, a reptili usque ad volucres coeli; poenitet enim me fecisse eos* [I will eradicate, I say, the humans I have created, from the face of the earth, from humankind, to the animals, from the reptiles to the birds of the sky, for I regret having made them—Gen 6:7]. Thus God repented having granted benefits to us that had served for our greater grief. Therefore, it was a greater demonstration of his love for him not to grant benefits. Oh, my Lord and my God, how dimwitted and blind we are not to recognize the species of negative benefits that you award us!

If someone is very much down on his luck, we say that it is a punishment from God. When God punishes, the punishment is also a benefit, because it is done in view of our correction, and God punishes those he loves. But it is not only punishing that he does for our benefit but also exempting us from the greater debt. If you are in poor health it appears to you that God is deaf, because he does not hear your complaints. But this is not the case; rather, he is granting you the benefit of not giving you health, because you use it badly. We envy our neighbors their good fortune and their natural gifts. Oh, what a mistake it is to envy people because of such things! We ought rather to pity them because of the great burden for which they have to give account! And if we want to envy, let us not envy the graces that God gives others, but rather the good that corresponds to them, which is what gives them merit. This alone is what we should envy, not their having received it, which is a burden. Let us consider the benefit God does for us in not granting us all the gifts that we would like and also those that his Majesty would like to give us but withholds in order to not make us more accountable. Let us give thanks and let us praise the beauty of divine Love in whom reward is a benefit, punishment is a benefit, the suspension of benefits is the greatest benefit, and not to demonstrate love the greatest demonstration of love. And if this is not the case, tell me: God who gave the world his only begotten Son, who became incarnate and died for us, what could he deny us? Nothing. He himself says: *Quis est ex vobis homo, quem si petierit filius suus panem, numquid lapidem porriget ei? Aut si piscem petierit, numquid serpentem porriget ei? Si ergo vos, cum sitis mali, nostis bona data dare filiis vestris: quanto magis Pater vester, qui in coelis est, dabit bona petentibus se?* [Who is there among you, if your son asks for bread, will give him a stone? And if he asks for a fish will give him a snake? If you who are evil know to give good things to your children, how much more will your Father who is in heaven give good things to those who ask for them?—Matt 7:9–11]. Well, why Lord, when the mother of the sons of Zebedee asked for the seats at your right and left hands in glory, did you not give them to her? (Matthew 20:20–23). Because they did not know what they were asking, and because for God, who is by nature generous and powerful, it is a greater demonstration of love not to give us what would not be good for us.

Thus I judge this the greatest demonstration of love that God does for us. May his Majesty give us the grace to recognize his benefits, and to respond to them, which shows a greater understanding. May he grant that when we consider benefits we do not remain at the level of speculative argument but go on to practical service, turning negative benefits into positive ones creating a disposition worthy to open the dam of our ingratitude, which restrains and holds in check the torrents of divine generosity.

May the Lord keep Your Grace for many years. Again I submit all that I have said above to the censure of our Holy Mother the Catholic Church, as her most obedient daughter. *Iterum vale* [Again, farewell].

LETTER OF "SOR PHILOTEA"

My Lady,

I have seen the letter in which you contest the demonstration of Christ's love that the reverend Father Antonio de Vieira in his sermon for Holy Thursday had discussed with such subtlety that even for the most learned it seemed that another Angel of the Apocalypse had arisen in this singular genius, following in the footsteps of the illustrious César Meneses,[1] a talent of the first order in Portugal. In my judgment, however, those who read your arguments will not be able to deny that your pen was cut finer than both of theirs, and that they might boast to see themselves challenged by a woman who is the honor of her sex.

I, at least, have admired the liveliness of your ideas, the subtlety of your proofs, the energetic clarity—that inseparable companion of wisdom—with which you pursue the matter. The first word pronounced by the divine Word was "light," because without clarity wisdom has no voice. Even the voice of Christ, when he spoke of the greatest mysteries beneath the veil of parables, was not admired in the world. Only when he spoke clearly did he merit the acclaim of knowing everything (John 16:29–30). This is one of the many benefits you owe to God, because clarity of mind is not acquired with work and diligence, but rather is a gift infused in the soul.

So that you will see yourself more clearly through your writing, I have printed this, in the hope that you will recognize the treasures that God has deposited in your soul, and as your understanding grows, so also your gratitude, since gratitude and understanding are always born of the same delivery. As you yourself have said in your letter, the more one receives from God the more one is obligated to him. I fear you are in arrears in your payment of what you owe God, as few creatures have received as many natural gifts as you. If you have used your talents well up to now (as I must believe of someone who is a professed religious), I hope you will use them even better in the future.

My judgment is not such a severe censor that it would criticize your writing of poetry, for which you have seen yourself celebrated, since St. Teresa, Gregory of Nazianzen, and other saints have through their poetry canonized this accomplishment. I would, however, wish that you imitate them, as much in your choice of subjects as you do in your choice of verse.

I do not approve the vulgarity of those who deny women learning, since so many women have applied themselves successfully to study, and not without the praise of St. Jerome. It is true that St. Paul says that women should not teach, but he does not command them not to study for the purpose of attaining knowledge (1 Tim 2:12). He only wished to warn against the danger of pride in our sex, predisposed as it is to vanity. Divine Wisdom took a letter away from the name Sarai, and added one to the name of Abram, not because a man was supposed to be more lettered than a woman, as many maintain, but because the *i* added to Sara's name expressed puffed up pride and domination (Gen 17:15). Sarai is interpreted as *Señora mía* (my lady). Thus it was not appropriate in that sense that someone in the role of subordinate in the house of Abraham should be called lady.

Letters engendering pride in women are not pleasing to God, although the Apostle does not disapprove of them if they do not take women beyond their status of due obedience. It is well known that study and knowledge have kept you contained in a state of subjection and have served to perfect the beauty of your obedience. Since other religious sacrifice their will to obedience, you, as captive of your mind, have a more difficult and agreeable sacrifice to offer on the altars of religious life.

I do not ascribe to the judgment that you modify your genius by renouncing books, but only that you improve it by sometimes

250

reading the book of Jesus Christ. None of the evangelists called the genealogy of Christ a book except St. Matthew (Matt 1:1), because in his conversion our Lord did not want to change his inclination, but rather improve upon it, so that if previously as a tax collector he had busied himself with his books of accounts and interest, later the apostle improved his inclination by exchanging the books of his destruction for the book of Jesus Christ. You have wasted much time in the study of philosophers and poets; now it would be right for you to perfect your use of time and improve your choice of books.

What people were more learned than the Egyptians? They were the first to discover writing in the world, and their hieroglyphics are the subject of admiration. In high praise of the wisdom of Joseph, holy scripture describes him as having the consummate learning of the Egyptians.[2] This being said, the Holy Spirit says very openly that the people of Egypt were barbaric, because the more all their wisdom penetrated the movement of the stars and the heavens, the less it served to restrain their disordered passions. All their science had for its purpose to perfect man in political life, but it did not serve to attain eternal life. Wisdom that does not enlighten the way to salvation, God, who knows everything, qualifies as foolishness.

Justus Lipsius (that marvel of erudition),[3] as he was close to death and final reckoning, when the mind is clearest, and as his friends were consoling him by mentioning the many learned books he had written, said to them making a sign of the cross: *Study that is not of the crucified is foolishness and mere vanity.*

I do not reproach you for reading these authors, but I recommend to you what Gersón[4] advised: Lend, do not sell yourself to, nor let yourself be robbed by these studies. Humane letters are slaves and can serve divine letters, but they should be condemned when they rob human understanding of divine Wisdom, lording over it when they are destined to serve it. They are commendable when from the motivation of curiosity, which is a vice, they progress to studiousness, which is a virtue.

St. Jerome was whipped by angels because he read Cicero obsessively and not freely, preferring the delights of his eloquence to the solidity of holy scripture.[5] However, this holy doctor is to be praised because he took advantage of his knowledge and the profane erudition that he had acquired from such pagan authors.

You have spent no little time on these curious studies. Move on, like the great Boethius, to take advantage of them, combining the subtleties of natural science with the usefulness of moral philosophy.[6]

It is a pity that your great mind should become confused by the despicable things of the earth and not desire to penetrate the things of heaven. As it is already bent down to the earth, let it not lower itself further, bearing in mind what goes on in hell. And if you sometimes have sweet and tender insights, turn your mind to Mount Calvary, where, seeing the demonstrations of love of the Redeemer and the ingratitude of the redeemed, you will find a great field for praising the excesses of an infinite love and for forming arguments, not without tears, in view of the extreme depth of this ingratitude. Oh, how profitable it will be on other occasions if you allow the rich galleon of your genius to set sail on the deep ocean of divine Perfection! Then I have no doubt that will happen which happened to Apelles. That is, when he painted Campaspe's portrait, each line of the brush across the canvas pierced his heart with the arrows of love, so that by the time he had finished it he was mortally wounded with love of the original.[7]

I am very certain and confident that if you, with the lively arguments of your mind, would form and paint an idea of divine Perfection (to the degree possible given the darkness of faith), at the same time you would see your soul illuminated and your will inflamed and sweetly wounded with the love of your God, in order that this Lord who has so abundantly showered positive natural benefits on you will not be obliged to grant you only negative supernatural benefits. Furthermore, that which your wit would call demonstrations of love, I consider punishments. The only thing that can be considered as a benefit is what God does to the human heart when he prepares it with his grace so that it can respond with gratitude, disposing it with a benefit that is acknowledged, so that it may respond unchecked to ever greater divine generosity.

This I desire for you, as one who since the time I first met you many years ago has lived enamored of your soul, which neither distance nor time has the power to cool, because spiritual love does not suffer the afflictions of inconstancy, nor does it recognize as pure anything that does not further its growth. May his Majesty hear my pleas and make you very holy, and keep you in prosperity for me.

From the Convent of the Holy Trinity of Puebla of Los Angeles, November 25, 1690.[8]

I kiss your hands, your affectionate servant, Philotea de la Cruz

RESPONSE TO THE VERY ILLUSTRIOUS "SOR PHILOTEA"

Very illustrious Lady, my Lady: It is not my will, my poor health, or my just fear that has postponed my response for so many days. Is it any wonder I was delayed when at the first step my clumsy pen encountered two impossible tasks to trip it up? The first one (and for me the most important) is the impossibility of knowing how to respond to your most learned, most witty, most holy, and most loving letter. If I consider that the angel of the schools, St. Thomas Aquinas, when asked about his silence in the company of his teacher, Albertus Magnus, replied there was nothing he could say worthy of him, how much more reason do I have to be silent, not as the saint was, out of humility, but because in reality I know nothing worthy of you. The second impossibility is to know how to thank you for such an excessive, unexpected favor, namely, the publication of my scribblings. This favor was so unmerited, surpassing the most ambitious hope, the most fantastic desire, that as a rational being it never entered my thoughts. In short, it was of such magnitude that it not only stretches the limited capacity of speech but exceeds the bounds of gratitude, as much because of its magnitude as for its unexpectedness, as Quintilian said: *Minorem spei, maiorem benefacti gloriam pereunt* [Hope produces minor glories, benefits greater ones].[1] And so the beneficiary is struck dumb.

SOR JUANA INÉS DE LA CRUZ

When the mother of the Baptist, once happily sterile only to become miraculously fertile, saw a visit to her house so disproportionate as that of the Mother of the Word, her mind became darkened and her speech was suspended. Thus, instead of thanking her she burst forth with doubts and questions: *Et unde hoc mihi?* [Whence comes such a thing to me?—Luke 1:43]. The same happened to Saul when he was elected and anointed king of Israel: *Numquid non filius Iemini ego sum de minima tribu Israel, et cognatio mea novissima inter omnes de tribu Beniamin? Quare igitur locutus es mihi sermonem istum?* [Am I not a son of Benjamin, the smallest tribe of Israel and is my family not least among the tribe of Benjamin? Why have you spoken these words to me?—1 Sam 9:21]. And so I say, whence comes, venerable Lady, whence comes to me such a favor? Could it be that I am more than a poor nun, the least creature in the world and most unworthy of being the focus of your attention? So *quare locutus es mihi sermonem istum? Et unde hoc mihi?* [Why have you spoken these words to me? Why me?].

To the first impossibility I can respond nothing more than that I am in no way worthy in your eyes. To the second I can merely respond with amazement in place of thanks and admit myself incapable of thanking you for even the tiniest bit of what I owe you. It is not affected modesty, my Lady, but the sincere truth from the depth of my soul, when I say that when the letter that you saw fit to name *Athenagoric,*[2] was delivered into my hands I burst into tears—a thing I do not do easily—of confusion at your kindness, which appeared nothing less than a reproach from God to the wretched way I respond to him. Others he corrects through punishments; me he wants to reprimand through benefits.[3] In my case it is a special favor to know myself indebted to his immense goodness in an infinite number of ways, but especially for the way in which he puts me to shame and confusion. His most exquisite means of punishment has been to make me, with my knowledge of myself, my own judge, leaving me to censure and condemn my own ingratitude. When I ponder this within myself, I am moved to say: "Blessed are you, Lord, not only did you not want judgment of me to fall into the hands of any other creature, including even my own, but you reserved this judgment for yourself. So doing you liberated me from myself and from the sentence that I would have imposed, which, given my knowledge of myself, could not have been less than condemnation. This judgment, however, you reserved for your mercy, because you love me more than I can love myself."

Forgive this digression, my Lady, which the force of truth has torn from me. I confess I was looking for a subterfuge that would allow me to evade the difficulty of responding to you. I had nearly determined to let silence be my response. But silence is a negative thing, and although it explains much through its emphasis on not explaining, it is necessary to affix some brief label to it so that it is understood to be signifying silence. Without this label silence would not say anything, because its proper office is to say nothing. The Sacred Vessel of Election (Acts 9:5) was ravished up to the third heaven, and having seen the mysterious secrets of God said: *Audivit arcane Dei, quae non licet homini loqui* [I heard the hidden things of God that cannot be uttered—2 Cor 12:4]. He does not reveal what he saw, but that such things cannot be spoken. For of those things that cannot be spoken, it is necessary to say so, in order that one's silence will not be misunderstood as meaning one has nothing to say, instead of that the many things in question cannot be put into words. St. John says that if all the signs and wonders that our Redeemer did were written down, the world would not be large enough to hold all the books (John 21:25). Vieira says that in this one verse the evangelist expressed more than in everything else he wrote. Here the Lusitanian phoenix is right. (But when does he not speak eloquently, even though what he said may not have been right?) In this verse St. John says everything he omitted to say and expressed everything he omitted to express. And so I, my Lady, can only respond that I do not know what to respond. I can only thank you by saying that I am not capable of thanking you. I will say as a brief indication of what I leave to silence, that it is only with confidence of your favor and under protection of your patronage that I dare even to speak to your greatness. If this is foolish, forgive me, for folly is the crown jewel of felicity. Through it I will supply more matter for your kindness, and you will give greater form to my gratitude.

Because he stuttered, Moses did not consider himself worthy to speak to pharaoh. Later, seeing himself so greatly favored by

God, he became filled with such courage that not only did he speak with God, but he dared ask impossible things of him, such as *Ostende mihi faciem tuam* [Show me your face—Exod 33:18]. The same is true for me now. My Lady, no longer do the two things that I mentioned in the beginning seem impossible considering the degree to which you have favored me. Who printed the *Letter* without consulting me? Who gave it its title? Who bore the costs of publication? Who honored it to such an extent (it being of itself and in its author, unworthy)? What would she not do? What not forgive? What would she leave undone, and what would she leave unpardoned? And thus presuming that I speak with the safe-conduct of your protection and with the guarantee of your kindness, and considering that you, like another Ahasuerus (Esth 5:2), have given me the tip of the golden scepter of your affection to kiss as a sign of granting me the benevolent license to speak and to present arguments in your venerable presence, I say that I have taken to heart your saintly admonition to apply myself to the study of holy scripture. Though it was clothed as advice, it will have for me the substance of a command. It is no small consolation that, even before this, it appears that my obedience had anticipated your pastoral suggestions and guidance, as can be inferred from the subject and the proofs of that same *Letter*. I know very well that your dear warning cannot possibly be referring to it, but rather to many things concerning human affairs that I have written. Thus what I have said is no more than an attempt to make good with the *Letter* the lack of application to sacred subjects that you have quite rightly inferred in other writings of mine. Speaking more precisely, I confess to you with the candor that I owe you and with the truth and clarity that have always been natural and customary for me that my not having written much of sacred things has not been because of a lack of affection or diligence, but from the great fear and reverence owed to holy scripture, which I know myself incapable of understanding and taking up into my unworthy hands.

I always hear resounding in my ears with no little horror that threat and prohibition of the Lord to sinners like me: *Quare tu enarras iustitias meas, et assumis testamentum meum per os tuum?* [Why do you speak of my commandments and put my covenant in your mouth?—Ps 49:16, Vulgate]. This question held me back, in addition to seeing that even learned men are prohibited from reading the Song of Songs and even the book of Genesis until they are over thirty years old, as my great father St. Jerome understood very well. (Genesis because of its obscurity, the Song of Songs so that sweetness of the wedding songs not be the occasion for imprudent youth to turn the meaning to carnal love.) He recommended that the Song of Songs be the last book to be studied for the same reason. *Ad ultimum sine periculo discat Canticum Canticorum, ne si in exordio legerit, sub carnalibus verbis spiritualium nuptiarium Epithalamium non intelligens, vulneretur* [Lastly they should read, without danger, the Song of Songs. It may be that if they read it at the beginning of their studies, they will not understand the wedding songs as spiritual beneath the carnal words, and will suffer harm].[4] And Seneca says, *Teneris in annis haut clara est fides* [Faith is not strong in the young].[5]

How, then, could I dare to take holy scripture into my most unworthy hands, thereby contradicting my sex, my age, and, above all, custom? And thus I confess that many times this fear has taken the very pen from my hand and has made me withhold from my mind the understanding of these subjects to which it was drawn. Profane subjects presented no such problems, since the Holy Office does not punish heresies against art, which are punished by the condescending smiles of the initiated and the censure of the critics. Therefore, whether *iusta vel iniusta, timenda non est* [rightly or not, it is not to be feared], as it does not affect whether one is permitted to go to communion or hear Mass, it concerns me little or not at all. Since, according to the judgment of those who malign me, I have neither the obligation to know nor the aptitude to succeed, therefore if I err, it is not a fault, nor does it harm my reputation. It is not a fault because I have no obligation, nor does it discredit me, because I have no possibility of succeeding and *ad impossibilia nemo tenetur* [No one is obliged to do the impossible]. In truth, I have never written anything where I was not forced against my will, and only at the pleasure of others, not only without pleasure, but with positive repugnance, for I have never judged myself to be learned or to have that kind of genius that carries with it the obligation to write. This is my usual response to those who urge me to write, and even more so when sacred subjects are involved. What understanding do I have, what course of studies, what material, or knowledge of it, except four superficial certificates? I leave these things to those who understand them. I do not want any trouble with the Holy Office. I am ignorant and tremble at the thought of making a statement that sounds heretical or of twisting the genuine meaning of any text. I do not study in order to write, and even less to teach (which would be for me disproportionate pride), but only in order to see if by studying I become less ignorant. This is my response; these are my sentiments.

To write has never been my own decision but the result of forces beyond myself, so that in truth I could say to them: *Vos me coegistis* [You have forced me—2 Cor 12:11]. What is true and what I will not deny (for one thing because everyone knows it, and for another because although it be counted as a strike against me, God has given me the grace of a great love of truth) is that from the first moment the light of reason shone upon me, the inclination to study was so vehement and powerful that neither persecution from without (of which I have had much) nor my own reflections (of which there have been not a few) have been enough to cause me to cease following this natural impulse that God has placed in me. His Majesty knows why and for what purpose, and he knows that I have pleaded with him to extinguish the light of my reason, leaving only enough for me to be able to keep his law, since any more is too much for a woman, at least according to some. There are even those who would say that it harms them. His Majesty also knows that having not succeeded in extinguishing the light of my reason, I had intended to bury my mind with my name, offering it up only to the one who gave it to me. This was my only motivation for entering religious life, notwithstanding the fact that the freedom and quiet that my scholarly bent required conflicted with the practices and companionship of community life. And afterward, once in the community, the Lord knows, as well as does the only person in the world who should know it, how hard I tried to hide my name. But this person did not permit it, saying that it was a temptation.[6] And in truth it would have been. If I were able to repay you some part of what I owe you, my Lady, I believe that I do so now by revealing this very thing, because the words have never before crossed my lips except to whom they should be said.

But now that you have crossed the wide open doors of my heart, now that I have made you party to its deepest secrets, you know my trust is commensurate to the debt I owe your venerable person and your excessive favors.

Proceeding with the narration of my inclination, of which I want to give you a complete account, I had not even reached my third birthday when my mother sent one of my older sisters to learn to read at a school for girls called *amigas*. I tagged along after her out of affection and high spirits. When I saw that she was being taught a lesson, the desire to learn to read burned within me to such an extent that, thinking I was fooling the teacher, I told her that my mother had arranged for her to teach me to read too. This she did not believe, because it was not believable, but in order to indulge my fantasy she went along with it. I continued to go and she continued to teach me, no longer as a game but because experience had undeceived her. I learned to read in such a short time that I already knew how by the time my mother found out. The teacher had kept it a secret in order to surprise her and also in order to receive payment in reward for the whole undertaking. I had kept quiet about it, believing that they would beat me for having done it without permission. The woman who taught me is still living (God keep her), and she can testify to this.

I remember that in those days, even though my appetite was normal for a child of that age, I gave up eating cheese because I had heard that it made you stupid. For me, the desire to know was stronger than the desire to eat, as powerful as it is in children. Later, when I was six or seven years old, already knowing how to read and write as well as all the other accomplishments of housekeeping and needlework that women learn, I heard that in Mexico City there was a university and many schools where many subjects were studied. Hardly had I heard this when I began to pester my mother to death with constant and inopportune pleas to dress me as a boy and send me to Mexico City to the home of some of her relatives so that I could study and take courses at the university. She did not want to do it, and it was a good thing too. However, I satisfied my desire to learn by reading the many and varied books that my grandfather had, and neither punishments nor reproaches were enough to hinder me. As a result, when I arrived in Mexico City people were astonished, not so much by my talent as by my memory and the amount of information I had learned by heart at an age when it appeared that I had hardly had time to learn to speak.

I began to learn Latin, taking, I believe, no more than twenty lessons. So intense was my concern that though women, especially those in the flower of youth, place a high value on the natural ornamentation of their hair, I cut mine four to six inches, measuring the length it had been before and imposing upon myself the rule that if I had not learned a certain amount by the time it had grown back, I would have to cut it off again in punishment for my stupidity. It happened my hair grew back and I did not meet my goal for learning, because my hair grew quickly and I learned slowly, with the result that I cut it again because of my stupidity. It did not seem right that a head bare of learning, the most pleasing adornment, should have hair as an ornament. I became a nun, because although I knew that there were things about this state in life (I am speaking of the incidental aspects, not of the form of life as a whole) that were repugnant to my temperament, all in all, given my total disinclination toward marriage,[7] it was the least disproportionate and the most decent state of life I could choose to assure my salvation as I desired.[8] To this latter motive, which was after all the most important, I surrendered and made subject all the little inconsequential traits of my character, such as the desire to live alone and not wanting obligations impinging on my freedom to study, nor the noise of a community, which would intrude on the peaceful silence of my books. This made me waver somewhat in my determination until certain learned people explained to me that it was a temptation, one that I conquered with divine help, and so I assumed the state that I now unworthily live. I thought that I was fleeing myself, but (miserable wretch that I am!) I brought myself with me and brought also my greatest enemy in this inclination that heaven has given me, which I do not know whether to consider a prize or a punishment. Far from being stopped or hindered by all the practices of religious life, it exploded like gunpowder, and in my case the saying *privatio est causa appetitus* [Deprivation increases the appetite] was proven to be true.

I returned, or rather more accurately, since I never stopped studying, I continued to study, which for me was not a chore but relaxation. In every moment that remained to me after fulfilling my obligations, I read more and more and studied more and more, with no teacher other than the books themselves. You can imagine how difficult it is to study only in the company of those soulless characters, without the live voice and explanation of a teacher. All the toil and suffering I endured was a pleasure to me because of my love of learning. Oh, had it been for love of God, which was my intention, how much merit I would have gained! I tried to elevate and direct as much as I could to his service because the goal to which I aspired was the study of theology. It seemed to me no small incompetence, being Catholic, not to know everything about the sacred mysteries that can be attained by the use of natural reason. Furthermore, being a nun and not of the world, I ought, because of my ecclesiastical state, profess learning, but even more so as a daughter of St. Jerome and St. Paula.[9] It would be truly disgraceful for such learned parents to have an ignorant daughter. This is what I determined on my own, and it seemed right to me. However, I may have done it (rather, as was most certainly the case) to flatter and applaud my own inclination by designating as obligation what was really my own pleasure.

So I proceeded always directing the steps of my study (as I have said) toward the summit of holy theology. To arrive there it appeared necessary to me to ascend the staircase of the secular sciences and arts. How could I understand the methodology of the queen of the sciences if I did not know the style of her handmaidens? How, without logic, would I know the general and particular methods with which holy scripture is written? How, without the study of rhetoric, would I understand its figures of speech, its tropes, its idioms? How know, without the physical sciences, many natural questions as to the nature of sacrificial animals, where so many things already professed are symbolized, and many other things are contained? How could I understand if the sound of David's harp was able to cure Saul by virtue of the natural power of music, or the supernatural power that God desired to infuse in David? (1 Sam 16:23). How, without the study of arithmetic, is it possible to understand the many computations of years, days, months, hours, and weeks as mysterious as those of Daniel, which require knowledge of the nature, concordance, and properties of numbers? (Dan 9:24–27). How, without geometry, is it possible to measure the holy ark of the covenant and the holy city of Jerusalem, whose mysterious dimensions equal a cube, and to understand the proportional distribution of all its marvelous parts? How, without architecture, could I understand the great Temple of Solomon, where God himself as the architect developed the floor plan and design, leaving only its execution to the wise king? (1 Kings 6—7). Here there was no pedestal without mystery, no column without its symbolism, no cornice without a reference, no architrave without significance. The same can be said for all the other parts of the Temple, so that even the least listel[10] was not only there to serve and complement art but also symbolized greater things. How, without a great knowledge of principles and epochs of which history consists, could I understand the historical books and the summaries that recount later events before the narrative of earlier ones? How, without knowledge of both profane and sacred legal systems, could I understand the books of the Law? How, without great erudition, understand the many events in profane history mentioned in sacred scripture, including many customs, rites, and idioms of the Gentiles? How, without many instructions and lessons from the writings of the holy fathers, could I understand the obscure expressions of the prophets? How, without being quite an expert in music, could I understand musical proportions and their beauty, which are to be found in so many passages. I am thinking especially of those petitions that Abraham made to God for the sake of the cities, when God says that, yes, he will spare the city if it has fifty just men; and from this number he goes down to forty-five, which is the sesquinone (from mi to re); and from there to forty, which is the sesquioctave (from re to mi); and from there to thirty, which is the sesquiterce or the diatessaron; from there to twenty, which is the proportion of the sesquialter, or diapente; from there to ten, which is the duple or diapason. And, as there were no more harmonic proportions left, Abraham went no further (Gen 18:24–32). How can this be understood without the study of music?[11]

In the book of Job, God says to him: *Numquid coniungere valebis micantes stellas Pleiadas, aut gyrum Arcturi poteris dissipare? Numquid producis Luciferum in tempore suo, et Vesperum super filios terrae consurgere facis?* [Are you perhaps capable of connecting the brilliant stars of the Pleiades, or can you stop the rotation of Arturus? Are you perhaps the one who can make the morning star and the evening star rise each at their proper time over the children of the earth?—Job 38:31–32]. This terminology would be impossible to understand without astronomy. And this is not only the case for the noble sciences. There is not one of the mechanical arts that is not mentioned. Finally, because this is the book that includes all books and the science in which all the sciences are included, all knowledge aids in understanding it. And after having studied them all (obviously, no easy task, nor even really possible), another circumstance is required that is more important than all the rest: continual prayer and purity of life in order to entreat of God the purification of will and the illumination of mind necessary for the understanding of such exalted matters. If this is lacking, the rest serves for nothing.

Of St. Thomas, the angelic doctor, Holy Church says these words: *In difficultatibus locorum Sacrae Scripturae ad orationem ieiunium adhibebat. Quin etiam sodali suo Fratri Reginaldo dicere solebat, quidquid sciret, non tam studio, aut labore suo peperisse, quam divinitus traditum accepisse* [When considering difficult texts of holy scripture, he joined fasting to prayer. And it happened that he said to his companion, Brother Reginald, that everything that he knew, he owed not so much to study and work but to what he had received from God].[12] How could I, so distant from virtue and learning, have the courage to write? In order to gain a foundation I continually studied diverse and varied subjects with no particular inclination to any one but rather to all of them in general. As a result, in those cases when I did study one subject more than another it has not been my choice, but because chance put more books on these subjects into my hands, not leaving a preference to my discretion. And since I had no particular interest that moved me, or limit of time that committed me to the continual study of one thing to prepare for examinations, I studied various subjects at the same time or would switch from one to the other. Although in all this I did observe a certain order, because some of them were for learning, others for fun. The latter gave me rest from the former. As a result, I have studied many things and know nothing, because some subjects were in competition with the others. This is primarily true for the disciplines requiring practice. For it is clear that while the pen is moving, the compass is at rest, and while playing the harp, the organ is silent, *et sic de caeteris* [and the same is true with the other subjects]. This is because since much use of the body is required to acquire the skill, no one who attempts the exercise of various skills of this kind can ever attain perfection in more than one. However, in those subjects that are formal and speculative, the opposite is the case. I would like to persuade all people, based on my own experience, that not only do they not obstruct one another, but they help one another, giving light and opening paths to one another, through variations and hidden connections. The wisdom of their Author put them in a universal chain, in such a way that they appear to correspond to one another and to be united with admirable consistency and agreement. This is the chain that the ancients imagined came from the mouth of Jupiter, through which all things were linked together. Reverend Father Athanasius Quirquerio [Kircher] demonstrated this in his curious book *De Magnete* [On the magnet]. All things come from God, who is the center and at the same time the circumference from which the lines of all created things come and to which they all tend.[13]

I, for my part, can assure you that whatever I do not understand from one author on one subject I am able to understand from another author on another subject that seems far removed. And these authors, as they explain themselves, employ metaphors from other disciplines. Mathematicians, for example, explain that the means in an equation functions as a measuring rod to the extremes. Similarly, we say that the arguments of the logician go in a straight line and those of the orator move like an arc along the longest path, but both are heading for the same point. The same is true when they say that the exegetes are like an open hand and the Scholastics like a closed fist. So there is nothing wrong, nor am I claiming that there is, in having studied such a variety of things, because the disciplines complement one another. Not having taken proper advantage of them was due to ineptitude on my part and the weakness of my understanding, not the fault of the variety of disciplines I studied. In my defense it could be said that there was an enormous amount of work involved, not only because of the lack of a teacher, but also the lack of other students with whom I could confer and review what I had studied. For teachers I have only mute books; for other students, an unfeeling inkwell. Instead of explanations and study sessions I have had many obstacles, not only those of my religious obligations (which all agree are a useful and advantageous use of time), but also those things incidental to community life. Sometimes when I am reading, the sisters in the adjacent cell take it into their heads to sing and play music. When I am studying, two of the maids who have been quarreling come to see me and ask me to mediate their quarrel. When I am writing something, a friend comes to visit me, thereby doing the worst thing possible with the best intentions in the world, so that in this case it is necessary not only to welcome the interruption but to appear thankful for the damage done. All this happens continually because since the times that I designate for my study are those remaining after the required community activities, these same times are available to the others to come and disturb me. Only those who have experience of life in community know how true this is. Here only the strength of my vocation and the great love there is between me and my beloved sisters can make this agreeable to my disposition. And since love is union, it knows no limits.

Yes, I confess it: my labor defies explanation. I envy those who say that the urge to study has cost them nothing. Blessed are they! For me, it has not been knowledge (which I still do not have), but rather the desire to know that has cost me dearly, so that I can say with my father, St. Jerome (although not profiting from it as he did), *Quid ibi laboris insumpserim, quid sustinuerim difficultatis, quoties desperaverim, quotiesque cessaverim et contentione discendi rursus inceperim; testis est conscientia, tam mea, qui passus sum, quam eorum qui mecum duxerunt vitam* [How much work I have undertaken, how many difficulties I have had to suffer, how many times I have despaired, and how many other times I have desisted and begun again because of my determination to learn, my conscience and the conscience of those who have lived with me bear witness].[14] Except for the companions and witness, for even this solace has been denied me, I can assure you of the truth of this. Such has been the strength of my black inclination that it has overcome all these obstacles!

Among other benefits for which I am indebted to God is a mild and affable nature, for which the nuns love me very much, since they are so good as not to consider my faults. They take great pleasure in my company, and knowing this and moved by the great love that I have for them, which is more justified by their virtues than is their love for me, I take even greater pleasure in their company. Frequently during our free time I comforted them and enjoyed their conversation. At the same time I was aware that during this free time I badly needed to study, and so I made a vow not to enter any sister's cell unless obliged by obedience or by charity. Without that severe restraint, love would have conquered my best intentions. Knowing my weakness, I would make this vow for a month or two weeks, and when that had passed I would allow one or two days of respite before renewing it again. These days served not so much as a rest for me (which not studying has never been), but so that I would not appear dour, withdrawn, and ungrateful in the face of the unmerited affection of my dear sisters.

How well this reveals the strength of my inclination! Blessed be God who wanted me to have an inclination to study and not to have another vice, which would have meant nearly insurmountable temptations. From the above can also be inferred the degree to which my poor studies have navigated against the current (or more precisely, have foundered). But these were not the most troublesome of my difficulties. Those I have mentioned thus far have only been obstacles due to obligation or chance, which only indirectly can be considered as such. I have not yet mentioned the intentional obstacles placed in my path to hinder and even to prohibit my studies. Who would not believe, seeing the general acclaim I have enjoyed, that I have not sailed on a sea of glass with the wind in my sails on a groundswell of universal approbation? God knows that this has not been the case, because among the bouquets of this very acclaim, there rose up and were awakened serpents of rivalry and persecutions beyond number. The most prejudicial and the most painful for me have not been those people who have persecuted me with open hatred and ill will, but those who loving me and desiring the best for me (and perhaps, God awards them merit for their good intentions) have afflicted and tormented me more than the others with the following judgment: *"These studies do not conform to holy ignorance, which is required of a religious. She will be ruined. In such a rarified atmosphere her own perspicacity and wit will cause her to be vain."* How much hurt I have experienced because of my resistance to this! What a rare species of martyrdom in which I was myself both martyr and executioner!

What grief have they not given me, grief continuing to the present, for the—in my case doubly unfortunate—talent for writing poetry, even sacred poetry? It is true, my Lady, that I sometimes think that the one who does something of significance or whom God (who alone can do it) renders significant, is welcomed as the common enemy because to some it appears that he is usurping the renown that they merit, or that his achievements diminish the exclamations of admiration to which they aspire. As a result they persecute him.

A politically barbaric law of Athens required that those with significant accomplishments and virtues be exiled from the republic, so that their example would not serve to tyrannize public liberty. This law continues intact today and can still be observed in our time, although not with the same motivation as for the Athenians. There is another law, no less efficient, although not as justified, because it is a maxim attributed to the impious Machiavelli: Hate the one who does something significant because he tarnishes the luster of the others.[15] This is the case today and has always been the case.

What other explanation is there for the Pharisees' intense hatred of Christ, when they had so many reasons to love him? If we behold his image, which quality is more lovable than divine beauty? Which with more power to enrapture the heart? If mere human beauty holds sway over free will, subjecting it with sweet, alluring violence, what would Christ's beauty with its many prerogatives and sovereign gifts not have had the power to do? What would the incomprehensible beauty of his lovely face, which as through a prism renders transparent the glory of the Divinity, do, or not do, move or not move? Who would not be moved by those features that beyond incomparable human perfections signified divine splendor? If merely conversing with God face to face made

Moses's countenance unbearable to behold (Exod 34:29–30), what would be the impact of this same God incarnate? Let us consider his other attributes. What more lovable than that heavenly modesty gently, tenderly, pouring forth mercy in his every move? Or his profound humility and meekness, or his words of eternal life and eternal wisdom? How is it possible that they were not enamored and transported, that their souls were not enraptured by him?

The holy mother, my mother, Teresa, said that after she saw the beauty of Christ she remained free of all inclination to any creature, because there was nothing that was not ugly by comparison.[16] How then could he have such contrary effects on people? And even if they were boorish and ignoble, possibly having no knowledge or appreciation of his perfections, were they not moved by their own self-interest, advantage, and profit when they saw the good works he did, such as healing the sick, resurrecting the dead, curing those afflicted with demons? How could they not love him? Oh, my God, for these very reasons they did not love him, for these reasons they hated him! They themselves have borne witness to it.

They gathered together in council and said: *Quid facimus, qui hic homo multa signa facit?* [What shall we do? This man has done many signs—John 11:47]. What kind of a reason is that? If they had said: This man is a criminal, a transgressor of the law, a rebel who, by deceiving them, causes the people to riot, they would have lied as they did lie when they said such things. But these were reasons that fit the request they were making, that is, to take his life. But to give as a reason for his prosecution that he had done significant things does not seem to reflect the level of such learned men as the Pharisees. However, when learned men become passionately involved, such inconsistencies in their reasoning are bound to occur. It is true that this was the only reason they gave for condemning Christ to death. You men, if you can be called such after being so brutal, how could you arrive at such a cruel decision? Their only answer remains, because *multa signa facit* [he has done many signs]. God preserve me! To think that achieving significant things would be grounds for the penalty of death! How does this *multa signa facit* resonate with *radix Iesse, qui stat in signum populorum* [the root of Jesse, which will be a sign among the nations—

THEOLOGICAL WORKS

Isa 11:12] and *in signum cui contradicetur* [a sign of contradiction— Luke 2:34]. He is a sign? Well, let him die! Designated? Well, let him suffer; this is the reward for significant achievement!

It is the custom to decorate the pinnacle of churches with figures of the four winds and of fame, and in order to protect them from the birds, to cover them with iron barbs. Though this is done ostensibly to protect the figures, in reality they are an essential property. No figure can be in a high place without being pierced by such barbs. There it encounters the ill will of the wind and the rigor of the elements. There lightning bolts unleash their rage. There it is the target of stones and arrows. O unhappy height, exposed to so many hazards! O sign, that makes you a target of envy and an object of contradiction! Any eminence, whether it is due to dignity, nobility, wealth, beauty, or wisdom suffers from this drawback, but reason suffers most. In the first place because it is the least capable of defending itself. Power and wealth punish those who dare to challenge them, which is not the case with reason, because reason, even though higher in rank, is more modest and long-suffering and less able to defend itself. Also because, as Gracian has said with much erudition, the advantages of reason are in the order of being.[17] Angels are greater than we are for no other reason than that they are more rational creatures. Likewise our superiority over the beasts is based on our superior reason. Therefore, since none of us wants to be less than another, none of us willingly admits others are more reasonable, because they will be greater on the level of being. We may suffer and admit that someone is nobler than we are, wealthier, more beautiful, even more learned, but there are hardly any of us who will willingly admit someone is more reasonable. *Rarus est, qui velit cedere ingenio* [It is a rare person who admits the superiority of another's mind].[18] This is why the assault on this quality is so effective.

When the soldiers mocked, amused, and diverted themselves with our Lord Jesus Christ, they brought an old crimson cloak, a hollow reed, and a crown of thorns for his mock coronation. The reed and the purple cloak were insulting but not painful. Why was it only the crown that was painful? Was it not enough that, as was the case for the other devices, it resulted in scorn and ignominy, since that was its purpose? No, because the sacred head of Christ and that divine brain were the deposit of wisdom. And for the world, it is not enough that the wise brain is scorned, it has to be injured and mistreated. A head that is a storehouse of wisdom can hope for no other crown than that of thorns. What garland can human wisdom expect seeing, what divine wisdom attained? Roman pride crowned the different exploits of its captains with different crowns: the one, civic, for those who had defended the citizens; the other, military, to those who broke into an enemy camp; another, mural, to those who scaled the escarpments; one, "obsidional," to the one who liberated a walled city, a besieged army, or an encampment. Or they crowned them with the naval, or the oval, or the triumphal crown according to other exploits, as Pliny and Aulus Gellius report.[19] When I saw the many different types of crowns, I wondered which kind Christ's would be. It seemed to me that it must be the obsidional, which (as you know, my Lady) was the most honorable. It was called obsidional from *obsidio*, meaning siege, and was a crown made not with gold or silver but rather with the very grass or weeds that grew in the field in which the campaign was waged. Christ's exploit was to raise the siege of the Prince of Darkness, which held all the earth under siege, as is said in the book of Job: *Circuivi terram et ambulavi per eam* [I roam around the earth and wander over it—Job 1:7], and as St. Peter said: *Circuit, quaerens quem devoret* [He roams the earth seeking someone to devour—1 Pet 5:8]. Then came our leader and raised the siege: *nunc princeps huius mundi eiicietur foras* [now the prince of this world has been cast out—John 12:31]. This was the reason the soldiers crowned him, not with gold or silver, but with the natural fruit that the battlefield of the world produced after the curse of God: *spinas et tribulos germinabit tibi* [thorns and thistles shall you bring forth—Gen 3:18]. And thus it was most fitting that they be the crown of the valiant and wise conqueror crowned thus by his mother, the Synagogue. Coming out to see this sorrowful triumph, reminiscent of the triumph of that other Solomon, the daughters of Zion, then joyful but now sorrowful, celebrated him with weeping, corresponding to the manner in which wisdom triumphs (Luke 23:28). Christ, as king of wisdom, wearing that crown for the first time, sanctified it on his temples and took away the horror of it for those who are wise, demonstrating that they should aspire to no greater honor.

The Lord of life wanted to go to give life to the dead Lazarus. The disciples, who were ignorant of his intent, responded: *Rabbi, nunc quaerebant te Iudaei lapidare, et iterum vadis illuc?* [Rabbi, now the Jews want to stone you, and you still want to go there?—John 11:8]. The Redeemer responded to their fear saying: *Nonne duodecim sunt horae diei?* [Are there not twelve hours in the day?—John 11:9]. Up to this point the disciples had been afraid, having previously seen those who wanted to stone him because he had reproached them for being thieves and not shepherds. Thus the disciples feared that if he did the same thing now his life would be in danger, since reprimands and reproaches, no matter how justified, are generally poorly received. After they are enlightened and aware that he is going to give life to Lazarus what could have moved Thomas, here taking courage as Peter did in the Garden, to say: *Eamus et nos, ut moriamur cum eo?* [Let us go and die with him—John 11:16]. What are you saying, holy apostle? The Lord is not going to die, so what do you fear? Christ is not going to denounce them but to perform a pious work, and as a result they cannot hurt him. Those very Jews could have assured you of this. When they later reconvened to stone him, he said: *Multa bona opera ostendi vobis ex Patre meo, propter quod eorum opus me lapidatis?* [I have done many good works among you from my Father. For which of my works are you stoning me?—John 10:32]. They answered: *De bono opere non lapidamus te, sed de blasphemia* [We are not stoning you because of your good works but because of blasphemy—John 10:33]. If they said they did not want to stone him for his good works, and now he is going to do a work so good as to give life to Lazarus, what is to be feared or why? Would it not be better to say: We are going to enjoy the fruit of gratitude for the good work that our Master is going to do, to see him applauded and thanked for his good deed, and to see the wonder that the miracle will cause? This, rather than saying something as they did, which seems so out of place as: *eamus et nos* [Let us go—John 11:16]. But, oh! The saint feared as an advisor and spoke as an apostle. Was not Christ going to perform a miracle? What danger is greater? It is less intolerable for pride to hear reproaches than for envy to see miracles. In all that I have said, venerable Lady, I do not want to imply (such a crazy thing would never occur to me) that I have been persecuted for my learning, but only for having a love of wisdom and of learning and not because I have achieved either one or the other.

There was a time when the prince of the apostles found himself far removed from wisdom as this phrase emphasizes: *Petrus vero sequebatur eum a longe* [Peter then followed him at a distance— Luke 22:54]. So far from the applause of the learned was he, that he was given the title of ignorant: *nesciens quid diceret* [not knowing what he said—Luke 9:33]. Even when examined about his knowledge of Wisdom, he said that he did not have the slightest notion: *Mulier, nescio quid dicis. Mulier, non novi illum* [Woman, I do not know what you are saying—Luke 22:60. Woman, I do not know him—Luke 22:57]. And what happened to him? In spite of his reputation as one of the ignorant, he did not have their good fortune but suffered the afflictions of the wise. Why? No other reason is given than this: *Et hic cum illo erat* [And he was with him—Luke 22:56]. He loved Wisdom and carried it in his heart; he walked according to her ways; he prized himself as being a follower and lover of Wisdom. Even though this was so much *a longe* [at a distance] that he had not understood or attained it, his proximity was sufficient for him to incur its torments. There was no lack of a soldier to afflict him, nor a servant woman to affront him. I confess that I have found myself very distant from the goals of Wisdom, and that I have desired to follow her, although *a longe*. However, everything has conspired to draw me closer to the fire of persecution, to the crucible of torment. This persecution has been so extreme that some people requested that I be prohibited from studying.

One time they achieved it through a very holy and simple mother superior who believed that study would get me in trouble with the Inquisition and ordered me not to do it. I obeyed her for the three months that she was in office in as far as I did not touch a book, but as far as absolutely not studying, this was not in my power. I could not do it, because although I did not study in books, I directed my study to all the things God has made. They became my letters, and my book was the machinery of the universe. There was nothing I saw that I did not reflect upon. There was nothing I heard that I did not ponder, even the smallest and most material of things. Because there is no creature, no matter how lowly, in which the *me fecit Deus* [God made me] cannot be found. There is not one that does not fill the mind with wonder if considered as it deserves. And so I repeat, I observed and admired them all. Even the people I spoke to, and what they said to me, gave rise to thousands of reflections. What was the source of all the variety of personality and talent I found among them, since they were all one species? What temperament and hidden qualities caused their differences? If I saw a figure, I would combine the proportion of its lines and by means of mental calculation convert it into different ones. Sometimes I would pace in front of the fireplace in one of our large dormitories and notice that, though the lines of its two sides were parallel and its ceiling level, to our vision it appears as though the lines are inclined toward each other and that the ceiling is lower in the distance than it is nearby. From this it can be inferred that the lines of our vision run straight, but not parallel, to form the figure of a pyramid. And I wondered if that was the reason that the ancients questioned whether the earth was a sphere or not. Because although it seemed so, their vision might have deceived them, showing concave shapes where there were none.

This facility of analyzing everything transpired and continues to do so without my willing it; rather, it makes me angry because it makes my head tired. I believed that the same thing, including composing poetry, happened to everyone until experience demonstrated the contrary. This natural inclination or custom is so strong that there is nothing I see that I do not reflect upon. Once I saw two girls playing with a top, and hardly had I seen the movement and the shape when I began, in my insane way, to consider the easy movement of the spherical shape and how long the momentum, once established, remained independent of its original cause, the distant hand of the girl. Not content with this I had flour brought and sprinkled on the floor in order to discover whether the spinning top would describe perfect circles or not. It turned out that they were not perfect circles but spirals that lost their circular shape to the degree that the top lost momentum. Others girls were playing a game of pickup sticks (childhood's most frivolous game). I drew near to examine the figures that they formed. As chance would have it, three sticks fell into a triangle, and I immediately set about linking one thing to another, recalling that this, they say, was the shape of Solomon's mysterious ring, in which could be discerned distant lights and representations of the holy Trinity, enabling Solomon to work many wonders and marvels. David's harp whose music cured Saul was said to be the same shape, as is the case with harps even to this day.

What could I tell you, my Lady, of the secrets of nature that I have discovered while cooking? I observed that an egg unifies and fries in butter or oil, but to the contrary dissolves in syrup; that in order to keep sugar liquid it suffices to throw on it a very little bit of water flavored with quince or another bitter fruit; that the yolk and white of the same egg when separated and combined with sugar have an opposite effect, and one different from when they are both used together. I do not mean to tire you with such foolishness, which I only recount to give you a complete picture of my nature and because I think it will amuse you. But, my Lady, what can women know except philosophy of the kitchen? Lupercio Leonardo has said it well: it is possible to philosophize while preparing dinner.[20] As I often say on observing these this little things, If Aristotle had cooked, he would have written much more.

But to continue with the manner of my cogitations, I say that they are so incessant that I have no need of books. On one occasion, because of a serious stomach ailment, the doctors prohibited my studying. After I had spent some days in that state I convinced him that it was less harmful to allow me to study, because my cogitations were stronger and more vehement, consuming more spiritual energy in a quarter of an hour without books than with them over the course of four days. As a result they reconsidered and allowed me to read. Furthermore, my Lady, not even in sleep am I free from the continual movement of my imagination. Rather, then, it habitually operates more freely and unencumbered, sorting through with greater clarity and tranquility the matters it has stored up from the day, arguing and composing poems (of which I could make you a long list) as well as some of the arguments and subtle distinctions that I developed better in my sleep than awake.

But I will omit them so as not to tire you. What I have said suffices for your discretion and perspicacity to penetrate and grasp perfectly my natural disposition in its entirety as well the origins, methods, and present state of my studies. If these, my Lady, were merits (as I have seen such celebrated in men), they would not have been such for me because they operate of necessity. If they are a fault, for the same reason I believe that I am not at fault. Moreover, all things considered, I have always been so mistrustful of myself that neither in these or other matters do I trust my own judgment. Therefore, I refer the decision to your sovereign intelligence, submitting myself immediately to your judgment in the matter without opposition or aversion, since this has been nothing more than a simple narrative of my inclination to study.

I confess also, this being true, as I have said, that I did not need models, since many books, secular and sacred, have continued to help me.[21] I see Deborah giving laws, both military and political, and governing a people with many learned men (Judg 4—5). I see the wise queen of Sheba, who was so learned that she dared to test the wisdom of the greatest of wise men with riddles and was not reprimanded for doing so; rather, because of it she became the judge of unbelievers (1 Kings 10; 2 Chron 9). I see so many women and so many illustrious women: some adorned with the gift of prophesy, like Abigail (1 Sam 25); others with the gift of persuasion, like Esther; still others with piety, like Rahab (Josh 2); others with perseverance, like Hannah, mother of Samuel (1 Sam 1—2), and an infinite number of others excelling in other types of accomplishments and virtues.

If I turn to the pagans the first that I find are the Sibyls,[22] selected by God to prophesy the principal mysteries of our faith in learned and elegant verses that filled all with admiration. I see a woman like Minerva, daughter of the great Jupiter, expert in all the wisdom of Athens, worshiped as goddess of the sciences. I see Polla Argentaria, who helped her husband, Lucanus, write about the great battle of Pharsalia. I see the daughter of divine Tiresias, more learned than her father. I see Zenobia, queen of the Palmyrans, as wise as she was valiant, and Arete, daughter of Aristippus, a most learned woman; and Nicostrata, who invented Latin letters and was most erudite in the Greek letters as well. I see Aspasia Milesia, who taught philosophy and rhetoric and was the teacher of the philosopher Pericles; Hypatia, who taught astronomy and lectured for a long time in Alexandria; Greek Leoncia, who challenged the philosopher Theophrastus and convinced him. I see Julia, Corina, Cornelia, and finally the great multitude of those who would merit being named, Greeks, muses, oracles, all those were no more than learned women, recognized, celebrated, and also venerated as such in antiquity, without mentioning the infinite number of others of which books are full. I see the Egyptian Catherine lecturing and confounding the wisdom of the wise men of Egypt. I see Gertrude lecture, write, and teach. So as not to search for examples beyond home, I see my most holy mother Paula, learned in Hebrew, Greek, and Latin, and with a gift for interpreting scripture. As her biographer, the great St. Jerome, who hardly considered himself worthy to be such, said with the lively praise and efficacious energy characteristic of his style: "If all the members of my body were tongues, they would not suffice to publish the wisdom and virtue of Paula."[23] Blesilla, widow, and the enlightened virgin Eustoquium, daughters of St. Paula, both receive similar praise. The former was called Wonder of the World for her learning. Fabiola of Rome was also very knowledgeable in holy scripture.[24] Proba Falconia, a Roman woman, wrote an elegant book with verses from Virgil that illustrated the mysteries of our holy faith. It is known that our Queen Isabella, wife of Alfonso X, wrote about astrology, not to name others whom I omit so as not to copy what others have said (a vice I have always hated). In our times we see that such women as the great Christina Alexandra, queen of Sweden, as learned as she is courageous and magnanimous,[25] as well as the most excellent ladies the duchess of Aveyro[26] and the countess of Villaumbrosa, are flourishing.[27]

The venerable doctor Arce (worthy professor of scripture for his virtue and his learning), in his *Studioso Bibliorum* raises this question: *An liceat foeminis sacrorum Bibliorum studio incumbere? eaque interpretari?* [Is it permitted for women to study the holy Bible? To interpret it?].[28] As evidence to the contrary, he quotes many opinions from the writings of the saints, especially that of the apostle Paul: *Mulieres in Ecclesiis taceant, non enim permittitur eis loqui, etc.* [Women should be silent in the church. It is not permitted for them to speak there—1 Cor 14:34]. Then he quotes as evidence other opinions, including the passage by the same apostle from his letter to Titus: *Anus similiter in habitu sancto, bene docentes* [Older women likewise of holy demeanor...teachers of what is good—Titus 2:3] and interpretations of the holy fathers. Finally, he concludes with all due care that teaching publicly from the position of a university chair and preaching from the pulpit are not permitted to women. However, studying, writing, and teaching privately are not only permitted but are very beneficial and useful. Clearly this is not to be understood as being the case for all women, but with those to whom God has given special virtue and prudence, who are very mature, learned, who have the talent and prerequisites necessary for such a sacred task. This does not apply only to women, generally held to be incompetent, but is also true for men who think that they are wise merely by virtue of being men. Men who are not learned, or virtuous, without receptive intellects and good inclinations should be forbidden to interpret sacred scripture. Many such men have become fanatics, and their teachings are at the root of many heresies. For many men study increases their ignorance, especially if they are of an arrogant nature, restless and proud, friends of novelties of the Law, which rejects such novelties, to the point that they are not happy until they have said something no one else has said, even if it is a heresy. Of these the Holy Spirit says: *In malevolam animam non introibit sapientia* [In the evil soul wisdom cannot enter—Wis 1:4]. Learning causes them more damage than ignorance does. As one wit has said, he who does not know Latin is not a total fool, but he who does can qualify as such. I would add that it would perfect his foolishness (if it is possible to speak of perfecting foolishness) to have studied a little philosophy and theology, and to have some knowledge of languages, so that he is able to be foolish in many disciplines and languages. For a great fool the mother tongue is not sufficient. For such as these study is dangerous because it is like putting a sword in the hands of a raging maniac. What is of itself a noble instrument meant for defense in his hands can cause his own death and the deaths of many others. Such were holy scriptures in the power of the perverse Pelagius and the obstinate

Arius, the perverse Luther, and all the other heretics, including our own Doctor Cazalla (who was neither our own nor a doctor).[29] There are those who are harmed by wisdom because, although it is the best food and life source of the soul, if the stomach is of a bad constitution and excessively hot, the better the foods it receives, the more dry, fermented, and perverse are the humors that it creates. So it is with these perverse men; the more they study the worse the opinions they generate. Their mind is obstructed by the very thing that it needs for nourishment. As a result, they study much and digest little, since they do not restrict themselves according to their minds' limited capacity. In this connection the apostle Paul says: *Dico enim per gratiam quae data est mihi, omnibus qui sunt inter vos: Non plus sapere quam oportet sapere, sed sapere ad sobrietatem; et unicuique sicut Deus divisit mensuram fidei* [I say by the grace that has been given me to all of you: Do not strive to know more than is necessary, but to know what is fitting for you each according to the faith that God has measured out to you—Rom 12:3]. In truth, this is what the apostle says not to women, but to men. And so the *taceant* [being silent] is not only meant for women, but also for all those who are not adept at learning. Should I want to know as much or more than Aristotle or St. Augustine, if I do not have the aptitude of St. Augustine or Aristotle, were I to study more than both of them, not only would I not achieve this goal, but I would weaken and obstruct the operation of my weak mind through the disproportionate greatness of the object of study.

Oh, if only all who endeavor to study, and I count myself first among them, ignorant as I am, first took the measure of our talents before we begin! What is even worse is to write with the greedy ambition of equaling or surpassing others. How little courage would remain and how many errors we would have avoided, and how many twisted theories would not be circulating! I place my own theories in first place, because if I knew myself as I ought, I would not even be writing this. I protest that I am only doing it to obey you, and with such great reluctance that you owe me more for having taken up my pen in the face of this fear than you would owe me if I had sent you more perfect works. But it is just as well that this is going to you for corrections. If you eradicate it, rip it up, and reprimand me, I will appreciate that more than all the vain applause others may give me. *Corripiet me iustus in misericordia, et increpabit; oleum autem peccatoris non impinguet caput meum* [If the just person corrects and rebukes me it is a work of mercy. May the oil of sinners not anoint my head—Ps 140:5, Vulgate].

Returning to our Arce, who uses the following from my father St. Jerome to support his opinion: *Adhuc tenera lingua psalmis dulcibus imbuatur. Ipsa nomina per quae consuescit paulatim verba contexere; non sint fortuita, sed certa, et coacervata de industria. Prophetarum videlicet, atque Apostolorum, et omnis ab Adam Partriarcharum series, de Matthaeo, Lucaque descendat, ut dum aliud agit, futurae memoriae praeparetur. Reddat tibi pensum quotidie, de Scripturarum floribus carptum* [Imbue her tongue from an early age with the sweetness of the psalms. Let the very names from which she learns to form phrases, not be accidental, but deliberately chosen such as those of the prophets and the apostles. Let the series from Adam through the patriarchs in the genealogies of Matthew and Luke serve as a preparation of her memory for the future. Her daily exercise shall include gathering the flowers of scripture that she shall repeat to you].[30] Well, if this is how the saint wishes that a girl who has just begun learning to speak be educated, how much more would he want his nuns and his spiritual daughters to be educated? The references to Eustochium and Fabiola, to Marcela,[31] her sister Pacatula, and other women whom the saint honors in his letters, exhorting them to this holy exercise, are well known. We can see from the letter quoted above where I have noted *reddat tibi pensum* [she shall review with you] that it reinforces and is in concordance with the *bene docentes* [older women teaching well] of St. Paul. And the *reddat tibi* of my great father makes it clear that the teacher of the girl should be the same Laeta, her mother.

Oh, how much harm could have been avoided in our nation if our older women were as learned as Laeta and knew how to teach as St. Paul and my father St. Jerome mandate! And not, as is the case for lack of this and the extreme negligence that has been the lot of our poor women, that parents seeking to educate their daughters beyond the usual level are forced by necessity and the lack of educated older women to hire male tutors to teach their daughters to read, write, and count, play instruments, and other accomplishments. This has resulted in no little harm, as we experience every day in the pitiful examples of unequal unions caused by the immediacy of the relationship and the connection over time that makes easy that which was thought impossible. For this reason many parents would rather leave their daughters uncultured and uneducated than expose them to the well-known danger of familiarity with men. All this could be avoided if there were learned women, as St. Paul wants, who from one generation to the next would pass on their expertise in teaching as they now do in needlework and other things it is customary for women to learn.

What harm could there be in having a mature woman, educated in the liberal arts, and of holy company and morals, in charge of the education of young women? And not as is currently the case that they perish for want of education or from the dangerous expedient of a male tutor. Even if the risk were no more than the impropriety of having a modest girl, who still blushes when her own father looks her in the face, sitting beside a strange man who treats her with the familiarity of a member of the household and the frankness of a teacher, her embarrassment in the company of men and their conversation would suffice to forbid it. I do not find this manner of men teaching women without danger, unless it is in the severe tribunal of the confessional, in the distant teaching from the pulpit, or through the remote knowledge in books, but not in ruinous palpable proximity. Even though everyone knows that this is true, it is permitted only because there are no mature women qualified to teach them. Clearly not having them is very destructive. Those wedded to the passage *Mulieres in Ecclesia taceant* [Women should be silent in the church] should take this into account when they slander women by saying that they may not study and teach. As if it were not the very same apostle Paul who said: *bene docentes!* Furthermore, this prohibition needs to be considered in the historical context as related by Eusebius. In the primitive church women began teaching each other doctrine in the church building. Because the sound of their teaching embarrassed the apostles as they preached, they ordered them to be quiet. Something similar occurs today when one is not permitted to pray aloud while the preacher is preaching.

There is no doubt that much knowledge of history, customs, ceremonies, proverbs, and idioms of the times in which they were written is necessary in order to know the nature of the references and allusions in many passages in holy scripture. *Scindite corda vestra, et non vestimenta vestra* [Rend your heart and not your garments—Joel 2:13]. Is this not an allusion to the ceremony in which the Hebrews had to rend their garments as a sign of grief, as did the evil high priest when he said that Christ had blasphemed? (Matt 26:65). Do not the many passages of the apostle Paul concerning the help for widows also reflect the customs of those times? The passage about the valiant woman, *Nobilis in portis vir eius* [Her husband is praised at the gates—Prov 31:23], does that not allude to the custom of the courts sitting in judgment at the city gates? The *dare terram Deo* [give the land to God], does it not mean to make some kind of vow? *Hiemantes* [those wintering], is not this what they called public sinners who did penance in the open air, as distinguished from those who did penance in the doorway of the churches? The reproach that Christ made to the Pharisee for his failing to kiss him in greeting and to wash his feet, was it not based on the custom among the Jews to do these things? There are an infinite number of passages, not only in sacred texts but also in secular ones, where at every step we encounter expressions such as *adorate purpuram* [venerate the purple], which signifies to obey the king; *manumittere eum*, which signifies to set free and refers to the custom and ceremony of slapping a slave when setting him free; *intonuit coelum* [the heavens sounded] of Virgil, which refers to the omen of thunder from the west, which was considered a sign of good fortune; *tu nunquam leporem edisti* [you never ate rabbit, that is, you never said anything clever] of Martial,[32] which not only had the graceful double meaning of *leporem* (rabbit/clever) but also is an allusion to the property that eating rabbit is said to confer.[33] The proverb *Maleam legens, quae sunt domi obliviscere* [Sailing around Malea can make you forget the things of home][34] refers to the great danger to ships of the promontory of Laconia. The response of the chaste matron to her bothersome suitor—*For me, a door hinge will not be greased or torches burn*—to say that she did not want to marry refers to the ceremony of oiling the doors with butter and lighting nuptial torches at weddings. Today we would say: For me, no one should spend a dowry or priest dispense the blessing. In like manner there is much that needs to be explained in Virgil and Homer and in all poets and orators. In addition to this, what difficulties are not to be found in sacred passages, even in connection with grammar, for example, using the plural for the singular, changing from the second to the third person, as in the passage in the Song of Songs: *Osculetur me osculo oris sui: quia meliora sunt ubera tua vino?* [Let him kiss me with the kisses of his mouth, for your lips are sweeter than wine—Song 1:1]; or the habit of using adjectives in the genitive instead of in the accusative, as in *Calicem salutaris accipiam* [I will take up the chalice of salvation—Ps 115:13, Vulgate]; putting a feminine for a masculine, or to the contrary, calling any sin adulterous?

All this requires more study than some think, who, remaining at the level of grammar, or at most using the four basic principles of formal logic, think they can interpret scripture and cling doggedly to *Mulieres in Ecclesiis taceant*, without knowing how it should be understood. As to the other passage, *Mulier in silentio discat* [Woman shall learn in silence—1 Tim 2:11], this passage is more in favor than against women, since it requires them to study, and while they study it is clear that they need to be silent. We also read: *Audi Israel, et tace* [Hear, Israel, and be silent].[35] There, the whole assembly of men and women is addressed, and all are commanded to be silent, because for those hearing and learning it is only right for them to be attentive and silent. If this is not the case, I would like those interpreters and exegetes of St. Paul to explain to me how they understand *Mulieres in Ecclesia taceant*, based on their conception of church, which in the material sense can be pulpits and lecterns, or in the formal sense the universality of the faithful. If they understand it in the first sense, which is, in my opinion, its true meaning in this instance, because we see that in effect it is not permitted that women teach publicly or preach, why should those women who study in private be reprimanded? If church is understood in the second sense, and the prohibition of the Apostle applied in the most far-reaching sense so that women are not allowed even in secret to write or study, how can it be that the church has permitted women like Gertrude, Teresa, Bridget, the nun of Ágreda, and many others to do so? And if they tell me that these were saints, though that is true, it does not nullify my argument. In the first place, because St. Paul's proposition is absolute, including all women without excepting holy ones, because in his time there were holy women such as Martha and Mary, Marcela, Mary, the mother of Jacob and Salome, and many others who participated with fervor in the primitive church, and Paul did not exclude them in his statement. Today we see that the church permits both women saints and those who are not to write, since the nun of Ágreda and María de la Antigua[36] are not canonized and their writings circulate. Neither were St. Teresa and the others canonized at the time they were writing. Therefore St. Paul's prohibition aims only at the public nature of the pulpit, because if the Apostle had prohibited all writing to women, the church would also not permit it as it does today. I, myself, do not dare to teach; for me, that would be boundless presumption on my part. Furthermore, writing requires a greater talent than mine, as well as much reflection. As St. Cyprian said: *Gravi consideratione indigent, quae scribimus* [What we write demands painstaking consideration].[37] The only thing I have desired is to study in order to be less ignorant. As St. Augustine wrote, some things are learned for practical application, others for the sake of knowledge itself: *Discimus quaedam, ut sciamus; quaedam, ut faciamus* [Some things we learn in order to know, others in order to do].[38] So what has been my offense if it is legitimate for women to teach through their writing? I do not do so because I know that I do not have the means to do it, according to the advice of Quintilian: *Noscat quisque, et non tantum ex alienis praeceptis, sed ex natura sua capiat consilium* [Those who would learn should consider not so much the rules of others, but the capacities of their own natures].[39]

If there were a crime associated with the *Athenagoric Letter,* was it more than simply to report my opinion with all the permissions I owe to our Holy Mother Church? Because if she, with her most holy authority, does not forbid me doing so, why should others prohibit me? It was impudence on my part to develop an opinion contrary to Vieira's, but it was not impudence on the part of Father Vieira to contradict three holy fathers of the church? Is my mind, such as it is, not as free as his, since it is descended from the same source? Is his opinion one of the revealed truths of our holy faith that we are required to believe blindly? Furthermore, I never failed to give what respect is due to a man such as he, as his defender has failed to do when he forgot the words of Titus Livius: *Artes committatur decor* [The arts are to be respected].[40] Nor did I lay a finger on the Society of Jesus.[41] Nor did I write anything that went beyond the judgment of the one who suggested it to me. And according to Pliny, *non similis est conditio publicantis, et nominatim dicentis* [It is one thing to say something, another to have it published].[42] Had I believed it would be published, it would not have been as slipshod as it was. If it were heretical in the opinion of my critic, why did he not denounce it? In that case he would remain avenged, and I would be happier to be appreciated as I ought with the name of Catholic and obedient daughter of my Holy Mother Church than with many accolades as a learned woman. If the letter is rough, as you rightly point out, you may laugh, although it will be a forced laugh. I'm not asking for your approval, since I was free to disagree with Vieira, just as anyone is free to disagree with my findings.

But what has possessed me, my Lady? This is not appropriate here, nor is it meant for your ears; rather, I have been considering those who attack me and, as I was reminded of one of their judgments just published, imperceptibly my pen ran on, and I began to respond to him in particular, although my intention was to speak in general. And so to return to our Arce, who mentions two nuns he knew in this city. One, from the Regina Convent, knew the Breviary so well that in her conversation she was able to apply its verses, psalms, and the texts of the homilies of the saints with great diligence and appropriateness. The other, from the convent of the Conception of Mary, was so accustomed to reading the letters of my father St. Jerome, and knew his particular expressions so well, that Arce said of her: *Hieronymum ipsum hispane loquentem audire me existimarem* [Hearing her I thought I heard Jerome himself speaking Spanish]. Only after her death, he said, did he discover her translations of Jerome's letters into Spanish. He grieves that such talents could not have been employed for higher studies based on scientific principles. Without saying the names of either of them, he uses them to confirm his position, that not only is it permitted but most useful and necessary for women to study sacred scripture and even more so for nuns. Likewise your wisdom exhorts me to do the same, and many other arguments support this position.

If I turn my eyes again to that much maligned facility for composing poetry—which for me is so natural that I do violence to myself not to write this letter in verse—I could say, *Quidquid conabar dicere, versus erat* [When I want to say something, poetry results]. Seeing this facility condemned and blamed so much by so many, I searched very deliberately for the harm it could cause, without being able to find it. Rather, I have seen poetry applauded in the mouths of the sibyls and sanctified through the writing of the prophets, especially King David, of whom the great exegete and beloved father of mine, St. Jerome, gave an account of the meters of his verses: *In morem Flacci et Pindari nunc iambo currit, nunc alcaico personat, nunc sapphico tumet, nunc semipede ingreditur* [In the manner of Horace and Pindar, now runs the iambic, now the alcaic rings out, now the sapphic swells, and now it advances on half-feet].[43] Other books of sacred scripture contain poetry, such as the canticle of Moses (Exod 15:1–18); and the book of Job, as St. Isidore says in his *Etymologies*, was written in heroic verse. Solomon used it in his wedding songs, as did Jeremiah in his lamentations. As Casiodorus says: *Omnis poetica locutio a Divinis scripturis sumpsit exordium* [Every poetic form had its origin in holy scripture].[44] Not only does our Holy Catholic Church not disdain poetry, but she uses it in her hymns and recites those of St. Ambrose, St. Thomas Aquinas, St. Isidore, and others. St. Bonaventure was so fond of it that there is hardly a page of his that does not contain poetry. It is clear that St. Paul studied the poets, because he quotes them and translated the poetry of Aratus:[45] *In ipso enim vivimus, et movemur, et sumus* [In him we live, move, and have our being—Acts 17:28], and he refers to Parmenides: *Cretenses semper mendaces, malae bestiae, pigri* [Cretans are always liars, as bad as beasts, lazy gluttons].[46] St. Gregory of Nazianzen disputed questions of marriage and virginity in elegant verses. Why belabor the obvious? The Queen of Wisdom and our Lady with her holy lips intoned the Canticle of the Magnificat (Luke

1:46–55). Since I am using her as an example, it would be insulting and goes beyond necessary proof to use profane examples, even those of serious and learned men. Knowing the elegance of Hebrew cannot be pressed into Latin meter, the holy translator [St. Jerome], more attentive to the importance of the meaning of the text, omitted the meter of the Psalms but retained the number and division into verses. What harm then can there be in poetry? The ill use of something is not the fault of art, but of the bad practitioner who falsifies it and makes it a snare of the devil. This is true for all subjects and disciplines.

If the evil consists in women writing poetry, we have already seen that many women have used poetry in a praiseworthy fashion. What then is the harm in my doing so? Of course, I admit I am base and vile, but I do not believe that anyone has seen a single indecent couplet of mine. Moreover, I have never written anything of my own free will, but rather because of the entreaties and commands of others, so that I cannot recall having written anything for my own pleasure except a little scrap of a thing they call *El Sueño* [The dream]. The letter that you, my Lady, have so honored, I wrote with greater reluctance than any other, as much because it concerned sacred matters for which (as I have said) I have reverence and awe, as because it might have the appearance of intending to spark controversy, something for which I have a natural aversion. I believe, had I been able to anticipate the fortunate destiny for which it was born—like another Moses, after I had thrown it out to be exposed to the waters of the Nile of silence, where it would be found and cherished by a princess such as you— I believe, I repeat, that if I had understood this would be its fate, I would have strangled it with my own hands at the moment of birth, for fear that my clumsy, ignorant scribbling would appear before the light of your wisdom. The magnitude of your kindness is revealed since your will praises precisely what must be repugnant to your enlightened mind. But since destiny cast it on your doorstep, a foundling and an orphan, so that you even gave it a name, it grieves me that among all its shortcomings, it also bears the defects of hasty composition. Because of my continual poor health, because of the many occupations imposed on me by obedience, because I lack someone to help me copy my writing and must write everything in my own hand, because it goes against my disposition not to comply with the express wish of one I could not disobey, I could not foresee ever finishing it. As a result I neglected to include entire arguments and many proofs that presented themselves to me in order to be done with it. If I had known they would be printed I would not have omitted them for the sake of satisfying some objections, since raised, which could have been put to rest. However, I will not be so discourteous as to put such indecent objects before your pure eyes. It is enough that I offend you with my ignorance, without setting before you the insolence of others. If on their own these objections flew to you (and they are so lightweight they might have), you will tell me what I need to do. Unless you command the contrary, I will never take up my pen in my defense, because it seems to me unnecessary to respond to someone who by the very act of hiding his identity is revealing his error. As my father St. Jerome says, *bonus sermo secreta non quaerit* [what is well said does not seek secrecy],[47] and St. Ambrose, *latere criminosae est conscientiae* [to hide is the property of a guilty conscience].[48] Neither do I consider myself to be accused, since a rule of law says: *Accusatio non tenetur si non curat de persona, quae produxerit illam* [An accusation cannot be sustained without the participation of the person bringing the accusation].[49] What is surprising is the effort he spent to have copies made. What a rare form of madness this: to expend more effort to deny credit than to attain it? My Lady, I did not want to respond at all, although others have done so without my knowing it. It is enough that I have seen some manuscripts, one very learned, which I am sending to you, so that by reading it you will be partly recompensed for the time you have wasted by reading mine. If it be your pleasure, my Lady, I would do the opposite of what I have just proposed to your judgment and opinion. At the least indication of your desire I would cede, as is right, my decision, which was, as I have told you, to remain silent, because although St. John Chrysostom says: *calumniatores convincere oportet, interrogatores docere* [It is necessary to convince those who malign us, and to teach those who question us]. I see also that St. Gregory says: *Victoria non minor est, hostes tolerare, quam hostes vincere* [To tolerate one's enemies is no less a victory than to vanquish them].[50] Patience conquers through

287

tolerance and triumphs through suffering. The pagan Romans had the following custom. At the height of their glory, conquering generals entered the city in triumph, dressed in purple and crowned with laurel, at the head of the conquered nations, whose kings, their crowns still on their heads, taking the place of beasts of burden, drew their chariots. They were accompanied by spoils of the riches of the entire world. The conquering armies, adorned with the insignias of their exploits, marched behind them. As they heard the acclamations of the crowds crying out such honorable titles of fame as fathers of the nation, pillars of the empire, walls of Rome, guardians of the Republic and other glorious titles—in this zenith of glory and human felicity—a soldier would say to the conqueror, as his own opinion and by order of the Senate: Behold, you are mortal. Behold, you have this and that defect. This was done without excepting even the most shameful, as happened in the triumphal parade of Caesar, when the most lowly of soldiers said within his hearing: *Cavete romani, adducimus vobis adulterum calvum* [Beware, Romans, we bring you one who is bald, and adulterous].[51] This was done so that in the midst of so much honor the victor would not become conceited because the ballast of these insults would be a counterweight to the sails of so much adulation and the ship of judgment would not be endangered by the winds of acclaim. If this is what some of the pagans do, I say, with only the light of natural law to guide them, how much more ought we Catholics, with the commandment to love our enemies, to tolerate those who insult us?

I, for my part, can assure you that slander has sometimes served to mortify me but has never harmed me, because I hold the person to be very foolish who, having the occasion to gain merit, passes up the labor and loses the merit. It is like those who do not want to resign themselves to dying and finally die without their resistance to death having prevented their dying, but without reaping merit from their resignation. As a result, they make a bad death out of what could have been a good one. Thus, my Lady, I think those things are advantageous rather than harmful, and I hold the risk of fame a great one for human weakness, which is apt to appropriate that which is not its own. It is necessary to proceed with great caution and have engraved in one's heart these words of the Apostle: *Quid autem habes quod non accepisti? Si autem accepisti, quid gloriaris quasi non acceperis?* [What do you have that you have not received? And if you have received, why do you glory in it as if you have not received it?—1 Cor 4:7]. These words should serve as a shield against the spearhead of praise, which when we do not attribute it to God, to whom it belongs, like the thrust of a lance takes life out of us, makes us thieves of the honor due to God, usurpers of the talents we were given and of the gifts lent to us for which we will be held strictly accountable. And thus, my Lady, I fear praise more than blame, because blame, with one simple act of patience, is converted to a benefit. Praise, on the other hand, requires many reflective acts of humility and knowledge of oneself in order not to cause harm. For myself, I know and recognize it as a special favor of God that I understand this, so that I know how to conduct myself when praised or blamed according to the words of St. Augustine: *Amico laudanti credendum non est, sicut nec inimico detrahenti* [Neither the friend who praises, nor the enemy who berates is to be believed].[52] Although my nature is such that most often I ruin the opportunities or mix it with such defects and imperfections that I spoil what by itself would have been good. Thus in the little I have published, not only my name, but not even the permission for publication has been a decision of my own, but the decision of others beyond my control, such as happened with the *Athenagoric Letter*. As a result, only the *Exercises for the Incarnation* and the *Offerings for the Sorrows* were printed with my permission for public devotion, but without my name. I will send you some copies of them so that, if it seems good to you, you can distribute them among our sisters, the religious of your holy community, and moreover of your city. I can only send you one copy of *Sorrows* because the rest have been used up and no more can be made. I only wrote them for the devotion of my sisters many years ago, and afterward they were published. Their subjects are so disproportionate to my tepid heart and to my ignorance that it was only their subject, our great Queen, that helped me. There is something about the consideration of most holy Mary that is bound to inflame the coldest heart. I would like, my venerable Lady, to send you works worthy of your virtue and wisdom, but as the poet says:

Ut desint vires, tamen est laudanda voluntas:
hac ego contentos, auguror esse Deos.

[Although lacking in strength, one still must praise the
intention.
I think that the gods will be happy with it.][53]

If I write other little things in the future, they will always seek
refuge at your feet and the security of your correction, since I have
no other jewel with which to pay you, and in the opinion of
Seneca, the one who begins to bestow benefits is obliged to continue them. Thus I will pay you back by making more demands on
your generosity, because only in so doing can I remain worthily
freed of my debt, without being guilty of what that same Seneca
calls: *Turpe est beneficiis vinci* [It is shameful to be conquered by
benefits].[54] It is gallant for a generous creditor to give poor debtors
the wherewithal to satisfy their debts. This is what God did for the
world, by making the impossible debt to him payable through the
gift of his Son, so that he could be sacrificed for just repayment.

Venerable Lady, if the style of this letter has not been to your
liking, I beg pardon for its homely familiarity or less than due
respect since, while I have been treating you as a veiled religious,
my sister, I have forgotten the distance between myself and your
illustrious person. If I were to see you without the veil, that would
not happen. But you, with your common sense and your kindness,
will make up for and correct the terms in question. If the *Vos* seems
incongruous to you, I used it because it seemed to me that out of
the reverence that I owe you it would be irreverent to address you
as *Your Reverence.* Change it from what appeared appropriate to
what you deserve.[55] I dared not exceed the limits of your style or
violate the margin of your modesty.

Keep me in your good graces in order to beseech divine
favors for me. May the Lord grant you much increase and keep
you safe, as I beg of him and need.

From the convent of our father St. Jerome in Mexico City,
the first day of March sixteen hundred and ninety one.

Your most favored servant, Juana Inés de la Cruz

NOTES

Introduction

1. In the seventeenth century Anne Bradstreet was also known as the "tenth muse." For a comparison of the two, see Stephanie Merrim, *Early Modern Women's Writing and Sor Juana Inés de la Cruz* (Nashville, TN: Vanderbilt Univ. Press, 1999), 138–90.

2. Plays inspired by her life include Electa Arenal, "This Life within Me Won't Keep Still," in *Revinventing the Americas*, ed. Bell Gale Chevigny and Gari Laguardia (Cambridge: Cambridge Univ. Press, 1986), 158–202; Antonio Arenas, *El Fénix del Nuevo Mundo*; Isabela del Campo, *Me persigue Sor Juana: juguete poetico psicodramatico en once entrevistas* (Mexico: Federacion Editorial Mexicana, 1974); Lois Hobart, *Dream of Sor Juana* (El Paso, TX, 1985); Karen Zacarias, *Sins of Sor Juana* (Woodstock, IL: Dramatic Publishing Co., 1990). See also Frederick Luciani, "Recreaciones de Sor Juana en la narrativa y teatro hispano/norteamericanos, 1952–1988," in *"Y diversa de mí misma entre vuestras plumas ando": Homenaje internacional a Sor Juana Inés de la Cruz*, ed. Sara Poot-Herrera (Mexico: Colegio de Mexico, 1993), 395–408. Film: María Luisa Bemberg, *Yo, la peor de todas* (I, the worst of all), 1997. Novel: Alicia Gaspar de Alba, *Sor Juana's Second Dream* (Albuquerque: University of New Mexico Press, 1999).

3. Collections of essays based on conferences include Stephanie Merrim, ed., *Feminist Perspectives on Sor Juana Inés de la Cruz* (Detroit: Wayne State Univ. Press, 1991); Sergio Fernández, ed., *Los empeños: Ensayos en homenaje a Sor Juana Inés de la Cruz* (Mexico City: UNAM, 1995); *Memoria del Coloquio Internacional: Sor Juana Inés de la Cruz y el pensamiento novohispano 1995* (Mexico City: Instituto Mexiquense de Cultura, 1995); Sara Poot-Herrera, ed., *Sor Juana y su mundo: una mirada actual* (Mexico City: Universidad del Claustro de Sor Juana, 1995); and Poot-Herrera, *"Y diversa de mí misma entre vuestras plumas ando."*

4. Octavio Paz, *Sor Juana Inés de la Cruz*, or *The Traps of Faith*, trans. Margaret Sayers Peden (Cambridge, MA: Harvard Univ. Press, 1988), 480.

5. Diego Calleja, "Aprobación del Reverendissimo Padre Diego Calleja, de la Companía de Jesus," in *Juana Inés de la Cruz: Fama, y obras póstumas/del fénix de México, décima musa, poetisa americana Sor Juana Inés de la Cruz* (Madrid: Ruiz de Murga, 1700), Digitale Rekonstruktion der Printausgabe, "unnumbered," page 13. Available online.

6. "Ballad to a Gentleman from Peru" (OC 1:148ff.). Sor Juana Inés de la Cruz, *Obras Completas*, vols. 1–4: *Lírica personal; Villancicos y letras sacras; Autos y loas; Comedias, sainetes y prosa (1951–57)*, ed. Alfonso Méndez Plancarte (vols. 1–3) and Alberto G. Salceda (vol. 4.), 3rd reprint (Mexico: Fondo de Cultura Económica, 1995). *Complete Works* or *Obras Completas* are referred to as OC followed by volume and page number. One of her poems prefaced the first published volume of poetry of a Swedish woman, Elizabeth Sophia Brenner. See Amy Katz Kaminsky, "Nearly New Clarions: Sor Juana Inés de la Cruz Pays Homage to a Swedish Poet," in *In the Feminine Mode Essays on Hispanic Women Writers*, ed. Noël Valis and Carol Maier (Lewisburg, PA.: Bucknell Univ. Press, 1990), 31–53.

7. Marie Cécile Bénassy-Berling, *Humanisme et religion chez Sor Juana Inés de la Cruz: La femme et la culture au XVII siècle* (Paris: Editions Hispaniques, 1982). This also exists in a Spanish translation: *Humanismo y religión en Sor Juana Inés de la Cruz*, trans. Laura López de Belair (Mexico City: Universidad Nacional Autónoma de México, 1983). See also, George Tavard, *Juana Inés de la Cruz and the Theology of Beauty: The First Mexican Theology* (Notre Dame, IN: University of Notre Dame Press, 1991); Pamela Kirk, *Sor Juana Inés de la Cruz: Religion, Art, and Feminism* (New York: Continuum, 1998); Michelle A. Gonzalez, *Sor Juana. Beauty and Justice in the Americas* (Maryknoll, NY: Orbis Books, 2003).

8. Jean Franco, "Sor Juana Explores Space," in *Plotting Women: Gender and Representation in Mexico* (New York: Columbia Univ. Press, 1989), 23.

9. For a summary of the controversy about the dating and circumstances of Sor Juana's birth, see Paz, *Sor Juana*, 64–66. I support Paz's earlier dating of her birth to 1648 rather than 1651, as a minority of scholars maintain (Kirk, *Sor Juana*, 14–15).

10. Calleja, in *Fama*, "unnumbered," 16–17.

11. Ibid., "unnumbered" 19.

12. Ibid., "unnumbered" 20.

13. A recent study reveals that this convent was deeply divided in 1661, which may have influenced Sor Juana's decision not to stay there. One sister had summoned others before the Inquisition on charges of heresy, a charge eventually found to be unsubstantiated. Elisa Sampson Vera Tudela, "Chronicles of a Colonial Cloister: The Convent of San José and the Mexican Carmelites," in *Colonial Angels: Narratives of Gender and Spirituality in Mexico, 1580–1750* (Austin: University of Texas Press, 2000), 14–34, 118–47.

14. Isabel Ramírez, Sor Juana's mother, in her will written in 1687, a year before her death, describes herself as an unmarried woman (*soltera*) who had six children by two different men. Convent records, however, and Sor Juana's earliest biographer describe Sor Juana as the legitimate daughter of Isabel Ramírez and the Basque Pedro de Asbaje y Vargas Machuca.

15. "They entertained bishops and Viceroys with their songs and music, sewed and embroidered ecclesiastical vestments and ritual linens, created what is known as Mexican cooking, and trained girls of all races, preparing them for the tasks appropriate to their station in life and enabling an isolated few to rise in social status from the acquisition of learning." Electa Arenal and Stacey Schlau, *Untold Sisters: Hispanic Nuns in their Own Works* (Albuquerque: University of New Mexico Press, 1989), 339. This entire volume contains extended examples of the writing of Hispanic nuns with commentary. For a short contextualization of female monastic life in Mexico, see Asunción Lavrin, "Unlike Sor Juana? The Model Nun in the Religious Literature of Colonial Mexico," in *Feminist Perspectives on Sor Juana Inés de la Cruz*, ed. Stephanie Merrim (Detroit, MI: Wayne State Univ. Press, 1991), 61–85; and Bénassy-Berling, *Humanismo y religión en Sor Juana Inés de la Cruz*, 36–55.

16. Alfonso Méndez Plancarte, editor of volumes 1–3 of the critical edition, attributes another ten anonymous series of *villancicos* to Sor Juana (OC 2:xlvii–li).

17. María del Carmen Reyna, *El convento de San Jerónimo. Vida conventual y finanzas* (Mexico City: Instituto Nacional de Antropología e Historia, 1990). For a brief description of the role of *contadora* and Sor Juana's relationship with her major domo, see Elías Trabulse, *Los años finales de Sor Juana: una interpretación (1688–1695)* (Mexico City: Centro de Estudios de Historia de México Condumex, 1995), 13–16.

18. Raquel Chang-Rodriguez, "A proposito de Sor Juana y sus admiradores novocastellanos," *Revista Iberoamericana* 51 (132–33) (1985), 605–19.

19. Juaquín Pérez Villanueve, "Sor María de Ágreda y Felipe IV: Un epistolario en su tiempo," in *La iglesia en la España de los siglos XVII y XVIII*, vol. 4 of *Historia de la Iglesia en España* (Madrid: Biblioteca de Autores Cristianos, 1979), 413–17. See also Paz, *Sor Juana*, 148–49, who gives some details about the countess's family tree, including the name of her mother.

20. Nina Scott, "'Ser mujer, ni estar ausente, no es de amarte impedimento': Los poemas de Sor Juana a la Condesa de Paredes," in Poot-Herrera, *"Y diversa de mí misma entre vuestras plumas ando,"* 168.

21. The most influential of these portrayals of Sor Juana in terms of the broad base of its audience is probably that of Argentinean director María Luisa Bemberg's film, *Yo la peor de todas* (I, the worst of all). The novel by Alicia Gaspar de Alba, *Sor Juana's Second Dream*, has as a central focus the erotic nature of the two women's relationship (see my review in *Journal of Hispanic/Latino Theology* 8 (4) (2001): 74–77.

22. Tavard, *Beauty*, 193–94.

23. Merrim, *Early Modern Women's Writing and Sor Juana Inés de la Cruz*, 68; Emilie Bergmann, "Ficciónes de Sor Juana: poética y biografía," in Poot-Herrera, *"Y diversa de mí misma entre vuestras plumas ando,"* 171–84.

24. Felipe B. Pedraza Jiménez and Milagros Rodrígues Cáceres, *Manual de literatura española*, vol. 4, *Barroco: teatro* (Pamplona: Cénlit: 1981), 347.

25. Tavard, *Beauty*, 34–100, includes analysis and translations of some of Sor Juana's *villancicos*. Méndez Plancarte (OC 2: vii–lxviii), in addition to giving a general introduction of the *villancico*, compares Sor Juana's treatment of the genre with that of her contemporaries. Aurelio Tello, "Sor Juana, la música y sus músicos," in *Memoria del Coloquio International*, 465–81; Xavier Cacho Vázquea, *Sor Juana y la liturgia (Una lectura de sus villancicos y letras sacras)* (Mexico City: Instituto de Estudios y Documentos Históricos, Claustro de Sor Juana, 1981). Latin American literary scholars have for the most part focused on their multilingual/ethnic aspect. Elias L. Rivers, "Diglossia in New Spain," *University of Dayton Review* 16 (2) (1983), 9–12; Georges Baudot, "La trova náhuatl de Sor Juana Inés de la Cruz," in *Estudios de folklore y literatura: dedicados a Mercedes Díaz Roig*, ed. Beatriz Garza Cuarón and Yvette Jiménez de Báez (Mexico City: Colegio de México, 1992), 849–59; Electa Arenal, "Sor Juana Inés de la Cruz: Speaking the Mother Tongue," *University of Dayton Review* 16 (2) (1983), 93–105; Yolanda Martínez-San Miguel, *Saberes americanos: subalternidad y epistemología en los escritos de Sor Juana*

(Pittsburgh: Instituto International de Literatura Iberoamericana, 1999), 151–65.

26. They were generally the "chapel masters" who were commissioned on a regular basis to write for the great cathedrals: José de Agurto Loaysa (Mexico City); Antonio de Salazar (Mexico City and Puebla); Miguel Matheo de Dallo y Lana (Puebla); Matheo Vallados (Oaxaca) (see Tello, "Sor Juana, la música y sus musicos," 474).

27. Ibid., 466–67.

28. Rivers, "Diglossia in New Spain," 11.

29. Baudot, "La trova náhuatl de Sor Juana Inés de la Cruz," 853.

30. Alejandro López López, "Sor Juana Inés de la Cruz y la loa al *Divino Narciso* (Raíces autóctonas en los escritos de Sor Juana)," in *Memoria del Coloquio International*, 222.

31. Valquiria Wey, "Sor Juana y el portugués: El *villancico* VIII de San Pedro de 1677," in Fernández, *Los empeños*, 229.

32. Kirk, *Sor Juana*, 143–47; Paz, *Sor Juana*, 321–22, 434–36; Tavard, *Beauty*, 31–33, 41–45.

33. Bénassy-Berling, *Humanismo y religión en Sor Juana Inés de la Cruz*, 206–8; Tavard, *Beauty*, 162–64.

34. OC 1:453–54; Tavard, *Beauty*, 163.

35. Paz, *Sor Juana*, 293–97; Tavard, *Beauty*, 136–36, 162–64; Bénassy-Berling, *Humanismo y religión en Sor Juana Inés de la Cruz*, 254–55; Martha Lilia Tenorio, "Algo sobre el romance 56 de Sor Juana," in Poot-Herrer, *"Y diversa de mí misma entre vuestras plumas ando,"* 201–8.

36. Tavard, *Beauty*, 12–24; Constance M. Montross, *Virtue or Vice? Sor Juana's Use of Thomistic Thought* (Washington, DC: University Press of America, 1981), 38–85.

37. Merrim, *Early Modern Women's Writing and Sor Juana Inés de la Cruz*, 54.

38. Merrim, *"Mores Goemetricae*: The 'Womanscript in the Theater of Sor Juana Inés de la Cruz,'"* in Merrim, *Feminist Perspectives on Sor Juana Inés de la Cruz*, 94–111, introduces the dramas with a feminist analysis. She does not include *La Segunda Celestina*, which is not in the *Obras Completas*. Most scholars agree that Sor Juana wrote two of its three acts. See Sor Juana Inés de la Cruz and Augustín de Salazar y Torres, *La segunda Celestina*, ed. Guillermo Schmidhuber de la Mora (Mexico City: Vuelta, 1990); Ángel Valbuena-Briones, "El auto sacramental en Sor Juana Inés de la Cruz," in Poot-Herrera, *"Y diversa de mí misma entre vuestras plumas ando,"* 215–25.

39. OC 3: vii–xcviii, again gives a history of the genre and situates Sor Juana's work in that framework.

40. Kirk, *Sor Juana*, 41–44; Paz, *Sor Juana*, 342–45; Tavard, *Beauty*, 52–53; Bénassy-Berling, *Humanismo y religión en Sor Juana Inés de la Cruz*, 335–55.

41. Kirk, *Sor Juana*, 47–48; Paz, *Sor Juana*, 345–48; Tavard, *Beauty*, 56–58; Michael McGaha, trans., "Sor Juana Inés de la Cruz: *Joseph's Scepter*," in *The Story of Joseph in Spanish Golden Age Drama*, ed. and trans. Michael McGaha (Lewisburg, PA: Bucknell University Press, 1998), 186–94.

42. Pamela Kirk, "Christ as Divine Narcissus: A Theological Analysis of 'El Divino Narciso' of Sor Juana Inés de la Cruz," *Word and World* 12 (2) (1992), 145–53; Kirk, *Sor Juana*, 37–40, 50–52; Paz, *Sor Juana*, 350–56; Gonzalez, *Beauty and Justice*, 63–90; Michelle A. Gonzalez, "Seeing Beauty within Torment: Sor Juana Inés de la Cruz and the Baroque in New Spain," in *A Reader in Latina Feminist Theology: Religion and Justice*, ed. María Pilar Aquino, Daisy Machado, and Jeanette Rodriguez, 11–22 (Austin, TX: University of Texas Press, 2002); Merrim, *"Mores Goemetricae,"* 94–123, analyzes the plays in terms of Sor Juana's literary construction of her identity; Bénassy-Berling ("Fábula y misterio: Eco y Narciso," in Bénassy-Berling, *Humanismo y religión en Sor Juana Inés de la Cruz*, 372–83) compares Sor Juana's treatment of the theme with that of Calderón de la Barca; see also the following chapter, "La fuente: encarnación y redención," for an analysis of the image of the fountain. See also María Esther Pérez, "Lo religioso," in *Lo Americano en el teatro de Sor Juana Inés de la Cruz* (New York: Eliseo Torres & Sons, 1975), 120–43.

43. Kirk, *Sor Juana*, 48–50; Paz, *Sor Juana*, 346–50; Bénassy-Berling, *Humanismo y religión en Sor Juana Inés de la Cruz*, 307–55; Pérez, *Lo Americano en el teatro de Sor Juana Inés de la Cruz*, 172–88; Martínez-San Miguel, *Saberes americanos*, 175–84; López López, "Sor Juana Inés de la Cruz y la loa al *Divino Narciso*," 221–40.

44. The characters Human Nature and Echo (representing fallen angelic nature) also claim authorship of the play.

45. For an example from Sor Juana's own time, see María de San José, *Word from New Spain: The Spiritual Autobiography of Madre María de San José (1656–1719)*, ed. Kathleen Myers (Liverpool: Liverpool Univ. Press, 1993).

46. Tavard, *Beauty*, 61–67; Margo Glantz, "Letras de San Bernardo: La excelsa fábrica," *Calâiope: Journal of the Society for Renaissance and Baroque Hispanic Poetry* 4 (1–2) (1998): 173–88.

47. Bénassy-Berling, *Humanismo y religión en Sor Juana Inés de la Cruz*, 234–61; Tavard, *Beauty*, 91–94; Kirk, *Sor Juana*, 60–65; Georgina

NOTES

Sabat de Rivers, *"Ejercicios de la Encarnación":* Sobre la imagen de María y la decisión final de Sor Juana," *Literatura mexicana* 1 (2), 349–71. Clark Colahan, *The Visions of Sor María de Ágreda: Writing Knowledge and Power* (Tuscon: University of Arizona Press, 1994), sets this woman in a broader context than has previously been the case. María of Ágreda was another religious who was very successful in her own lifetime (1602–65). A correspondent and confidant of the King Phillip IV, she wrote not only mystical texts but also a geography of the world and a cosmology. Sor María's work *The Mystical City of God* was on and off the index of forbidden books charged with supporting Mary as "co-Redeemer of the World" (OC 4: 660). She was also an ardent supporter of Mary's immaculate conception.

48. Tavard, *Beauty,* 90–91; Kirk, *Sor Juana,* 75–55.

49. Marie-Cécile Bénassy-Berling, "Más sobre la conversión de Sor Juana," *Nueva Revista de Filología Hispanica* 23 (2) (1983), 462–71, points out that the first edition of the *villancicos* for the feast of St. Catherine of Alexandria, published in Puebla a year after the critique of Father Vieira's sermon, contains lengthy laudatory prefaces of both of the ecclesiastical censors. These, she argues, demonstrate the support Sor Juana enjoyed in Mexico as well as in Spain even after the publication of the critique of Father Vieira's sermon.

50. Sor Juana's first biographer, Calleja, was also a Jesuit.

51. Paz, *Sor Juana,* 169–79; Pamela Kirk, "Political Simulation: Sor Juana's Monument *Neptuno Alegórico," Journal of Hispanic/Latino Theology* 2 (2) (1994): 30–40; Kirk, *Sor Juana,* 27–35; Tavard, *Beauty,* 147–49, 156–59; Martínez-San Miguel, *Saberes americanos,* 141–51.

52. Aureliano Tapia Méndez, *Carta de Sor Juana Inés de la Cruz a su confesor: Autodefensa espiritual* (Monterrey, Mexico: Universidad de Nuevo Leon, 1981), in the first edition of this letter, relates how he found it in a file of miscellaneous documents from the eighteenth century in the library of the archdiocesan seminary of Monterrey, Mexico. Since its publication it has been referred to variously as the *Letter of Monterrey, Spiritual Self Defense,* or just *Self Defense.* An easily accessible translation by Margaret Sayers Peden can be found in the appendix to Paz, *Sor Juana,* 495–502. See also Mabel Moraña, "Orden dogmático y marginalidad en la *Carta de Monterrey* de Sor Juana Inés de la Cruz," *Hispanic Review* 58 (2) (1990), 205–25; Josefina Muriel, "Sor Juana Inés de la Cruz y los escritos del Padre Antonio Núñez de Miranda," in Poot-Herrera, *"Y diversa de mí misma entre vuestras plumas ando,"* 71–83.

53. See OC 4:673–94 for a Spanish translation of Vieira's sermon.

54. Bénassy-Berling, *Humanismo y religión en Sor Juana Inés de la Cruz,* 218–31; Kirk, *Sor Juana,* 81–94; Tavard, *Beauty,* 137–56; Paz, *Sor*

SOR JUANA INÉS DE LA CRUZ

Juana, 389–96; Montross, *Virtue or Vice?*, 1–27; Mauricio Beuchot, "El universo filosófico de Sor Juana," in *Memoria del Coloquio Internacional,* 29–39; Gerardo Rivas, "El velo del templo," in Fernández, *Los Empeños,* 207–33; Florbela Rebelo Gomes, "Para una nueva lectura de la *Carta Atenagórica,* in Poot-Herrera, *"Y diversa de mí misma entre vuestras plumas ando,"* 287–300. Margarita Peña, "Teología, biblia y expresión personal en la prosa de Sor Juana Inés de la Cruz," in *"Y diversa de mí misma entre vuestras plumas ando,"* 279–85; Joaquim de Montezuma de Carvalho, Sor Juana Inés de la Cruz e o Padre António Vieira ou a disputa sobre as finezas de Jesus Christo (Mexico City: Vega, 1998); Hernani Cidade, "António Vieira et Sor Juana Inés de la Cruz," *Bulletin des Études Portugaises et de l'Institut Français au Portugal* 12 (1948): 1–34.

55. Antonio Alatorre, "Para leer la *Fama y Obras pósthumas* de Sor Juana Inés de la Cruz," *Nueva Revista de Filología Hispánica* 29 (1980): 499, points out that the title page of the first edition (Puebla, 1690) of *Critique/Athenagoric Letter* not only has "Sor Philotea" as the nominal author but also specifically attributes publication of the work to "her," a responsibility only a bishop could assume. In *Juana Inés de la Cruz* (1700) the letter of "Sor Philotea" is published as "The Letter of the…Archbishop of Puebla, under the name of Sor Pilotea" (*Juana Inés de la Cruz,* 1). In 1716 Fernández de Santa Cruz's biographer, Miguel de Torres, a nephew of Sor Juana, included the letter of "Sor Philotea" in a collection of the bishop's letters written to various nuns. Antonio Alatorre, "La Carta de Sor Juana al Padre Núñez, 1682," *Nueva Revista de Filolgía Hispánica* 35 (2) (1986): 642–71, sees Núñez rather than Santa Cruz as targeted in the *Response* based on textual connections between it and the earlier *Letter of Monterrey.* Elías Trabulse in *Los años finales de Sor Juana* published a new text presumed to be by Sor Juana, the *Carta de Serafina* (letter of Serafina). Though addressed to Santa Cruz, the Bishop of Puebla, by textual analysis Trabulse makes a case that the true addressee is again Sor Juana's confessor, Núñez de Miranda. Critical of this interpretation are Antonio Alatorre and Marta Lilia Tenorio, *Serafina y Sor Juana (con tres apéndices)* (Mexico City: El Colegio de México, Centro de Estudios Lingüísticos y Literarios, 1998).

56. Paz, *Sor Juana,* 414–24; Kirk, *Sor Juana,* 116–42; Bénassy-Berling, *Humanismo y religión en Sor Juana Inés de la Cruz,* 262–80; Nina Scott, "Sor Juana Inés de la Cruz: 'Let your Women Keep Silence in the Churches…,'" *Women's Studies International Forum* 8 (5) (1985), 511–19; Rosa Perelmutter Pérez, "La éstructura retórica de la *Respuesta a Sor Filotea,*" *Hispanic Review* 51 (2) (1983): 147–58.

NOTES

57. Kirk, *Sor Juana*, 94–115; Paz, *Sor Juana*, 389–424; Winifred Corrigan, "The Bishop and the Woman: 'Sor Filotea' and Sor Juana Inés de la Cruz," *Studia Mystica* 15 (2–3) (1992): 72–83; Sharon Larisch, "Sor Juana's *Apologia*," *Pacific Coast Philology* 21 (1–2) (1986), 48–53; Bénassy-Berling, *Humanismo y religión en Sor Juana Inés de la Cruz*, 161–78.

58. Sor Juana's first biographer, Calleja, in *Fama*, unnumbered pages 28–33, saw the end of her life in terms of a conversion and total retreat from the world into the convent. Méndez Plancarte and Salceda, editors of the critical edition, follow this interpretation. Salceda quotes another supporter of this view, Gabriela Mistral, the first Latin American to win the Nobel Prize for literature. She describes Sor Juana at the end of her life as freed from intellectual vanity with her face turned to Christ as the epitome of beauty and as supreme truth (OC 4:xliii–xlviii). See also Tavard, *Beauty*, 167–83.

59. See also Bénassy-Berling, "Más sobre la conversión de Sor Juana," 446, who argues that the bishop's letter may have been a vehicle for publishing the *Critique/Athenagoric Letter* as well as an excuse for Sor Juana to formulate the ideas expressed in the *Response* into a coherent whole.

60. In this I follow Bénassy-Berling, *Humanismo y religión en Sor Juana Inés de la Cruz*, 170.

61. Paz's analysis has been very influential. Building on work of Darío Puccini, *Sor Juana Inés de la Cruz: Studio d'una personalita del Barocco messicano* (Rome: Edizioni dell'Ateneo, 1967), he concludes that Sor Juana was the pawn used by Manuel Fernández de Santa Cruz, Bishop of Puebla, to humiliate Francisco Aguiar y Seijas, Archbishop of Mexico City, by publishing a woman's refutation of the work of the renowned Vieira, whom Aguiar admired and had published in Spanish in Mexico City.

62. Through a complex and detailed analysis Trabulse, in *Los años finales de Sor Juana*, comes to the conclusion that Sor Juana was put under direct official pressure from the Archbishop of Mexico City, which led to her return to her confessor Núñez, the sale of her books, and her abjuration of the world. Numerous scholars have followed him, including Margo Glanz, *Sor Juana: la comparación y la hipérbole* (Mexico City: CONACULTA, 2000), 105–6; Sara Poot-Herrera, *Los guardaditos de Sor Juana* (Mexico City: Textos de Difusión Cultural, UNAM, 1999); and Jean Michel Wissmer, *Las sombras de lo fingido; sacrificio y simulacro en Sor Juana Inés de la Cruz* (Toluca, Mexico: Instituto Mexiquense de Cultura, 1998).

63. Kirk, *Sor Juana*, 147–50.

64. In *Sor Juana* (p. 148) I set this year after her renewal of vows, so that it would end just before her death, based on Salceda's judgement (OC 4:671) that it "revealed the same state of soul" as the shorter pieces dated February of 1694. It now makes more sense to me that the year of self-examination would be in preparation for, rather than subsequent to, her renewal of vows. This dating also respects the chronology of Calleja's narrative.

65. Bénassy-Berling, *Humanismo y religión en Sor Juana Inés de la Cruz*, 175.

66. Trabulse, *Los años finales de Sor Juana*, 13–16, has brought this office into the discussion in a manner not attended to previously.

67. Though Sor Juana's *Exercises* are a novena leading up to the feast of the Annunciation, March 25, she refers to it as the "feast of the Incarnation." The whole premise of the devotion of all creatures to Mary is her immaculate conception.

68. Julien Stricher, *Le voeu du sang en faveur de l'Immaculée Conception: Histoire et bilan théologique d'une controverse* (Rome: Academia Mariana Internationalis, 1959).

69. Pérez Villanueve, "Sor María de Ágreda y Felipe IV," 455–60; René Laurentin, "The Role of the Papal Magisterium in the Development of the Dogma of the Immaculate Conception," trans. Charles Sheedy and Edward Shea, in *The Dogma of the Immaculate Conception: History and Significance*, ed. Edward Dennis O'Connor, 281–307 (Notre Dame, IN: University of Notre Dame Press, 1958).

70. Tavard, in *Beauty*, 37–38, 67–79, discusses a development in her understanding of the teaching.

71. According to Genesis 3:20, Eve is the mother of all the living.

72. The entire argument is replete with honoring the feminine. There is only Adam to blame for the first sin and no mention of Eve.

73. Gregory the Great, *Homily 16*, on Matthew 4:1–11.

74. Teresa of Avila, "The Book of Her Life," chap. 28, nos. 2–3, 9; chap. 29, nos. 1–2, in *The Book of Her Life: Spiritual Testimonies: Soliloquies*, vol. 1 of *The Collected Works of St. Teresa of Avila*, trans. Kieren Kavanaugh and Otilio Rodriguez (Washington, DC: ICS Publications, 1989), 237–38, 241, 246–47.

75. Teresa of Avila, *The Interior Castle*, VI, chap. 9, nos. 3–6, in *The Way of Perfection: Meditations on the Song of Songs: The Interior Castle*, vol. 2 of Kavanaugh and Rodriguez, *The Collected Works of St. Teresa of Avila*, 411–13.

76. Alan Trueblood (p. 216) traces this image to the Jesuit Athanasius Kircher (1602–80). He also mentions Macrobius's

NOTES

Commentary on the Dream of Scipio, chap. 14. See Alan S. Trueblood, trans., *A Sor Juana Anthology* (Cambridge, MA: Harvard University Press, 1988); Méndez Plancarte refers to the *Iliad* (8.14–18) and Lucian's *Dialogue of Ares and Hermes* (OC 4:651). See note in translation for more details on Kircher.

77. Dr. Juan Díaz de Arce taught sacred scripture at the University of Mexico for thirty years. He died in 1653.

78. Paz, *Sor Juana*, 500.

79. Ibid., 499.

80. Teresa of Avila, *The Interior Castle*, I, ch. 1, no. 1, in Kavanaugh and Rodriguez, *The Collected Works of St. Teresa of Avila*, 2:284.

81. Ibid. Though here she introduces the image of a "diamond or crystal," in its development she most often uses the word "crystal." An early biographer, Father Diego de Yepes, describes Teresa's telling him of her vision of "a most beautiful crystal globe like a castle" (ibid., "Introduction," in Kavanaugh and Rodriguez, *The Collected Works of St. Teresa of Avila*, 2:269.

82. Teresa of Avila, "The Interior Castle," I, ch. 2, no. 3 in Kavanaugh and Rodgriguez, *The Collected Works of St. Teresa of Avila*, 2:289. In I:2/3 she combines the images of crystal-clear flowing water and polished crystal.

83. Ibid., I, ch. 2, no. 2, in Kavanaugh and Rodriguez, *The Collected Works of St. Teresa of Avila*, 2:288.

84. John of the Cross's *Spiritual Canticle* is his inspired interpretation/translation of the Song of Songs. Sor Juana sets her own beautiful rendering of the Song of Songs in the mouth of Human Nature as she searches for Narcissus and in Narcissus's response to her. See Juan de la Cruz, "Cántico espiritual," Canticle XII, no. 1, in *Obras de San Juan de la Cruz, Doctor de la Iglesia* (Madrid: Editorial Apostolado de la Prensa, 1966), 623.

85. Juan de la Cruz, "Cantico espiritual," Canticle XII, no. 3, in *Obras de San Juan de la Cruz, Doctor de la Iglesia*, 624.

86. Bénassy-Berling, *Humanismo y religión en Sor Juana Inés de la Cruz*, 205–18, deals with the question of whether Sor Juana was a mystic or not. She concludes that it is impossible to say with certainty.

Section 1:
Villancicos and Devotional Poetry

1. November 21. The feast commemorates the tradition that Mary was taken by her parents to the temple to be consecrated and then live with other virgins in the temple. The primary source for this tradition is the apocryphal Gospel of Matthew (OC 1:459–60).

2. The feast was not yet named "Immaculate" Conception because this dogma was still in dispute.

3. I have omitted the introductory refrain.

4. The poem is a *jácara*, typically celebrating knights errant, adventurers, even criminals. It was very popular and was also applied to religious figures such as Augustine, Francis, and, as here, to Mary (OC 2:359–61).

5. Most Beautiful.

6. It is not clear whether this is an intentional reference to the *Song of Roland* or merely an example of a knight adventurer, one of the many who populated the tales of chivalry that Cervantes parodied in *Don Quixote*. St. Teresa reports that her mother was an avid reader of such tales, and that she herself was enthralled by them (Teresa of Avila, "The Book of Her Life," 1, ch. 2, no. 1, in Kavanaugh and Rodriguez, *The Collected Works of St. Teresa of Avila*, 1:57).

7. *Pupilos*, most often as here "orphans," can also mean prostitutes.

8. See Kirk, *Sor Juana*, 144–47, for a brief summary of the entire series. Translations of the obviously autobiographical poems are found in Sor Juana Inés de la Cruz, *The Answer/La Respuesta: Including a Selection of Poems*, ed. and trans. Electa Arenal and Amanda Powell (New York: The Feminist Press at The City University of New York, 1994), 161–63. See also Alan S. Trueblood, trans., *A Sor Juana Anthology* (Cambridge, MA: Harvard University Press, 1988), 137–45.

9. An indication of Sor Juana's devotion to Mary Immaculate. Here for the feast of the Assumption she addresses Mary in her dedication as "conceived in grace from the first moment of her being."

10. Titles of the poems were given by the first editors.

11. Literally, "the divine Lynx."

12. Today this would be the feast of the Annunciation.

Section 2: Drama

Loa to *Divine Narcissus*

1. Throughout I maintain the line numbering of the Mandez Plancarte/Salcedas edition.
2. A reference to the Spaniards' weapons.

Divine Narcissus

3. Sor Juana draws on the double myth of the origin of the hyacinth. Editor Mendez Plancarte explains that the first refers to the beautiful young man, Hyacinth, inadvertently mortally wounded by Apollo. In his grief Apollo turns him into a white flower tinged with purple markings that seem to spell *AI*, recalling the cry of grief "ay." The second story is of Ajax, hero of the Trojan war, whose blood was transformed into the hyacinth, which contains the first two letters of his name, *AI*. Christian poets saw the purple in the flower as reminiscent of the wounds of Christ, and the shape *AI* as alluding to his sufferings (OC III, 530).
4. The numbering of the verses I'm following is that of the critical edition of Méndez Plancarte, which misnumbered the lines, skipping ninety numbers at this point.
5. Basilisk *(régulo)* is the name of a legendary reptile whose breath and glance were fatal.
6. Roman Breviary, October 9. At that time, the feast of St. Dionysius.
7. Taken from Thomas Aquinas's *Pange, Lingua,* a hymn celebrating the Eucharist.

Section 3: Devotional Works

Devotional Exercises for the Nine Days before the Feast of the Most Pure Incarnation of the Son of God, Jesus Christ, Our Lord

1. Commonly called feast of the Annunciation. Sor Juana's title underscores its broader significance.

2. Sor Juana does not spell out her name in full, but suggests "agreda" in the phrase *agradecida*, which I translate "appreciated," losing the word play.

3. Mary of Jesus (of Ágreda), *The Incarnation*, vol. 2 of *The Mystical City of God: The Divine History and Life of the Virgin Mother of God*, trans. Fiscar Marison (a.k.a. George J. Blatter) (Washington, NJ: Ave Maria Institute, 1971), 25–92. María de Ágreda was a correspondent and confidant of King Phillip IV. Her *Mystical City of God*, the work Sor Juana refers to, was controversial. Sor Juana's contemporary Antonio de Robles in his *Diario*, entry for March 9, 1682, writes that "letters" had come to Mexico City commanding that all the books of the "nun of Ágreda" be collected. Sunday, September 24, 1690, he notes that three edicts of the Inquisition were read in the churches prohibiting her books (OC 4:660). Salceda calculates that the *Devotional Exercises* were written between 1684 and 1688 (OC 4:663). A comparison of *Devotional Exercises* and this portion of *The Mystical City of God* would make an interesting study.

4. María of Jesus (of Ágreda), *The Incarnation*, 1:69–92.

5. The apostle John, to whom Jesus gave his mother as they stood under the cross (John 19:25–27).

6. Salceda refers to a book of observances from Sor Juana's convent from 1831 which requires that the nuns observe "discipline the Fridays of Lent, and Wednesday, Thursday and Friday of Holy Week" (OC 4:664). The contextualization of practices such as *disciplina* usually referring to self-flagellation has yet to be written.

7. Here Sor Juana presumed the widely accepted view of the scientific community influential from the time of Aristotle and Ptolemy that there are a series of spheres in the heavens rotating around the fixed earth. See Herbert Butterfield, *The Origins of Modern Science, 1300–1800* (New York: Macmillan Company, 1960), 18–24.

8. This text was recited after each Mass and was called the Last Gospel.

9. A crown rosary with seven decades in honor of the virgin Mary (OC 4:664).

10. Again, Sor Juana presumes her readers have an earth-centered view of the cosmos.

11. According to Genesis 3:20, Eve is the mother of all the living.

12. Here Sor Juana is playing on the Latin root of humility (*humus* = dust). In the Magnificat (Luke 1:46–53) Mary calls herself God's humble servant, *humilitatem ancillae suae*, and she praises God as raising up the humble, *exaltavit humiles*.

NOTES

13. In his *Diario* Antonio de Robles wrote of several major earthquakes in 1682, including one on the feast of St. Joseph (OC 4:665). This would date the *Exercises* several years after the quake.

14. A type of rosary with only three decades (OC 4:665).

15. References to Mary as harbinger of salvation comparing her to winged creatures associated with salvation in the Bible. The reference to Samson's honeycomb (Judg 14:8) remains obscure.

16. Sor Juana's translation here of the Vulgate text leaves out some half verses.

17. An interpretive rendering of the Vulgate's *igitur perfecti sunt caeli et terra et omnis ornatus eorum.*

18. My way of rendering the tribute to Mary in Sor Juana's expression: "la hizo el Senor Senora de todos los hombres."

19. Texts suggested here, with the exception of the litany, are all from the Breviary. *Alma Redemptoris mater, Angelus Domini,* and *Gratiam tuam* are from the Office of the Virgin.

20. María de la Antigua (1566–1617), Spanish nun, writer, and poet.

21. A reference to María de Ágreda's *The Mystical City of God.* See note 3 above.

22. Power, wisdom, and love are three traditional attributes of the three Persons of the Trinity.

23. Pope Gregory, *On the Gospels,* XXXIV, 6, 7. Readings for matins on the feast of St. Michael the Archangel mention the nine orders of angels but not their division into three choirs.

24. Angels in the classic Scholastic teaching were pure intelligence. Their knowledge was complete, not mediated by physical matter, as is the case with human beings.

25. Antiphons to the Virgin Mary for Saturday vespers.

26. Hymn for vespers for the feast of St. Michael the Archangel, September 29.

27. Collect of the Mass of St. Gabriel, March 24.

28. Sor Juana's hymn includes themes from the hymn, response, and prayer of the *Ave, Regina Caelorum [Hail, queen of heaven],* one of the antiphons to the Virgin for Saturday vespers.

29. Responsorial prayer from the Breviary for feasts of the angels.

30. Antiphon to the Virgin Mary for Saturday vespers.

31. Hymn for vespers on All Saints' Day, November 1.

32. Hymn for lauds for the feast of St. Michael the Archangel, September 29.

33. Antiphon for lauds and vespers, also for the feast of St. Michael the Archangel.

34. Prayer for lauds and vespers for the feast of St. Michael.

35. Augustine, *De sancta Virginitatae*, I,3.3.

36. Bonaventure, *Expositio in Evangelium S. Lucae*, Cap XI, no. 27.

37. Hymn from the Common of the Blessed Virgin Mary.

38. Prayer for the feast of the Annunciation, March 25.

39. Based on Sor Juana's translation of the prayer above.

Offerings for the Rosary of the Fifteen Mysteries to Be Prayed on the Feast of the Sorrows of Our Lady, the Virgin Mary

1. As *Critique/Athenagoric Letter* shows, Sor Juana valued free will, but she also emphasizes that grace is necessary for salvation (See *Divine Narcissus*.) Here she focuses on the redemptive death of Christ, which makes salvation possible. Consequently, human merit pales in comparison.

2. This emphasis of Christ's divinity on the cross or of divinity "suffering" is also suggested in *Divine Narcissus*.

3. Mary in *Devotional Exercises* and Sor Juana's *villancicos* is related to God as mother, spouse, and "daughter" of the Creator.

4. Mary's suffering, even vicarious, becomes a source of merit for others.

Section 4: Theological Works

Critique of a Sermon of One of the Greatest Preachers, which Mother Juana called Response *because of the Elegant Explanations with Which She Responded to the Eloquence of His Arguments*

1. A reference to the proverbial boasting of the Portuguese (OC 4:632).

2. Neither Salceda's critical edition of Sor Juana's works nor the editions of Vieira's sermons I have been able to consult have indicated the sources of these positions. It is possible that Vieira was referring to generally held views in the seventeenth century of the position of the three

NOTES

authorities on the issue of the *finezas*, rather than to specific texts. This seems likely since not only does he refrain from mentioning a specific text of Augustine, Thomas Aquinas, or John Chrysostom, but instead in each case introduces their position in very general terms. Augustine's position is also that of "the many others who have followed him" (OC 4:675). Thomas Aquinas's "opinion" is also that "of many who before and after the Angelic Doctor" had the same position (OC 4:678). In the case of John Chrysostom, Vieira again says it is also the opinion "of other Doctors, ancient and modern who follow him" (OC 4:684).

3. OC 4:674. It is not known whether Sor Juana read Vieira's sermon in a Spanish edition or in Portuguese, which scholars think she knew fairly well because some of her *villancicos* contain characters who speak Portuguese (OC 4:633).

4. This is a composite quotation from John 19:30 (he bowed his head) and Matthew 27:50 (he gave up his spirit) (OC 4:633).

5. The quotation is from the canon of the Mass, which refers back to Luke 22:19 and 1 Corinthians 11:24.

6. From "Stabat Mater," a hymn to the Virgin Mary.

7. Sor Juana is assuming Mary of Bethany and Mary Magdalene were one and the same.

8. What follows is a discussion of the term *fineza*, which I have been translating most often as "demonstration of love," but also "gift of love" or "benefit of love," depending on the context. Since this paragraph is a discussion of the term and employs puns based on its sound in the original, I am using the Spanish word here.

9. In this case Sor Juana has translated the Latin.

10. Gregory the Great, *Homily 16*, on Matthew 4:1–11.

11. Sor Juana's translation.

12. Latin proverb.

13. Another name for Hercules. The story is told in Ovid, *Heriodas*, IX; Lucian, *Dialogue of the Gods*, XIII.

14. Macrobius, *Saturnalia*, V. 3.

15. Sor Juana's paraphrase of the above quotation.

16. St. Gregory the Great, *Commentary on the Gospel of St. Matthew*, *Homily 9*, on chapter 25. This passage is also part of the ordinary of the office of a bishop confessor from the Roman Breviary.

SOR JUANA INÉS DE LA CRUZ

Letter of "Sor Philotea"

1. Diogo César Meneses (1604–61), another Portuguese preacher, Vieira's mentor (Alan S. Trueblood, trans., *A Sor Juana Anthology* [Cambridge, MA: Harvard University Press, 1988], 199).

2. An apparent reference to Acts 7:22, where, however, Moses, not Joseph is described as having mastered the wisdom of the Egyptians (Trueblood, *A Sor Juana Anthology*, 201).

3. Justus Lipsius, a Flemish humanist and scholar (1547–1606) who considered himself a Stoic. Source of quotation not found.

4. Jean Gersón (1363–1429), chancellor of the University of Paris, an early humanist and spiritual writer. Reference not found.

5. Jerome describes a similar scene in "To Eustochium (Letter 22)," in *Handmaids of the Lord: Contemporary Descriptions of Feminine Asceticism in the First Six Christian Centuries*, ed. and trans. Joan M. Petersen (Kalamazoo, MI: Cistercian Publications, 1996), 196–97.

6. Boethius (480–524) in *The Consolation of Philosophy* argues that philosophical contemplation that leads to contemplation of Divinity is the highest form of knowledge. Given the conflicts caused in Sor Juana's life by her poetry, it is interesting to note that *The Consolation* is written partly in verse.

7. Apelles painted the mistress of Alexander the Great and then was allowed to marry her.

8. November 25, 1690, is also the date on which the Bishop of Puebla, Manuel Fernandez de Santa Cruz's permission for the publication of *Carta Athenagorica* was notarized by Br. Geronimo Lazcano. As such, it is another indication that Santa Cruz was indeed Sor Philotea, since had it been another author there would have been a gap between the date of the letter and the permission to publish it.

Response to the Very Illustrious "Sor Philotea"

1. Sor Juana may have been quoting from memory, as Alan Trueblood suggests (Alan Trueblood, trans., *A Sor Juana Anthology* [Cambridge, MA: Harvard University Press, 1988], 205). He found the following: *Quo minores opes fuerunt, maiorem benefactis gloriani parit* [The glory of good deeds may be enhanced by the smallness of their resources]. Quintilian, *Institutio Oratoria*, 3.7.13, Loeb Classics (Cambridge, MA: Harvard Univ. Press, 1969).

2. Most scholars see this title as referring to Athena, goddess of wisdom. Thus the letter is "worthy of Athena."

NOTES

3. A theme of the last section of *Critique/Athenagoric Letter* and of the poem: "Gentle lover of the soul" (OC 1:169–70).

4. "To Laeta: A Girl's Education," Letter CVII, 12, in *Select Letters of St. Jerome*, ed. and trans. F. A. Wright (Cambridge, MA: Harvard Univ. Press, 1975), 364.

5. Electa Arenal disputes the attribution of Salceda and Trueblood to Seneca's *De Beneficiis* [On Public Honors], maintaining it is from Seneca's *Octavia*, 1, 538 (see *The Answer/La Respuesta: Including a Selection of Poems*, ed. and trans. Electa Arenal and Amanda Powell [New York: The Feminist Press at The City University of New York, 1994], 111).

6. Most scholars consider this a reference to her confessor at the time of her entry into the convent, Antonio Núñez de Miranda, SJ.

7. A comparison with St. Teresa's description of her state of mind when considering entering the convent reveals interesting parallels. Teresa initially had "no desire to be a nun, and I asked God not to give me this vocation; although I also feared marriage. "Life," chap 3, no. 2, in *The Collected Works of St. Teresa of Avila*, trans. Kieren Kavanaugh and Otilio Rodriguez (Washington, DC: ICS Publications, 1989), 1:61.

8. "I saw that the religious life was the best and safest state, and so little by little I decided to force myself to accept it" (ibid., 1:63).

9. St. Paula was St. Jerome's student and friend. Sor Juana's order (Hieronymite) was inspired by St. Jerome, and her convent named in honor of St. Paula. St. Teresa recounts being inspired by reading the *Letters of St. Jerome* when she was struggling over whether to enter the convent ("Life," chap. 3, no. 7).

10. A narrow decorative band, for example, on a column.

11. Mendez Plancarte (OC 1:387) and Salceda (OC 4:649–51) refer to a book in the Mexican Library of Congress on musical theory by Pedro Cerone that contains marginal notes by Sor Juana. They also mention Sor Juana's manuscript on musical theory, *El Caracol* [The spiral], mentioned in a poem to her patroness and friend, the Countess of Paredes (OC 1:64).

12. Early editions identify this quotation as from the fifth reading of the Roman Breviary for the feast of St. Thomas Aquinas, March 7.

13. Athanasius Kircher (1602–80) was a German Jesuit with encyclopedic interests. Sor Juana appears to have abbreviated the title. Trueblood (*A Sor Juana Anthology*, 216) has traced this to two books of Kircher that have *magnet* in the title: *Magnes, sive de arte magnetica* [Magnet, or On the art of the magnet] (Rome, 1641), and *Magneticum Naturae Regnum* [Nature's magnetic realm] (Rome, 1667). Each has an image of Jupiter with a chain emerging from his mouth in the fron-

tispiece. He also mentions Macrobius's *Commentary on the Dream of Scipio*, chap. 14. See also the *Iliad* (8.14–18) and Lucian's *Dialogue of Ares and Hermes* (OC 4:651). God as center and circumference of the universe is from Nicholas of Cusa's *De Docta Ignorantia (On Learned Ignorance)* Book 2, chap. 2, par. 157.

14. "To Rusticus," Letter CXXV, par. 12, in Wright, *Select Letters of St. Jerome*, 419.

15. Not found by any of Sor Juana's editors. Perhaps "attributed to" is an important qualification here. In general Machiavelli praises excellence in rulers as a source of respect and admiration, even awe. See for example *The Prince*, XV–XIX.

16. Teresa of Avila, "The Interior Castle," VI, chap. 9, nos. 3–6 in Kavanaugh and Rodriguez, *The Collected Works of St. Teresa of Avila*, 2:411–13.

17. Balthasar Gracian SJ. (1601–58), *El discreto* "Genio e ingenio" (OC 4:653).

18. Martial, *Epigrams*, VIII, 18 (OC 4:653).

19. Aulus Gellius, *Noctes Atticae*, v.vi, contains a summary of the various types of crowns. Pliny, *Naturalis Historia*, viii–xxii, has random references to them.

20. According to Salceda, Sor Juana falsely attributes this to Lupercio. The verse is from Bartolomé Leonardo de Argensola's *Sátira primera*, vv. 143–44.

21. Electa Arenal indicates that Boccaccio's *De Mulieribus Claris* [concerning famous women] and probably Christine de Pizan's *Book of the City of Ladies* are sources (Arenal and Powell, *The Answer/La Respuesta*, 124).

22. Isidore of Seville, *Etymologies*, VII, 8, lists ten sibyls to whom much was revealed about God, Christ, and the gentiles (OC 4:655).

23. St. Jerome, "To Eustochium (Letter 108)," par. 1, in *Handmaids of the Lord: Contemporary Descriptions of Feminine Asceticism in the First Six Christian Centuries*, ed. and trans. Joan M. Petersen (Kalamazoo, MI: Cistercian Publications, 1996), 126.

24. St. Jerome praises her in "Letter to Oceanus," Letter CXXVII, par 7, in Wright, *Select Letters of St. Jerome*, 327.

25. Queen Christina abdicated on becoming Catholic. She moved to Rome, where she patronized artists and philosophers, including Descartes. Antonio Vieira, SJ, was her confessor while he was in Rome.

26. María Guadalupe Alencastre, duchess of Aveyro, to whom Sor Juana dedicated a poem (OC 1:37), was also a relative of her patroness,

the countess of Paredes (Arenal and Powell, *The Answer/La Repuesta*, 129).

27. The countess of Villaumbrosa supported a Dominican nun, Sor María de la Santísima Trinidad, in founding a convent in Spain. It is not known why Sor Juana would mention her here (ibid., 130).

28. Dr. Juan Díaz de Arce, *Questionarium expositium pro clariori intelligentia Sacrorum Bibliorum, liber quartus; sive de Studioso Bibliorum*, Quaestio 4 (Mexico, 1648). Arce (1594–1653) taught sacred scripture at the University of Mexico for thirty years.

29. Dr. Augustin Cazalla, b. 1510, a canon in Salamanca, and royal chaplain, became a Lutheran and died in an auto-da-fe in 1559.

30. St. Jerome, "To Laeta," Letter CVII, 4, in Wright, *Select Letters of St. Jerome*, 346.

31. Marcello, a Roman widow, whose life St. Jerome commemorated in "To Principia," Letter CXXVII, in Wright, *Select Letters of St. Jerome*, 438–66.

32. Martial, *Epigrams*, 5.30 (OC 4:659).

33. It was commonly thought that if one ate rabbit one remained beautiful for seven days (OC 4:659).

34. Isidore of Seville, *Etymologies* XIV.7; and the Odyssey II, 287, IV.514, IX.80, XIX, 187 (OC 4:660).

35. Not an exact quotation, it probably corresponds to the book of Job 33:31–33 (OC 4:660).

36. María de la Antigua. A Spanish nun (1544–1617) whose works were collected and published posthumously as *Desengaño de religiosos* (1678) (Arenal and Powell, *The Answer/La Repuesta*, 138).

37. Source not found.
38. Source not found.
39. Source not found.

40. Editions list this author as "Tito Lucio" (Titus Lucius) but cannot identify him. I suggest that the Roman historian Tito Livio (Titus Livius or Livy) (59 BC–AD 17) is intended, although I cannot find the quotation in question.

41. Vieira, of course, was a Jesuit, as was Sor Juana's confessor Antonio Núñez de Miranda. Archbishop Aguiar y Seijas and Carlos de Sigüenza y Góngora, though friendly with many Jesuits, were not Jesuits, as some maintain.

42. Source not found.

43. St. Jerome, "Preface," *Chronicles of Eusebius: Book II* (OC 4:661).

44. Source not found.

45. Third century BC poet from Cilicia, Aratus of Soli.

46. Scholars today think it was not Parmenides, but Epimenides, a Cretan prophet (sixth century BC) (OC 4:662).

47. St. Jerome, "To Pacatula, Feminine Training," Letter CXXVIII, par. 3, in Wright, *Select Letters of St. Jerome*, 474–75.

48. Source not found.

49. Source not found.

50. Source not found.

51. Suetonius, *The Twelve Caesars*, "Julius Caesar" 51 (OC 4:662).

52. Augustine, *Contra litteras Petiliani donatistae* 3.10/11.

53. Salceda presumes that in a moment of distraction Sor Juana attributed these verses of Ovid, *De Ponto*, 4.79–80, to the poet Virgil (OC 4:662).

54. Seneca, *De Beneficiis*, V, 2 (OC 4:662).

55. *Vos* is a form of the second person used to address equals, but with a suggestion of intimacy. Sor Philotea as Sor Juana's fictional respondent was her equal. The bishop, *reverencia* is one way he would be addressed, could not appropriately be addressed as an equal. Sor Philotea addresses Sor Juana as "Your Grace," which is more formal.

SELECT BIBLIOGRAPHY

Editions

Sor Juana Inés de la Cruz. "Carta de la Madre Juana Inés de la Cruz escrita al R.P.M. Antonio Núñez de la Companía de Jesús." In Aurelano Tapia Méndez, *Carta de Sor Juana Inés de la Cruz a su confesor: Autodefensa espiritual*, 14–25. Monterrey, Mexico: Universidad de Nuevo León, 1981.

———. *Carta de Serafina de Cristo, 1691*. Edited by Elías Trabulse. Mexico City: Instituto Mexiquense de Cultura, 1996.

———. *Fama, y obras póstumas / del fénix de México, décima musa, poetisa americana Sor Juana Inés de la Cruz*. Madrid: Ruiz de Murga, 1700. Digitale Rekonstruktion der Printausgabe. Available online.

———. *Inundación castálida*. Edited by Georgina Sabat de Rivers. Madrid: Editorial Castalia, 1983.

———. *Obras Completas*. Vols. 1–4: *Lírica personal; Villancicos y letras sacras; Autos y loas; Comedias, sainetes y prosa* (1951–57). Edited by Alfonso Méndez Plancarte (vols. 1–3) and Alberto G. Salceda (vol. 4). Mexico City: Fondo de Cultura Económica, 1995.

———. *Obras completas*. Prologue by Francisco Monterde. Mexico City: Editorial Porrúa, 1989.

Sor Juana Inés de la Cruz and Augustín de Salazar y Torres. *La segunda Celestina*. Edited by Guillermo Schmidhuber de la Mora. Mexico City: Vuelta, 1990.

Translations

Sor Juana Inés de la Cruz. *The Answer/La Respuesta: Including a Selection of Poems*. Edited and translated by Electa Arenal and Amanda Powell. New York: The Feminist Press at The City University of New York, 1994.

————. *Response to the Most Illustrious Poetess Sor Filotea de la Cruz.* Translated by Margaret Sayers Peden, 2–75. In *Poems, Protest and a Dream.* New York: Penguin Books, 1997.

————. "The *Reply to Sor Philotea.*" Translated by Alan S. Trueblood, 205–45. In *A Sor Juana Anthology.* Cambridge, MA: Harvard Univ. Press, 1988.

————. *El Sueño.* Translated by John Campion. Austin, TX: Thorp Springs Press, 1983.

————. *Sor Juana's Dream.* Translated by Luis Harss. New York: Lumen Books, 1986.

————. *La Carta Atenagórica.* Translated by Fanchón Royer. In *The Tenth Muse: Sor Juana Inés de la Cruz,* 86–120. Paterson, NJ: St. Anthony Guild Press, 1952.

————. "*Loa* to *Divine Narcissus.*" Translated by Willis K. Jones. In *Spanish American Literature in Translation,* vol. 1, 301–8. New York: Frederick Ungar, 1966.

————. "*Loa* to *Divine Narcissus.*" Translated by Margaret Sayers Peden, 195–239. In *Poems, Protest and a Dream.* New York: Penguin Books, 1997.

————. "Letter from Sister Juana Inés de la Cruz Written to the R[everend] F[ather] M[aster] Antonio Núñez of the Society of Jesus." Translated by Margaret Sayers Peden. In Paz, *Sor Juana Inés de la Cruz, or The Traps of Faith,* 495–502.

————. *The Divine Narcissus/ El Divino Narciso.* Translated and annotated by Patricia A. Peters and Renée Domeier. Albuquerque, NM: University of New Mexico Press, 1998.

————. "Sor Juana Inés de la Cruz: *Joseph's Scepter.*" In *The Story of Joseph in Spanish Golden Age Drama,* edited and translated by Michael McGaha, 186–225. Lewisburg, PA: Bucknell Univ. Press, 1998.

Works About

Alatorre, Antonio. "La carta de Sor Juana al Padre Núñez (1682)." *Nueva Revista de Filología Hispánica* 35 (2) (1987): 591–673.

————. "Para leer la *Fama y obras pósthumas* de Sor Juana Inés de la Cruz." *Nueva Revista de Filología Hispánica* 29 (1948): 428–508.

Alatorre, Antonio, and Martha Lilia Tenorio. *Serafina y Sor Juana (con tres apéndices).* Mexico City: El Colegio de México, Centro de Estudios Lingüísticos y Literarios, 1998.

Arenal, Electa. "Sor Juana Inés de la Cruz: Speaking the Mother Tongue." *University of Dayton Review* 16 (2) (1983): 93–105.

SELECT BIBLIOGRAPHY

Arroyo, Anita. *Razón y pasión de Sor Juana*. Mexico City: Porrúa y Obregón, 1952.

Azar, Héctor. "Sor Juana y el descubrimiento de América." In *Memoria del Coloquio Internacional: Sor Juana Inés de la Cruz y el pensamiento novohispano, 1995*, 9–15. Toluca, México: Instituto Mexiquense de Cultura, 1995.

Bénassy-Berling, Marie Cécile. *Humanisme et religion chez Sor Juana Inés de la Cruz: La femme et la culture au XVIIe siècle*. Paris: Editions Hispaniques, 1982.

———. *Humanismo y religión en Sor Juana Inés de la Cruz*. Translated (from the French) by Laura López de Belair. Mexico City: UNAM, 1983.

———. "La mitificación de Sor Juana Inés de la Cruz en el mundo hispánico (finales del siglo XVII-principios del siglo XVIII)." *Revista de Indias* 55 (205) (1995): 541–50.

———. "Sobre el senequismo moral de Sor Juana Inés de la Cruz." In *Pensamiento europeo y cultura colonial*, edited by Karl Kohut, 238–44. Madrid: Iberoamericana, 1997.

———. "Sor Juana frente al mundo infernal." In *Memoria del Coloquio Internacional: Sor Juana Inés de la Cruz y el pensamiento novohispano, 1995*, 17–28. Toluca, México: Instituto Mexiquense de Cultura, 1995.

———. "Sor Juana Inés de la Cruz en Europa." *Colonial Latin American Review* 4 (2) (1995): 215–26.

Bergmann, Emilie. "Sor Juana Inés de la Cruz: Dreaming in a Double Voice." In *Women, Culture, and Politics in Latin America: Seminar on Feminism and Culture in Latin America*, edited by Emilie Bergmann, 151–72. Berkeley and Los Angeles: University of California Press, 1990.

Beuchot, Mauricio. "Los autos de Sor Juana: tres lugares teológicos." In Poot-Herrera, *Sor Juana y su mundo*, 353–92.

———. "Sister Juana Inés de la Cruz." In *The History of Philosophy in Colonial Mexico*, translated by Elizabeth Millán, 125–37. Washington, DC: The Catholic University of America Press, 1998.

———. *Sor Juana, una filosofía barroca*. Mexico City: UNAM, 1999.

———. "Sor Juana y el hermetismo de Kircher." In Fernández, *Los empeños*, 1–9.

———. "El universo filosófico de Sor Juana." In *Memoria del Coloquio Internacional: Sor Juana Inés de la Cruz y el pensamiento novohispano 1995*, 29–40. Toluca, Mexico: Instituto Mexiquense de Cultura, 1995.

SOR JUANA INÉS DE LA CRUZ

Bravo Arriaga, María Dolores. *La excepción y la regla: estudios sobre espiritualidad y cultura en la nueva España*. Mexico City: UNAM, 1997.

Buxó, José Pascual. *Sor Juana Inés de la Cruz y las vicisitudes de la crítica*. Edited by José Pascual Buxó. Mexico City: Universidad Nacional Autonóma de México, 1998.

Cacho Vázquea, Xavier. *Sor Juana y la liturgia (Una lectura de sus villancicos y letras sacras)*. Mexico City: Instituto de Estudios y Documentos Históricos, Claustro de Sor Juana, 1981.

Chang-Rodriguez, Raquel. "A proposito de Sor Juana y sus admiradores novocastellanos." *Revista Iberoamerícana* 51 (132–33) (1985): 605–19.

Chávez, Ezequiel A. *Sor Juana Inés de la Cruz, su misticismo y su vocación filosófica y literaria*. Mexico City: Asociación Civil Ezequiel A. Chávez, 1968.

Cidade, Hernani. "António Vieira et Sor Juana Inés de la Cruz." *Bulletin des Études Portugaises et de l'Institut Français au Portugal* 12 (1948): 1–34.

Corrigan, Winifred. "The Bishop and the Woman: 'Sor Filotea' and Sor Juana Inés de la Cruz." *Studia Mystica* 15 (2–3) (1992): 72–83.

Fernández MacGregor, Genario. *La santificación de sor Juana Inés de la Cruz*. Mexico City: Editorial Cultura, 1932.

Fernández, Sergio, ed. *Los empeños: Ensayos en homenaje a Sor Juana Inés de la Cruz*. Mexico City: UNAM, 1995.

Glantz, Margo. "Letras de San Bernardo: La excelsa fábrica." *Calâiope: Journal of the Society for Renaissance and Baroque Hispanic Poetry* 4 (1–2) (1998): 173–88.

Glantz, Margo, ed. *Sor Juana Inés de la Cruz y sus contemporáneos*. Mexico City: Centro de Estudios de Historia de México, 1998.

Gonzalez, Michelle A. *Sor Juana: Beauty and Justice in the Americas*. Maryknoll, NY: Orbis Books, 2003.

Kaminsky, Amy Katz. "Nearly New Clarions: Sor Juana Inés de la Cruz Pays Homage to a Swedish Poet." In *In the Feminine Mode: Essays on Hispanic Women Writers*, edited by Noël Valis and Carol Maier, 31–53. Lewisburg, PA.: Bucknell Univ. Press, 1990.

Kirk, Pamela. "Christ as Divine Narcissus. A Theological Analysis of *El Divino Narciso* of Sor Juana Inés de la Cruz." *Word and World* 12 (2) (1992): 145–53.

———. "Political Simulation: Sor Juana's Monument *Neptuno Alegórico*." *Journal of Hispanic/Latino Theology* 2 (2) (1994): 30–40.

———. *Sor Juana Inés de la Cruz: Religion, Art, and Feminism*. New York: Continuum, 1998.

Larisch, Sharon. "Sor Juana's *Apologia.*" *Pacific Coast Philology* 21 (1–2) (1986), 48–53.

Lavrín, Asunción. "Cotidianidad y espiritualidad en la vida conventual Novohispana: siglo XVII." In *Memoria del Coloquio Internacional: Sor Juana Inés de la Cruz y el pensamiento novohispano,* 1995, 203–19. Toluca, Mexico: Instituto Mexiquense de Cultura, 1995.

———. "Espiritualidad en el claustro novohispano del siglo XVII." *Colonial Latin American Review* 4 (2) (1995): 155–79.

———. "Sor Juana Inés de la Cruz: Obediencia y autoridad en su entorno religioso." *Revista Iberoamericana* 61 (172–73) (1995): 605–22.

———. "Values and Meaning of Monastic Life for Nuns in Colonial Mexico." *The Catholic Historical Review* 58 (October 1972): 367–87.

———. "Vida conventual: rasgos históricos." In Poot-Herrera, *Sor Juana y su mundo,* 33–91.

Leonard, Irving A. "A Baroque Poetess." In *Baroque Times in Old Mexico: Seventeenth-Century Persons, Places, and Practices.* Ann Arbor, MI: University of Michigan Press, 1959.

Long, Pamela H. "Sor Juana as Composer: A Reappraisal of the *Villancicos.*" In *Critical Essays on the Literatures of Spain and Spanish America,* edited by Luis T. González-del-Valle and Julio Baena, 161–69. Boulder, CO: Society of Spanish and Spanish American Studies, 1991.

Merrim, Stephanie. *Early Modern Women's Writing and Sor Juana Inés de la Cruz.* Nashville, TN: Vanderbilt Univ. Press, 1999.

———, ed. *Feminist Perspectives on Sor Juana Inés de la Cruz.* Detroit: Wayne State Univ. Press, 1991.

———. "*Mores Goemetricae*: The 'Womanscript' in the Theater of Sor Juana Inés de la Cruz." In *Feminist Perspectives on Sor Juana Inés de la Cruz,* edited by Stephanie Merrim, 94–123. Detroit, MI: Wayne State Univ. Press, 1991.

———. "Narciso *desdoblado*: Narcissistic Stragegems in *El Divino Narciso* and the *Respuesta a sor Filotea de la Cruz.*" *Bulletin of Hispanic Studies* 64 (2) (1987): 111–17.

Miranda, Ricardo. "Sor Juana y la música: una lectura más." In *Memoria del Coloquio Internacional: Sor Juana Inés de la Cruz y el pensamiento novohispano 1995,* 253–70. Toluca, Mexico: Instituto Mexiquense de Cultura, 1995.

Montañez, Carmen L. "La literatura mariana y los ejercicios devotos de Sor Juana Inés de la Cruz." *Revista Iberoamericana* 61 (172–73) (1995): 623–30.

SOR JUANA INÉS DE LA CRUZ

Montross, Constance M. *Virtue or Vice? Sor Juana's Use of Thomistic Thought.* Washington, DC: University Press of America, 1981.

Moraña, Mabel. "Orden dogmático y marginalidad en la *Carta de Monterrey* de Sor Juana Inés de la Cruz." *Hispanic Review* 58 (2) (1990): 205–25.

Muriel, Josefina. "La vida conventual femenina de la segunda mitad del siglo XVII y la primera del XVIII." In *Memoria del Coloquio Internacional: Sor Juana Inés de la Cruz y el pensamiento novohispano 1995,* 285–93. Toluca, Mexico: Instituto Mexiquense de Cultura, 1995.

———. "Sor Juana Inés de la Cruz y los escritos del Padre Antonio Núñez de Miranda." In Poot-Herrera, *"Y diversa de mí misma entre vuestras plumas ando,"* 71–83.

Myers, Kathleen, ed. *María de San José, Word from New Spain: The Spiritual Autobiography of Madre María de San José (1656–1719).* Liverpool: Liverpool Univ. Press, 1993.

———. "The Mystic Triad in Colonial Mexican Nuns' Discourse: Divine Author, Visionary Scribe, and Clerical Mediator." *Colonial Latin American Historical Review* 6 (4) (1997): 479–524.

———. "Sor Juana's *Respuesta:* Rewriting the Vitae." *Revista Canadiense de Estudios Hispánicos* 14 (3) (1990): 459–71.

———. "Sor Juana y su mundo: La influencia mediativa del clero en las vidas de religiosas y monjas." *Revista de Literatura* 61 (121) (1999): 35–59.

Paz, Octavio. *Sor Juana Inés de la Cruz, or The Traps of Faith.* Translated by Margaret Sayers Peden. Cambridge, MA: Harvard Univ. Press, 1988.

Peña, Margarita. "Teología, biblia y expresión personal en la prosa de Sor Juana Inés de la Cruz." In Poot-Herrera, *"Y diversa de mí misma entre vuestras plumas ando,"* 279–85.

Perelmuter Pérez, Rosa. "La estructura retórica de la *Respuesta a Sor Filotea.*" *Hispanic Review* 51 (2) (1983): 147–58.

Poot-Herrera, Sara. *Los guardaditos de Sor Juana.* Mexico City: Textos de Difusión Cultural, UNAM, 1999.

Poot-Herrera, Sara, ed. *Sor Juana y su mundo: una mirada actual.* Mexico City: Universidad del Claustro de Sor Juana, 1995.

———, ed. *"Y diversa de mí misma entre vuestras plumas ando": Homenaje Internacional a Sor Juana Inés de la Cruz.* Mexico City: El Colegio de México, 1993.

Powell, Amanda. "Women's Reasons: Feminism and Spirituality in Old and New Spain." *Studia Mystica* 15 (2–3): 59–69 (1992).

SELECT BIBLIOGRAPHY

Puccini, Darío. *Sor Juana Inés de la Cruz: Studio d'una personalita del Barocco messicano.* Rome: Edizioni dell'Ateneo, 1967.

Ricard, Robert. "António Vieira et Sor Juana Inés de la Cruz." *Bulletin des études portugaises de l'Institut Français au Portugal* 12 (1948): 1–34.

Rivas, Gerardo. "El velo del templo." In Fernández, *Los empeños*, 207–33.

Sabat de Rivers, Georgina. "El tema bíblico de Adán y Eva en la obra de sor Juana Inés de la Cruz." In *El monacato femenino en el imperio español,* edited by Manuel Ramos Medina, 83–92. Mexico City: Centro de Estudios de Historia de México, 1995.

———. "Mujeres nobles del entorno de Sor Juana." In Poot-Herrera, *"Y diversa de mí misma entre vuestras plumas ando,"* 1–19.

Scott, Nina M. *"La gran turba de las que merecieron nombres*: Sor Juana's Foremothers in *La Respuesta a Sor Filotea."* In *Coded Encounters: Race, Gender and Ethnicity in Colonial Latin America,* edited by Javier Cevallos-Candau, 206–23. Amherst, MA: University of Massachusetts Press, 1994.

———. "Sor Juana Inés de la Cruz: 'Let Your Women Keep Silence in the Churches.'" *Women's Studies International Forum* 8 (5) (1985): 511–19.

Soriano Vallés, Alejandro. *La invertida escala de Jacob: Filosofía y teología en* El sueño *de Sor Juana Inés de la Cruz.* Toluca, Mexico: Instituto Mexiquense de Cultura, 1996.

Tavard, George H. *Juana Inés de la Cruz and the Theology of Beauty: The First Mexican Theology.* Notre Dame, IN: University of Notre Dame Press, 1991.

Tello, Aurelio. "Sor Juana, la música y sus músicos." In *Memoria del Coloquio Internacional: Sor Juana Inés de la Cruz y el pensamiento novohispano 1995,* 465–81. Mexico City: Instituto Mexiquense de Cultura, 1995.

Tenorio, Martha Lilia. *Los villancicos de Sor Juana.* Mexico City: El Colegio de México, 1999.

Trabulse, Elías. *Los años finales de Sor Juana: una interpretación (1688–1695).* Mexico City: Centro de Estudios de Historia de México Condumex, 1995.

———. *El enigma de Serafina de Cristo: acerca de un manuscrito inédito de Sor Juan Inés de la Cruz (1691).* Toluca, Mexico: Instituto Mexiquense de Cultura, 1995.

———. *La muerte de sor Juana.* Mexico City: Centro de Estudios de Historia de México Condumex, 1999.

Weber, Alison. *Teresa of Avila and the Rhetoric of Femininity.* Princeton, NJ: Princeton Univ. Press, 1990.

INDEX

INDEX